The Birth of
the National Park Service

Howe Brothers

SALT LAKE CITY   CHICAGO

an Institute of the American West Book

1985

The Birth of
the National Park Service

The Founding Years, 1913–33

Horace M. Albright
as told to Robert Cahn

Volume Two in the series
INSTITUTE OF THE AMERICAN WEST BOOKS
Alvin M. Josephy, Jr., Acquiring Editor

Howe Brothers
Salt Lake City, Utah

Manufactured in the United States of America

second printing 1986

title page photograph: The Three Tetons, Grand Teton National Park.
George A. Grant, National Park Service

chapter opening illustrations and line drawings from
Outing magazine (Vols. 10–40) and *Scribner's Monthly* (Vols. 2-3),
courtesy University of Utah Marriott Library Special Collections

LIBRARY OF CONGRESS CATALOGING-IN-PUBLICATION DATA
    Albright, Horace Marden, 1890–
        The birth of the National Park Service.
        "An Institute of the American West book."
        Includes index.
        1. United States. National Park Service—History.
    2. Albright, Horace Marden, 1890-   . 3. United States.
    National Park Service—Officials and employees—Biography.
    I. Cahn, Robert, 1917-   . II. Title.
    SB482.A4A367   1985   353.0086'32   85–19743
    ISBN 0-935704-32-9
    ISBN 0-935704-33-7 (pkb.)

Contents

to my beloved Grace
who made my whole life possible

Acknowledgments

MANY INDIVIDUALS HAVE CONTRIBUTED TO THE CREATION OF THIS BOOK. I would like particularly to acknowledge the contributions of my daughter, Marian Schenck, who has devoted months, perhaps years, of her life to organizing, cataloging, and filing the materials and memorabilia of my long lifetime. Her help was indispensible in preparing this book. Also indispensable was Pat Cahn, who has been an active partner throughout the interviews as well as the writing and editing of the book.

I would also like to thank Rita Matthews Mastin, who transcribed many of the taped interviews; National Park Service historians Edwin Bearss and Barry Mackintosh, who read the manuscript, made editorial suggestions, and verified factual points; Yellowstone National Park historian Timothy Manns, who checked material concerning the Yellowstone era; Verne E. Chatelain, one of the few living colleagues of those old days, who read for accuracy those portions of the book relating to the period from 1930–33; and Raymond Tretheway III, who indexed the transcripts.

Unless a reference is given, all quoted material comes from letters and documents in my possession or in records I have given to the library of the University of California at Los Angeles.

Horace M. Albright

Foreword

ON THE OPENING DAY OF THE SECOND WORLD CONFERENCE ON NA-
TIONAL PARKS IN 1972 AT YELLOWSTONE NATIONAL PARK, I noticed
a number of people congregating around an elderly man. I soon discovered that the focus of attention was the legendary Horace Marden
Albright, one of the founders of the National Park Service, its second
Director, and the first superintendent of Yellowstone after thirty years
of military administration. Then eighty-two, Albright was more avidly
interested in parks than many conference participants a third his age.

Over the two weeks of the meeting, my wife, Pat, and I (who
work as an editorial team), had several long talks with Albright and
his spunky, bright-eyed wife, Grace, and we took some auto trips with
them around Yellowstone and down to Grand Teton National Park.
I was brimming with questions, but found little chance to ask them
because Albright had his own barrage of questions, trying to find out
from this reporter what I thought was going on in the national parks.
When I did manage to ask a few of my own, I was struck by Albright's
almost superhuman power of recall. He could tell about events that
happened fifty years earlier with an accuracy and fullness of detail you
or I might fail to muster regarding an event that happened the day
before yesterday. It was then that I started to get my first real appreciation of the tremendous story that lay behind the founding years of
the National Park Service.

As we drove through Grand Teton Park Albright recounted how
he had seen the awesome, snow-capped mountains and the beauti-

ful valley that is Jackson Hole in 1916, during a short trip to the area
with Stephen T. Mather, and how they both vowed then to add the
Teton area to Yellowstone. He pointed out to Pat and me the hill
where, in 1926, he and John D. Rockefeller, Jr. had sat for an hour
watching the sunset. Albright recalled how he had poured out to the
philanthropist the idea of bringing the Grand Tetons and Jackson
Hole into the national park system and how Rockefeller soon afterward organized a land-purchasing organization that secretly assembled
over thirty thousand acres to give to the government to complete the
Grand Teton National Park, his vision of which became a reality
twenty-four years later.

I was enthralled with other revelations that came out in our continuing conversations — the story behind Mather's decision in 1915
to take on the task of getting a national park system started, and how
he agreed to accept the job only after the Secretary of the Interior
promised him the assistance of a twenty-five-year-old member of the
Secretary's staff named Albright. I began to find out about the 1916-
style wheeling and dealing involved in getting Congress to pass the
National Parks Act authorizing establishment of the National Park
Service. I heard the story behind Albright's appointment as superintendent of Yellowstone National Park in 1919, after the army had
left. And I learned how a three-hour drive with President Franklin
Delano Roosevelt in 1933 led to a presidential executive order that
added more than fifty military parks, historical sites, and national
monuments to the national park system, elevating it overnight from a
small bureau managing natural areas mostly in the West to a truly
national system in charge of the nation's natural, historical, and cultural heritage.

My journalistic curiosity having been aroused and a family friendship having blossomed between the Cahns and the Albrights, Pat
and I found ourselves stopping by to visit with Horace and Grace
whenever our work took us to southern California. I would always
have my tape recorder with me, and as the pile of cassettes grew I
began to realize that Albright's recollections of those founding years of
the National Park Service needed to be assembled in a book.

When I first broached the idea to Horace of publishing *his* story of
those historic times, I learned that the noted book publisher Alfred A.
Knopf had been after him for a quarter-century to do just that. But
Albright had always declined. Although he was willing to help any-

one who wanted to write *about* these events, he was unwilling to put the story in his own words. The reason for this reticence, I finally discovered, was that Albright did not want to take anything away from the place Mather holds in history as the "founder" of the National Park Service. Albright's deep and abiding respect for Mather was the stumbling block to his telling his own story in print. I argued that the truth would not harm the Mather record in the least, and that for the historical record to be complete, he needed to give his firsthand account of those eventful days, including the story of how he stepped in during Mather's illness to organize the Park Service in 1917 and 1918. I also appealed to his personal dedication to American history and education and the Park Service itself, and suggested that he had an obligation to fill out the record of those early days.

Although I continued to gather material from Albright from 1979 through 1984, it was not until he began to see the story take shape on paper in 1984 that he finally relented and agreed to let it be "his" story, as told to me, a journalist and friend. There had never been any question in my mind: no historian or journalist writing *about* the events could do justice to the story — it had to be told by the one who took part in the events himself.

Confining the book to Albright's career with the National Park Service, rather than making it a personal life story, does present some drawbacks. His colorful boyhood and youth in turn-of-the-century California has to be left out, as does the story of his second career, in industry. Also, the fifty years of activism in conservation and national parks from 1934 to the present can be covered only briefly. But perhaps Horace, as he pecks away on his old Smith-Corona portable typewriter, will yet fill in those historical gaps.

Another element that does not fit into this format is the full story of Grace Noble Albright, the continual inspiration and buoyancy she lent to Horace and the role she played in events throughout the sixty-five years of their marriage. Grace had a significant though unmeasurable influence in the development of the National Park Service. Her death in 1980 after a few months' illness was a blow that almost toppled Horace.

Albright's struggle against physical problems in the five years since then has been difficult, but has not hampered his mental agility. At ninety-five, he remains mentally alert and still avidly interested in the welfare of the national parks. Though his physical condition necessitates living at a convalescent home in North Hollywood, California, his daughter, Marian, and her husband, Roswell Schenck, live nearby and tend to his needs. Their home is the scene of many family gatherings, birthday parties, and press and television interviews. He also goes home to dinner once or twice a week and still uses his office there on occasion, although he carries on most of his writing and voluminous correspondence sitting on the edge of his bed and banging on the trusty old typewriter that he puts on his bedside table.

Because of Albright's reticence about tooting his own horn, it is not possible to include in his narrative the credit others have given him for his unique place in history, or the many awards that have been bestowed on him. For instance, he does not include being knighted by King Gustav V of Sweden with the Order of the Northern Star in 1933 for achievements in management of national parks, and receiving the Pugsley Gold Medal from the American Scenic and Historic Preservation Society in 1929 for achievements in resource conservation. He has three honorary Doctor of Laws degrees — from the universities of Montana, California, and New Mexico. He was given the Camp Fire Club of America's Gold Medal for wildlife conservation (1962); the Garden Club of America's Hutchinson Medal for his work in saving of redwoods (1959); the Theodore Roosevelt Memorial Association's Roosevelt Medal for resource conservation and wildlife protection (1959); the Audubon Medal for wildlife conservation (1969); the Department of the Interior Conservation Service Award (1953); the American Forestry Association's Distinguished Service Award for conservation activity (1968); and the Cosmos Club Award (1974). He has been elected as an honorary vice-president of the Sierra Club every year since 1937, and served on the board of trustees of the National Audubon Society (1933–37), the board of trustees of Colonial Williamsburg (1935–1958), and the board of directors of the Jackson Hole Preserve (1940–1977). He was the first president of Resources for the Future and board chairman from 1953 to 1962. In 1952 the University of California Alumni Association named him Alumnus of the Year for his leadership in establishing Resources for the Future.

In 1984 a plaque was installed at the Pacific Tropical Botanical Garden in Hawaii in recognition of Albright's achievements as chairman at the time it was being organized in 1965, and for raising contributions for it from then until 1971. In 1959, some friends donated sixty thousand dollars to establish the annual Horace M. Albright Conservation Lectureship at his alma mater, the University of California, Berkeley. Among the twenty-three lecturers so far have been Rene Dubos, David Brower, Stewart Udall, Russell Train, Barry Commoner, Ansel Adams, and Michael Frome, and I was fortunate to have been selected as the 1980 Albright lecturer.

The honors that are the most satisfying and most enduring to him are the designation in 1981 by the state of California of a ten-acre tract of redwoods in the South Calaveras State Park as "The Horace and Grace Albright Grove" to commemorate his securing the last one million dollars for acquiring this magnificent giant redwood forest, and the naming of the major school for training of National Park rangers the Horace M. Albright Training Center in Grand Canyon National Park. And in 1980 President Jimmy Carter awarded him the nation's highest civilian honor, the Presidential Medal of Freedom. The citation accompanying the medal states:

> The President of the United States of America awards the Presidential Medal of Freedom to Horace M. Albright, a living monument like the Grand Tetons he has fought so hard to preserve. Horace Albright has been a driving force for conservation in this country during most of the 20th Century. A founding father of the National Park Service, he is a champion of nature's causes and a defender of America's most precious inheritance.

Robert Cahn

1

Go East, Young Man

As I rode the train eastward I kept my face at the window every hour there was light. I was twenty-three years old, had grown up in the small California town of Bishop, and except for a few trips around California and to Reno, Nevada, I had never been anywhere. As I gazed at the wonders of the United States passing by, I also wrestled with myself over the decision that had put me on that train. Was I crazy to leave Berkeley just a year short of getting my law degree and go off to Washington, D.C.?

The events in May 1913 that had led to my being on this train, now only a few miles from the nation's capital, had been set in motion by Adolph C. Miller, the ranking professor in the Department of Economics in the University of California. A man with a national reputation in banking and finance, Miller had been picked by the new Woodrow Wilson administration to be a top assistant to Secretary of the Interior Franklin K. Lane, and had gotten permission to bring along "a young fellow who has been working for me."

I was a reader for Professor Miller at the time, working my way through law school. When he offered me the job, my reaction was pretty negative. I enjoyed my law studies and had worked out what I thought was a perfect situation for my final year, with the promise of a job as an assistant in economics (my undergraduate major had been economics), that would cover all my expenses.

"A year away from California is a broadening experience that you need," Professor Miller argued. "Working at the Department of the

Interior would give you wide experience. It would be interesting and exciting, and since you are planning to specialize in land and mining law, it's a chance to work right there where much of this law is made."

At last I began to see the possibilities and ventured to ask what kind of salary the job would pay. I told him I didn't see how I could afford the train fare, since I didn't even have enough to make a trip up to Inyo County to visit my parents.

"Don't worry," Miller said. "I'll loan you the money to pay your travel costs, and you can pay me back over a period of months or years, as you can." And he said he could guarantee that the job would pay one hundred dollars per month.

I told him I would think it over, and spent most of the next week talking with various confidants, especially William E. Colby, one of my law professors who had become a good friend. Colby was secretary of the Sierra Club, and I had learned quite a bit about conservation from him, even though at that time parks and conservation were not primary interests with me. He had even taken me to San Francisco once to meet the great John Muir. (Muir died in 1914.) Colby assured me, as had everyone else, that the experience in Washington would be good for me and for my career.

When I went over to Miller's home to tell him that I had decided to accept, we arranged that I would get ready and go right away, even though he would not wind up his university duties for another month. He asked if I had proper clothes for Washington. My school clothes were pretty worn, but I told him I thought what I had would be all right on the job. "I hope I won't have to get dressed up, though," I said, "because I don't have those kind of clothes."

"Wait a minute," he said. Then he brought out a full dress suit which he said he no longer used, and gave it to me. Judging by its style, I think it probably was the one he had worn for his graduation from the university in the class of 1887. But it was beautifully tailored in fine material, fit me well, and it looked just fine to me.

As word of my move to Washington got around, I noticed that some of my campus friends began to look at me in a new light. It was quite a mark of distinction for a California youth to get the chance to go east to a job in Washington. Their reaction gave my ego such a boost that I finally got up the courage to call on the girl I had been worshipping from afar for a long time.

Grace Noble was pretty, charming, and popular, and although we knew each other by name, I had never dared ask her for a date. At the time I first met her I had been working in the registrar's office, and sneaked a look at her records. Among other bits of information, I learned that her grade average was better than mine. "I'd never have a chance with her," I thought. "She's not only charming and popular, she's smarter than I am." But now, with my new-found self-assurance, I went over to her house my last afternoon in Berkeley. She seemed genuinely friendly, and we talked a long time. As I was leaving, Grace said, "Drop me a line some time." I could hardly believe my ears. I happily responded, "Of course I will."

I boarded the train the next day, and now, at 7:30 Saturday morning, May 31, 1913, I was arriving at Washington, D.C.'s Union Station. The elaborate building astonished me with its size and beauty. I checked my bags, emerged into the dewy morning light, and found myself gazing straight at the dome of the Capitol of the United States. I bought a city map and guidebook, ate a light breakfast, and began the ten-block walk to the U.S. Patent Office Building (now the U.S. Portrait Gallery), where the Department of the Interior was housed at that time. In those days government offices were in full swing on Saturdays.

As I neared the imposing building (it occupied two full city blocks in the heart of the city, between F and G Streets extending from Seventh to Ninth Streets, Northwest), I became more conscious of the rumpled appearance of my one suit, a blue serge that I had had about three years. I passed a tailor's shop and stopped in to see if he could press the suit and sponge off any spots, and do it quickly. I took off the suit, he sat me in a chair and threw a rug over my legs, and spruced up the suit in no time.

Promptly at 9:00 I presented myself at Secretary Lane's office where I was cordially welcomed by Herbert A. Meyer, secretary to the Secretary, and by Edward Kemper, his assistant. They talked with me a few minutes about my background and education and took me to the appointment clerk, Ronnie C. Shelse. I learned that my position was not under Civil Service rules and had the title "confidential clerk to the Secretary," and that my salary would be sixteen hundred dollars per year! Dr. Miller had mentioned something like one hundred dollars a month, so I was gratified at this high starting salary.

Kemper took me to the big room adjacent to the Secretary's office that would be Dr. Miller's, and where I would have my desk. He gave me some materials about the Interior Department that I was to read, but I explained that I did not want to work that day because I had to find a place to live. He warned that by not staying at the office I would lose not only that day's pay but Sunday's as well, for I wouldn't get on the payroll until Monday. But I felt it was important to get settled.

I found a nice room at the YMCA for sixteen dollars per month and arranged to get two good meals a day at Mrs. Travis' boarding house on G Street, not far from the Y, for thirty-five dollars per month. Lunches cost about thirty cents a day. So I felt like a prince with only sixty-one dollars per month living expenses and a monthly salary of roughly $133.

Monday morning I began the long, confusing process of learning the ways of the bureaucracy. Talking with other employees, I found out that Miller would have responsibility for many of the areas and subjects over which the Interior Department had jurisdiction: the Bureau of Education, then a part of Interior, the eleemosynary institutions (what we would now refer to as welfare or family services), the territories of Alaska and Hawaii, certain legislative matters, all of the departmental inspectors, and the national parks. In fact, it soon became clear that the parks would be the main part of Miller's job.

When Lane became Secretary in March of that year, he had promised to concentrate on getting a national park service established and to bring some order to the chaos that surrounded the administration of the eleven existing national parks, seventeen national monuments, and two comparable reservations under Interior. It was expressly for tackling the problems of the national park system that Lane had wanted to bring Miller to Washington. Not only was Miller a man of reputation, but he was quite wealthy and could afford, in the public interest, to work at the ridiculous salary of $2,750 — all that Interior had available.

The new Woodrow Wilson administration was aware of the problems besetting the national parks. But there had been no big public outcry and no particular congressional interest, so no pressure was being exerted on the Secretary to address the problems. Nevertheless, Lane was determined to help the national parks. Possibly he felt embarrassment at the role he had played, shortly after taking office in 1913, in putting through the Hetch Hetchy Act that allowed a dam to be built in Yosemite National Park just to provide additional water for San Francisco.

I had been very much opposed to the Hetch Hetchy plan, and one of the most heartbreaking tasks I had to perform when I first started my job was signing the Secretary's name to hundreds, I suppose even thousands, of answers to letters that came in protesting the dam.

I knew very little about national parks or other protected areas at that time, even though I often heard about current conservation issues from Colby and other Sierra Club friends. I had never even been in a national park, except an area around the Minarets in the eastern Sierra that at one time was a part of Yosemite. Now, as it became clear that parks would be a major subject in my work, I set out to learn what I could about their current status.

The national parks of the nineteenth century — Yellowstone, established in 1872; Yosemite, Sequoia, and General Grant (later enlarged and renamed Kings Canyon), all started in 1890; and Mount Rainier, 1899 — had been created thanks to a handful of conservation advocates. The congressional actions that established those first parks could be attributed to the absence of any concerted opposition, more than to any particular strength of the few conservationists who advocated their designation as national parks. Crater Lake had been established in 1902, mostly through a seventeen-year crusade by William Gladstone Steel. Mesa Verde, one of the nation's great archeological sites, was added in 1906, and Glacier, a real wilderness park in Montana, in 1910. Wind Cave, a small area in South Dakota, had been set aside by Congress in 1902, but some government officials felt that it should not have been a national park, and Congress appropriated virtually no funds for it. Also there were two tiny parks — Platt in Oklahoma, and Sullys Hill in North Dakota — established in 1902 and 1904, respectively, with less than one thousand acres each. Both were totally lacking in national park qualifications. They had been established because of the parochial enthusiasm of local politicians.

Some of the national monuments, such as Grand Canyon in Arizona and Mount Olympus in Washington, had natural values equal to national parks, but were administered as multiple-use areas by the Forest Service of the U.S. Department of Agriculture, with timber harvest the primary use. Later they would become Grand Canyon and Olympic National Parks.

The designation "monument" puzzled me at first, as it has many people over the years. The term makes people think of historical memorials of granite or other man-made structures. To add to the confusion, the term has been given various interpretations over the years since 1906, when the Antiquities Act was passed, with its provision allowing the President to set aside "historic landmarks, historic and prehistoric structures, and other objects of historic or scientific interest" on public lands by proclaiming them national monuments.* It is generally known as the Lacey Act, for its author, Iowa Congressman John F. Lacey. At its inception, the legislation was primarily intended to allow a President to provide protection for prehistoric archaeological remains.

President Theodore Roosevelt used the Lacey Act to good advantage, although he aroused controversy when he used it to preserve huge natural areas such as the eight hundred thousand acres of Arizona Territory he proclaimed as Grand Canyon National Monument in 1908. Making his first trip to the Grand Canyon five years earlier, he had said, "Do nothing to mar its grandeur. . . . keep it for your children, your children's children, and all who come after you, as the one great sight which every American should see." Roosevelt and many presidents after him have used the Lacey Act when Congress was unwilling to pass legislation. And many areas thus protected have later been designated by Congress as national parks.

As I continued my on-the-job research, I learned that few people were going to the parks and monuments. They were hard to get to and had limited accommodations. Yellowstone, for instance, was getting only twenty thousand visitors a year. The little management that existed was split among the Interior, Agriculture, and War departments. A cavalry unit of the army controlled Yellowstone throughout the year, and in the summer army troops were sent in to administer Yosemite and Sequoia. There was little or no communication among the three departments. Even within Interior, there was no coordination among the areas it administered. One assistant attorney, W. Bertrand Acker, spent part of his time shuffling papers concerned with national parks and monuments, and two or three of his clerks and accountants spent part of their time on it. Interior had a superintendent in charge of each national park, with a minimum of help. Many of the superintendents owed their jobs to patronage from a senator or congressman, and none had had any experience in natural area management.

* Public Law No. 209, 59th Congress.

Secretary of the Interior Franklin K. Lane. National Park Service.

National park problems had been given attention briefly at a conference held at Yellowstone in September 1911 by Walter L. Fisher, who was Secretary of the Interior during the last two years of President William Howard Taft's term. The first conference ever held to discuss parks, its purpose was twofold: to foster the development needed in order to attract the public to the parks, and to consider better ways of administering the parks. The seventy participants included Interior Department officials, superintendents or custodians of the national parks, and a few officials from other federal agencies. There were representatives from railroads and other transportation companies serving the parks, concessioners, and a few of the leading private sector advocates, such as J. Horace McFarland. As president of the American Civic Association, he was spearheading an effort to establish a bureau of national parks within the Interior Department.

The railroad people at the conference made it clear that it wasn't their fault more people weren't going to Yellowstone, because their rates were as low as one and one-half cents per passenger mile. Much of the discussion centered on whether to remove the rules then in effect restricting automobiles and other motor vehicles from some parks.

That year President Taft had sent a special message to Congress recommending the establishment of a bureau of national parks and, at the American Civic Association's annual meeting, Taft had made a speech advocating a parks bureau. McFarland also had spoken at the meeting, noting that the parks and monuments were drawing barely two hundred thousand visitors a year, and were not ready for visitors. "The parks have just happened," he said. "They are not the result of such an overlooking of the national domain as would, and ought to, result in a coordinated system. There is no adequately organized control of the national parks. With forty-one national parks and monuments [some monuments were administered by agencies other than the Department of the Interior] aggregating an area larger than two sovereign states, and containing priceless glories of scenery and wonders of nature, we do not have as efficient a provision for administration as is possessed by many a city of but forty thousand inhabitants for its hundred or so acres! In a lamentable number of cases, the administration consists solely in the posting of a few warning notices!"

That just about described the situation in June 1913, as far as I could find out, when Professor Miller arrived to assume his job. In July he joined Lane for a tour of Yellowstone, Glacier, Mount Rainier, and Yosemite. Miller returned from the trip fired up about the need for establishing a national park service. But he could not generate similar enthusiasm on the part of Congress.

One day David Curry appeared at our office for an appointment with Miller, accompanied by both U.S. senators from California and two congressmen from the area around Yosemite National Park. Curry, a rugged and fiery-tempered entrepreneur, had gone to Yosemite in 1898 and established Camp Curry. He was known for his loud, lusty voice, and was called "The Stentor of the Yosemite." Each night at the Camp Curry campfire he would bellow, "Let the fire fall." An assistant at the top of Glacier Point, thirty-five hundred feet above and a mile away, would then push a huge bonfire over the edge of the cliff, giving the Camp Curry visitors a show of natural fireworks. At the nightly campfire programs, Curry frequently made abusive remarks about the Secretary of the Interior and other officials, partly because the government allowed him only a year-to-year permit, while the major camp concessioner at Yellowstone, W. W. Wylie, had been given a ten-year franchise.

Curry started off by demanding a five-year contract. Miller let him and the congressmen say their piece. Then he looked Curry in the eye and said, "Mr. Curry, I'm not going to give you any of the things you asked for. Furthermore, I'm going to take something away from you. I'm going to stop the firefall."

The congressmen and senators tried to persuade Miller not to take the action, but he did. There were no firefalls for the next several years. Curry continued to get his franchise to operate Camp Curry renewed for only one year at a time.

Then Miller got diverted from his work on parks. The Wilson administration wanted to establish a Federal Reserve Board, and Miller, as one of the nation's top experts in finance, found himself on loan to the Treasury Department to work on drafting legislation to create the board and promote the bill in Congress.

Late in 1913, realizing that he would not have time to work on creating an administrative framework for the national parks, Miller hired a young San Francisco architect he knew, Mark Daniels, also a graduate of the University of California, to work on the parks. Miller gave him the title general superintendent and landscape engineer for national parks. Although Daniels had no government experience whatever, and no expertise in national parks, Miller felt he could do the job.

Daniels set up an office in San Francisco and hired an assistant. Since there was no legislative authority or appropriation for any of this, Interior Department attorneys had to find the money some other way. They did it by reducing the budgets of each of the parks. Needless to say, this did not go over very well with the superintendents. Nor did the fact that Daniels was given general control of all park funds, and the superintendents had to report to Daniels rather than directly to Washington. And because Daniels had the title of general superintendent, all the superintendents of national parks had their titles changed to supervisor. Inasmuch as the men in charge of national forests were called "supervisors," it was considered a mark of distinction for the managers of national parks to be "superintendents," and this change was not appreciated in the field. Most of them ignored the order and went right on calling themselves superintendents. A further bone of contention was that Daniels was permitted to continue his private architectural practice.

The park structures Daniels designed were attractive, and he also designed the olive green uniform for park rangers. He proved to be an

Leslie, Dewey, Mary, George, and Horace Albright. Berkeley, California, Christmas 1915.
Albright collection.

able spokesman for parks when given the opportunity, but his igno-
rance of government got him into trouble when a bookkeeping system
he devised to build in depreciation and obsolescence was not com-
patible with the department's system. He even tried to place an economic value on the wear and tear on natural features of parks, such
as waterfalls.

Daniels also got himself in a jam with Louis W. Hill, president of
the Great Northern Railroad which had built hotels and roads in
Glacier National Park. Touring Glacier in 1914 with Daniels, Hill
pointed to the bald dome of Mount Henry, and mentioned in passing:
"That's the baldest mountain top I've ever seen. Why in the world do
you suppose nothing grows up there?"

Daniels looked in his notebook to find out what Glacier's annual
appropriation was, and then suggested to Hill that three thousand of
the thirty thousand dollar annual budget be used to plant trees on
Mount Henry's bald top to see if the cause of the problem could be
found. Hill was so appalled by Daniels' apparent willingness to waste
one-tenth of Glacier's minute appropriation for such a purpose that he
immediately called an end to the trip. Hill's formal complaint to

Washington forced Miller to recognize some of Daniels' shortcomings.

With Miller's time pretty well monopolized by his Federal Reserve legislation project, I found myself having to cope the best I could with all kinds of matters that came across his desk. It also brought me into closer contact with Secretary Lane than I would have been otherwise. I found him to be a forceful administrator and a crafty politician.

I made an effort to get acquainted with members of Congress and their staffs, and tried to interest them in supporting legislation to establish a national park service. I also found much of my time taken with coordinating the work of the Interior Department inspectors. The department's responsibilities covered such a vast geographic area and so many and varied fields of expertise that the department used a corps of eight so-called "inspectors" to keep an eye on the far-flung activities. They were highly qualified in different fields. For instance, one was a certified public accountant, and if a bookkeeping matter went wrong anywhere in Interior, he was detailed to help solve the problem. Another inspector had been chief of detectives in Manila, and if any question or charges came up against somebody, this fellow would be sent to handle the matter. Still another inspector, James McLaughlin, had written a book about Indians and knew their sign language and could communicate with almost every tribe. The eight inspectors reported to Miller. As his surrogate, I found myself spending quite a bit of time with them, and through them beginning to get a good grasp of the workings of the Interior Department. My job included acting as a go-between for them with the chiefs of the various bureaus of the department. I enjoyed the occasions when I was sent to handle some aspects of relations with congressmen.

My time in Washington wasn't all work, of course. I had settled comfortably in my room at the YMCA and was making many friends. You never knew who you would encounter at the Y in those days. For instance, running around the indoor track one rainy morning I met Senator George Norris of Nebraska. After work or on weekends I often rented a horse and rode in Rock Creek Park, where I sometimes talked with Senator William Borah of Idaho. He rode almost every day, and liked to talk with other riders, including me. I joined the District of Columbia chapter of the University of California Alumni Association, and was elected president. In the fall I enrolled in evening classes at Georgetown University Law School, determined not to lose any time getting my law degree.

I felt I was living in a place where history was being made every day, and I tried to take advantage of opportunities to be a part of events. For instance, I wanted to see President Wilson make his second personal appearance before Congress, delivering a special message on banking and currency reform. So I went to Capitol Hill and introduced myself to California Congressman John E. Raker, ostensibly to talk about the legislation he had introduced to establish a national parks bureau. Mr. Raker had been an acquaintance of my father through the Odd Fellows, and he greeted me warmly. After we finished talking, I asked if perhaps he might have an extra ticket for the gallery so I could hear President Wilson's speech. But it turned out that each congressman had been allotted only one ticket, and Raker had given his to his wife. He must have been a little amused by my youthful eagerness, however, because he told me he would see if he could smuggle me onto the House floor with him.

He looked me over, and said, "You're not too much younger than some of these new members of Congress. There are a lot of new members, and we have new doorkeepers. I believe we might be able to get you in. Now, when we get near the door, keep your head down and pound the fingers of your right hand into your left as if you were giving me the devil about something, and just keep going." Well, it worked, and I got into the House, and Raker would identify the important people to me as they came in. It was a great thrill to see the diplomatic corps and the cabinet members and the Supreme Court come in and take their seats, and then watch the pomp as a delegation went out to escort President Wilson into the chamber. Watching the President of the United States deliver his message to Congress was an experience I will never forget.

By the spring of 1914, I was well into my work and learning to take on even wider responsibilities, when the game suddenly changed. President Wilson appointed Miller to a ten-year term as one of the members of the new Federal Reserve Board, which had just been established through the legislation Miller had done so much to draft. He invited me to go along with him to the Federal Reserve, but I had become very involved in my work and felt I had a great deal to gain by continuing to learn more about the Department of the Interior and getting experience in the administration of land law.

In June I got my law degree, and passed the bar examination for the District of Columbia. When Will Colby wired from California to congratulate me, he included an offer to join his law firm. It was hard to resist the chance to get back to California and join such a prestigious firm, headed by Judge Curtis Lindley. But I concluded that I should stay and finish what I had started, a decision that was made a little easier when Secretary Lane urged me to remain and promised to let me do some legal work for the department.

By then I had earned a month's leave, and headed home to California for a vacation. I stopped off in Los Angeles for a visit with one of my law school buddies, Beverly Clendenin, and he happened to mention that the California bar examination was being given there two days later. I thought I might as well see if I could pass it. Although my head was full of District of Columbia and general law, I hadn't thought about California law for over a year. But I figured I had nothing to lose.

As it turned out, the bar exam was mostly oral. Strangely enough, although the other applicants were thrown questions about California laws, every single question directed to me had to do with constitutional or common law, with which I was quite familiar. I got through without a hitch, and could hardly believe my stroke of luck.

After spending a week in Bishop with my family, I headed for Berkeley to pursue one other bit of unfinished business that was very important to me — Grace Noble. The day I had left for Washington, over a year ago, the Oakland-San Francisco ferry had been delayed a few minutes, and I had used the time to phone Grace and ask once again if she really meant it when she promised to write to me. She assured me that she did, and when the train stopped at Ogden, Utah, I mailed my first post card to her. When I changed trains in Chicago, I sent another card, and when I got to Washington I sent a fourteen-page letter. Upon completing her graduate studies in the fall she got a job teaching fifth grade in Alameda, California. I continued to write once or twice a week for the entire year, and she answered them all. An increasingly warm relationship was growing between us — at least on paper. Now I could hardly wait to be with her.

For ten days, we picnicked and talked, went to the movies, spent nearly every day and evening together, and I was convinced that she was the one person in all the world I wanted to spend the rest of my life with. I still didn't really think I had a chance, but the night before I was to return to Washington, I asked her to marry me. To my astonishment she gave an unhesitating yes!

Having spent so much on our good times together, I didn't have enough money to buy her an engagement ring. I got her mother to measure Grace's finger with a piece of string so I could take it along and send her a ring as soon as I could afford it. We made tentative plans for a wedding about a year hence. By then I would be finished with my Washington adventure and ready to settle down to law practice in California.

Meanwhile though, there was a full year's work ahead if we were to accomplish the tasks Lane had in mind at Interior, particularly the goal of getting Congress to establish a bureau to bring together the administration of the national parks and monuments and straighten out their management.

2

Enter Stephen Mather

LIBERTY CAP (MT. BRODERICK.)

JUST FOUR MONTHS AFTER RETURNING TO WASHINGTON, I MET A MAN WHO CHANGED THE COURSE OF MY LIFE. It also marked the beginning of a new era for the national parks, though we did not realize it at the time.

When Secretary Lane was searching for the right person to replace Miller as his chief assistant, the name Stephen Tyng Mather had been mentioned. Lane found out that Mather had also gone to the University of California and had become a mountaineering buff after going on the Sierra Club's 1905 climb of Mount Rainier. Almost every year since then he had climbed some western peak of ten thousand feet or more and had made countless wilderness trips in national parks. On an expedition into the wild Kings River Canyon in 1912, he had encountered the legendary John Muir, then eighty, and Muir's plea for help in saving the Sierra country from loggers, miners, and dam builders had stirred the crusader in Mather. Revisiting Yosemite and Sequoia national parks in 1914, Mather had been shocked by what he saw — little protection, poor trails, and inadequate facilities for visitors. He also had discovered that privateers had taken over some of the groves of Giant Sequoia trees and were planning to log them on the fraudulent basis that because the land where they grew became a swamp each spring when the snows melted, they were open targets for logging under the outdated Swamp Act of the nineteenth century.

Secretary Lane had persuaded a close friend, John H. Wigmore, dean of the Northwestern University law school, who knew Mather

[15]

well, to arrange a meeting in Chicago so Lane could size up Mather. He was impressed, and asked Mather to write him about conditions he had found in the national parks. The letter Mather sent forthrightly criticized the condition and management of the national parks he had seen. Lane had written back, "Dear Steve: If you don't like the way the national parks are run, why don't you come down to Washington and run them yourself?" It was that challenge that had brought Mather to Washington on a cold mid-December day in 1914.

Mather had not come for the purpose of accepting the job, however. He told Lane that he was skeptical of whether he could be of any help, pointing out that he had no government experience and could not imagine himself sitting behind a desk running a departmental office.

"I'm not asking you to sit at a desk and run a department," Lane replied. "I'm looking for a new kind of public official, one who will go out in the field and sell the public on conservation, then work with Congress to get laws passed to protect the national parks. The job calls for a man with vision. I can't offer you rank or fame or salary — only a chance to do some great public service."

But Mather reaffirmed his reluctance to work in government under a lot of rules and regulations. With his freewheeling method of working, he told Lane, he would be in trouble before he had been on the job an hour.

"I'll give you a young fellow who knows the ropes and who'll handle the legal routine for you; he's another University of California man, by the way," Lane told Mather. At that point he picked up the phone and asked me to come to his office.

When I entered, a silver-haired man was sitting by the Secretary's big desk, and Lane introduced us. "I have asked Mr. Mather to take Mr. Miller's place," Lane said, "but he doesn't want to come. I want you to talk with him about it. Go sit over there by the fireplace, you fellows, and talk it over." So we went to the couch at the other end of the long room, and sat beside a crackling fire and talked for more than two hours.

Mather was unlike anybody I had met since coming to Washington. He was exuberant, warm, yet had an aura of authority about him that came, perhaps, from the fact that he was a successful businessman. He was forty-seven. I was only twenty-four, and a bit in awe of him.

He was like a wound spring. His reactions were sharp and un-

Cliff Palace, Mesa Verde National Park, looking east, 1929. George A. Grant photograph.
National Park Service.

guarded as I began to lay out the picture for him. He listened intently, plying me with questions that made it clear that he grasped the situation and cared deeply about what he was hearing. We talked about what needed to be done and about the strategies that would have to be followed in order to get Congress to pass legislation creating a national park service.

The more he heard about the challenging task it would be to put the national parks in order, the more enthused he became. We continued talking for another two hours. Finally he said: "I'll tell you what, let's make no promises today. But if you'll agree to stay for a year and help me, I'll consider coming down to Washington to run the parks for a year."

"But Mr. Mather," I protested, "I can't stay. I plan to leave soon and go back to California. I'm engaged to be married, and William Colby has offered me a job in his law firm out there. I'll be twenty-five next month, and I really need to get started practicing mining and land law. Besides," I rattled on, "I can't afford to go on here now that I'm going to get married. My sixteen hundred a year wouldn't be enough for the two of us, and there's no chance of promotion here either."

Mather said he could see why I was reluctant. But he said, "I would be more than happy to pay you an extra thousand myself, if I decide to take the job and you agree to stay with me. Think it over, and we'll get together after the holidays."

I wrote to Grace about meeting Mather, the decision he was about to make, and how it might affect me. She wrote back that it sounded like a fine opportunity, and that she didn't see any reason for it to spoil our plans for getting married at the end of 1915.

Early in January 1915, Mather told Lane that he would devote one year to organizing a national park service and getting the legislation for it passed in Congress. I agreed to stay and assist him. On January 21, the Secretary called in other officials of the department, introduced Mather and instructed the chief clerk to swear him in as assistant to the Secretary.

After everybody had departed except Lane, Mather, and I, Lane shook hands solemnly and departed for his own office, which was next to the one Mather and I shared, with only a stenographer's small office in between. Lane shut the door behind him, then immediately opened it again, stuck his round, smiling face in and said, "By the way, Steve, I forgot to ask your politics — are you a Democrat or a Republican?"

Lane, of course, knew full well that Mather was a Bull Moose Republican in this Wilson Democratic administration. But it was his way of assuring Mather that he would meet no political interference in getting his job done.

Steve Mather laid out a stiff set of objectives for the year the two of us expected to devote to government service before returning to the private sector. The most important need, of course, was to get the legislation passed to form a national park service and then get the service established. There were other activities tied into this goal. To persuade Congress to pass the national park service legislation we would need to build more public support for the parks. Public support would come only if we could generate more publicity for the parks and also make it easier for people to get to them. That would mean providing increased accommodations and facilities and better roads. Generating more public use was also necessary if we were to get money from Congress, which seemed reluctant to appropriate any significant funds to a park unless it was being used by a lot of people. Meantime, we would have to protect the areas already included in the park system, while at the same time trying to get Congress to add new areas that deserved to become parks. Also, there was the need to rid the parks of private holdings that were at odds with national park values.

Congress had started out 1915 in a helpful mood by establishing Rocky Mountain National Park in late January. It was not something we could take credit for, but was the result of a long-time effort by Enos Mills and other leaders in the Colorado area. They had been supported by the American Civic Association and other organizations such as the General Federation of Women's Clubs. Dealing with Congress was no bed of roses, however, as Mather found out when he came up against Representative John J. Fitzgerald, chairman of the House appropriations committee, an economy-minded Brooklyn congressman who was notoriously hard on witnesses.

Fitzgerald was overseer of the Sundry Civil Bill, a catch-all for miscellaneous parts of Interior and other departments that did not fall within the oversight of any particular congressional committee. Salaries for the national park staff and funds for road building and other construction had to be provided annually in the Sundry Civil Bill. When Mather prepared his budget, some senior bureau chiefs advised him to pad the estimates by one-third, knowing that the appropriations committee would arbitrarily cut it back. But Mather insisted on handling estimates for the national parks exactly the way he approached his finances in private business. "I'm not going to ask for more money than I need, and I'm going to spend the money as my estimate says I should," he argued.

Too late he learned that the Interior experts were right. Fitzgerald and the appropriations committee drastically cut his budget. He ran into a further problem in a provision established by Senator Irvine Lenroot of Wisconsin requiring special enabling legislation from Congress before appropriating more than ten thousand dollars for the maintenance or protection of Rocky Mountain National Park and which Lenroot later got Congress to apply to all new national parks.

Mather soon had another clash with "the system" when he sought to improve the old Tioga road from Mono Lake to Yosemite National Park. Two major expositions were to take place later in the year in San Francisco and San Diego, and they could draw several thousand people to Yosemite. Tioga was the only access to the park from the eastern side of the High Sierra. The toll road had been carved out of

Merced River, Yosemite National Park, 1917. Author, second from left; W. B. Lewis, Yosemite superintendent, at right. Albright collection.

the steep canyon walls in the 1880s to tap a gold mine, but it had fallen into a dangerous state of disrepair since the mining company that owned it had gone bankrupt. Mather discovered that government funds could not be used to repair a private road, so he decided that the government should buy the rights, which the owners were willing to sell for about fifteen thousand dollars.

"We've simply got to have that road," Mather told me.

"But the House has already finished its national park appropriations for this year," I explained, "so I'm afraid the road will have to wait."

"It can't wait," he insisted. "I'll buy the road rights myself and give them to the government." But he found out from Interior Department legal people that he couldn't even do that without first getting authority from Congress for the government to accept the gift.

"All right, let's draw up an enabling act and I'll present it to the appropriations committee," Mather said. So the lawyers wrote a simple clause saying, "Hereafter, the Secretary of the Interior is authorized to accept donations of money, rights of lands, and rights of way in our national parks."

When Mather took it before the appropriations committee, Fitzgerald viewed the proposal with suspicion. Why would anybody want to give anything to the government? He refused to accept the enabling legislation. Mather appealed to Senator James D. Phelan of California to include in the Sundry Civil Bill, then pending in the Senate, a provision permitting gifts just to Yosemite. With support from California congressmen, Mather finally persuaded Fitzgerald to drop his opposition. Mather got the Sierra Club, the Modesto, California, Chamber of Commerce, and a few of his wealthy California friends to put up half of the $15,500 purchase price. He contributed the rest himself and the road became a part of Yosemite.

Mather had found out soon after arriving that coping with the national parks presented an incredible variety of situations, including some that could provide a bit of humor. One morning three Blackfeet Indians from Montana presented themselves at Secretary Lane's office. The translator with them explained that the gentlemen wanted to protest the use of white man's names for mountains, rivers, and lakes in Glacier National Park. The Secretary sent them to Mather.

The three arranged themselves around Mather's desk in their beaded costumes and feathered war bonnets, and the interpreter introduced them: Wolf Plume, Bird Rattlers, and Curly Bear. (The fourth member of their party, Many Tail Feathers Coming Over the Hill, had taken ill and was unable to come.) Mather introduced Robert B. Marshall, chief geographer of the U.S. Geological Survey, who had been working with us. As an expert map maker, he might be able to help them.

Marshall explained that we had decided not to use the Indian names for the various places because people would not be able to pronounce or spell them, and that the nearest we could come would be translations such as "Almost a Dog Mountain." But he assured them that whenever possible, we would use English versions of the Indian names rather than name them after white men.

Then they got down to the name that had really been bothering them: Lake McDermott. Marshall explained that the Indian name for that particular lake translated "Jealous Woman's Lake," which we did not like. But he promised that we would change it from McDermott. And we did. It became Swiftcurrent Lake.

As they prepared to leave, Mather bade each man goodbye by name, then said with a grin: "Come to think of it, all of you have names that are English translations." The Indians chuckled delightedly as they left the office.

There had not been a conference of superintendents since 1912, and Mather decided that calling one now would serve a number of purposes. He could get acquainted with the heads or custodians of the national parks who were an unknown quantity to him. He could also get to know the major concessioners, and representatives of the railroads that served the parks. Some of the leading conservationists and public advocates would be invited, along with representatives of the Forest Service, Geological Survey, two California members of Congress, the superintendents or custodians of eleven national parks and four national monuments, and two army officers who still had responsibility for Yellowstone National Park.

We scheduled the conference for March 1915, and decided to hold it in Berkeley so that the participants could spend a day at the big Panama-Pacific Exposition in San Francisco. Mather arranged for the delegates to be housed at the Sigma Chi fraternity house (which he had helped to finance as an alumni member of the fraternity). The meetings would be held in the University of California chemistry building until the final day, when they would move to the Panama-Pacific Exposition.

Those of us based in Washington gathered with Mather in Chicago and made the trip west in a special Pullman car appropriately named "Calzona," a combination of California and Arizona. For the entire three-day train ride, Mather held talk sessions, learning all he could and listening to the Washington bureaucrats' ideas for dealing with park problems. I, too, picked up a great deal of information as I sat in on all of the sessions.

I found out that Major General Hugh L. Scott, U.S. Army chief of staff, was in another car en route to Colorado. I introduced myself to him, and took him to our car to meet Mather, and until we reached Colorado, Scott stayed in our car and participated in our meetings. Mather took advantage of the opportunity to talk with him about national park problems, and was surprised when the general mentioned that with war having started in Europe, he could think of better uses for his troops than taking care of Yellowstone (the only place where troops were still used for managing a park).

We all stopped off in San Diego, where another exposition was in progress, and Mather used the opportunity to win some friends for the parks. Then he went on to Los Angeles, where he urged southern California businessmen who were park enthusiasts to cooperate with northern Californians in raising capital to make it possible for a concessioner to provide food and lodging in Yosemite for the visitors he hoped to be attracting to the park.

The conference of superintendents produced no great policy decisions, but it did provide Mather with valuable information about natural resources and administrative problems. He had invited a number of natural scientists from other government agencies, because he wanted to get them involved in helping to protect the park resources. Realizing the intensity of opposition in Congress to adding large bureaus, Mather was advocating a national parks agency that would have only a small administrative staff, and then would "beg, borrow, or steal" experts from other bureaus to handle specific matters in the parks. He would get the Corps of Engineers to do the road building, for instance, and have the Biological Survey do the wildlife management, and get the Geological Survey and other bureaus to help in their areas of expertise.

The meeting also helped us to identify some of the staunch friends of the parks. One of the two women who participated, Mrs. John D. Sherman, conservation chairman of the General Federation of Women's Clubs, told how the Federation's two million members were working for the establishment of a national park service. They had played a part in getting Congress to pass legislation for a Rocky Mountain National Park. The Federation women of Arizona were working to get a Grand Canyon National Park established. "We want more national parks," Mrs. Sherman told the conference, "and we are going to keep right on working for them."

Contact with the park superintendents during the conference led Mather to conclude that some personnel changes were needed. Some of the superintendents were political appointees who had no qualifications for running parks. But to remove them, he would have to find a way to break through the system that allowed influential members of Congress to control some of the field appointments.

The conference also gave Mather a chance to assess Mark Daniels, whom Miller had named general superintendent and landscape engineer of national parks. Being set up in San Francisco, Daniels had not had direct contact with Mather, and although he showed himself to be a good salesman for the parks, he appeared to have little administrative capability.

When Mather had told me of his decision to hold the conference in Berkeley, I had been overjoyed at the prospect of seeing Grace. But Mather set such a breakneck pace for me all during that week, that I saw her only two or three times. She assured me, though, that she knew how important the work was, and her understanding attitude was very comforting, because Mather's activities, and my part in them, gathered even more steam as time went on.

He spent much of his energy for the next few months promoting the parks, especially working with his friends on eastern newspapers and getting to know some of the leading magazine editors, a number of whom became strong boosters of national parks. One of his first actions after taking the job had been to persuade Robert Sterling Yard, a friend from Mather's days on the *New York Sun*, to give up his job as editor of the Sunday magazine of the *New York Herald* and come to Washington to head up a national parks information office. Never mind that no government positions or funding were available for Yard or a publicity staff. Mather arranged for the Geological Survey (one of the bureaus of the Department of the Interior) to hire Yard for thirty dollars per month and detail him to Mather, who agreed to pay the rest of Yard's six-thousand-dollar-a-year salary himself.

Mather's own promotional efforts included taking an elite group of opinion makers on a wilderness trip in the California Sierra Nevada. Bob Marshall had helped survey both Sequoia and Yosemite national parks for the Geological Survey, and Mather asked him to plan the trip.

It was an imposing party of men who assembled in Visalia, California, on July 14, 1915, to start the journey into Sequoia National Park. They included Frederick H. Gillett of Massachusetts, ranking Republican on the appropriations committee and future speaker of the

The July 1915 Sequoia party. 1. Stephen Mather; 2. Gilbert Grosvenor; 3. Mark Daniels; 4. E. O. McCormick; 5. Clyde LeRoy Seavey; 6. Frederick H. Gillett; 7. Burton Holmes; 8. Henry Fairchild Osborn; 9. Emerson Hough; 10. George Stewart; 11. author. Albright collection.

House, Burton Holmes, the noted travel lecturer, Gilbert Grosvenor, editor of the *National Geographic*, Henry Fairfield Osborn, president of the American Museum of Natural History, Ernest O. McCormick, vice-president of the Southern Pacific Railroad, Emerson Hough and Peter Scott Macfarlane, both popular novelists and magazine writers, and Ben M. Maddox, owner and publisher of two influential California newspapers. Marshall, Daniels, and I, along with Mather, served as hosts.

Mather spared no expense for the outing. Each person had a new sleeping bag and air mattress, and each was assigned a horse. Pack mules were laden with supplies, including the fresh fruits and fine foods that expert Chinese trail cook Ty Sing served up.

Mather wanted the group to appreciate the magnificent Sierra scenery, but he also wanted them to learn something of the issues needing attention: private holdings within national parks that did not belong there and should be removed, and some public domain land that ought to be brought into national park status.

We camped amidst the Giant Sequoias (*sequoia gigantea*) in Giant Forest, which was at that time a private holding within Sequoia

National Park. We went on up to the summit of 14,494-foot-high Mount Whitney, highest peak in the continental United States (at that time under the jurisdiction of the Forest Service), then down to the eastern side of the Sierra to Bishop, where I had been born. We went up into the Mammoth country and across the Tioga Pass into Yosemite National Park, dedicating the opening of the Tioga Road on July 28. Even though I had lived in Bishop, such a short way off, I had never been to Yosemite Valley.

As the youngest member of the party, I was "elected" to pitch tents, set up camp, even inflate some of the air mattresses. Despite the twenty-odd-year difference in our ages, it was all I could do to keep up with Mather, who was always rushing off ahead of everyone to climb a canyon wall or explore some new trail.

As a promotional event, the trip was a success, and made firm park advocates of all the participants. It was Grosvenor's first trip west, and he was so taken with Giant Forest that he provided twenty thousand dollars in National Geographic Society funds to supplement a fifty-thousand-dollar congressional appropriation to buy the land and add it to the park. The trip also convinced most of the writers and politicians of the need for getting a national park service act through Congress. They agreed to support the expansion of General Grant National Park to include the Kings Canyon area.

In an article for the *Saturday Evening Post* Hough wrote that the Kings Canyon country "is too big for any man or men to own. . . . it belongs to humanity, as it is, unchanged and never to know change." Congressman Gillett also became a parks convert and gave a good deal of political support to park needs in future years.

When the Sierra trip was finished, Mather and I worked our way through most of the existing parks before returning to Washington. It was the quickest way to become familiar with each of them. McCormick gave us a ride as far as Seattle with him in the plush parlor car he had as a vice-president of the Southern Pacific Railroad. We transferred to an automobile at Klamath Falls, Oregon, and drove to Crater Lake.

William Gladstone Steel, who had dedicated his life to establishing Crater Lake as a park, and had been named superintendent, showed us around. The beauty of the place was breathtaking, but we were appalled at the condition of the concession facilities and paucity of park development. In the thirteen years that it had been a national park, practically no funds had been available for its improvement. Conditions were so difficult that few visitors were venturing into the park.

From Seattle we went to Mount Rainier, the fifth national park, established in 1899 after a five-year campaign led by five scientific and conservation groups: the American Association for the Advancement of Science, the National Geographic Society, the Geological Society of America, the Sierra Club, and the Appalachian Mountain Club. We found a good lodge at Longmire Spring, built by the Chicago, Milwaukee, and St. Paul Railroad, but at Paradise Valley, in the heart of the alpine part of the park, there was only a crude tent camp.

Mather decided to try to get the leaders in nearby Seattle and Tacoma (both of the cities claimed Mount Rainier National Park as "theirs") together and cooperatively back the formation of a concession for Paradise Valley. To promote the idea, he invited civic leaders of both cities to go on an eighty-five-mile pack trip around Mount Rainier National Park. Mather also visited Tacoma and Seattle and persuaded the leaders to join in forming the Rainier National Park Company to finance construction of an inn at Paradise Valley.

Continuing our inspection tour, Mather and I made a brief trip to the Olympic Peninsula to visit Mount Olympus National Monument. It was under the jurisdiction of the Department of Agriculture's Forest Service, but conservationists were advocating that it be designated a national park, and we felt we should take a look as long as we were so near.

We timed our arrival in Colorado so Mather could attend the ceremonial dedication of Rocky Mountain National Park on September 4. Enos Mills, the "father" of this park that had been created out of national forest lands, told us how important it was that Interior acquire the adjacent scenically majestic forest area that ought to be a part of the national park. The Forest Service, which had failed in its attempt to prevent establishment of Rocky Mountain National Park, had succeeded in excluding this vital area almost as large as the park itself.

We went on by train to Cody, Wyoming, then took a stage to Yellowstone. Along the road we overtook a group of autos struggling along through the mud toward the park. The group had started in Denver and were trying to blaze the first portion of a proposed park-to-park highway. Their destination was Mammoth Hot Springs, where Mather and I were to attend a conference on park highways.

Mather announced at the conference that a new National Park-to-Park Highway Association had been formed and that it would push for establishment of a permanent circle highway to link most of the national parks in the Rocky Mountain, North Cascade, Olympic, and Sierra ranges. The idea was for the highway to go from Denver to Rocky Mountain National Park, on to Yellowstone, Glacier, Mount Rainier, Crater Lake, Yosemite, and Sequoia, then east through Salt Lake City and back to Denver, a total of 3,500 miles.

Acting superintendent of Yellowstone Colonel L. M. Brett had participated in the Berkeley superintendents conference, and we discussed with him our mutual interests in the administration of the park. Brett was a distinguished soldier, and had won the Medal of Honor for valor in the Indian wars. In addition to the issue of whether the army should remove its troops from the park, there was an ongoing controversy over access by automobiles. Yellowstone had only been opened to motorized vehicles on August 1, and strict regulations were in place to prevent conflict with the horse-drawn stages and covered wagons. The automobile clubs had been pushing Congress to allow cars to enter the park, but the Yellowstone Park Transportation Company had opposed the move, arguing that the roads were impassable in some places, and that too many autos or buses would frighten the horses, thus threatening the safety of the visitors. The answer seemed to be for the mechanically-powered vehicles to follow the horse-drawn stages at scheduled intervals, but not be allowed to pass them or to go in the opposite direction. But Mather formed a committee consisting of Brett, Bob Marshall, and the secretary and manager of the American Automobile Association, A. G. Batchelder, to work out a better solution.

Blackfeet chiefs meeting with Stephen Mather to protest white names for Glacier topography, 1915. Author standing third from right. Albright collection.

The final leg of our parks inspection trip took us into northwest Montana to Glacier National Park. We arrived in time for the first snowfall of the season, just as the park was preparing to close down for the winter. Mather had planned a rugged three-day pack trip across the Continental Divide, but we were advised against it because of the heavy snow. Mather, however, discovered that an old Chicago friend, Frederic A. Delano, had started out over Gunsight Pass with his two young daughters only a few hours earlier. Mather did not want to be outdone, or hear later that he had been intimidated by weather that had not stopped Delano and the two girls. So he insisted on going ahead.

It was rough going, but we reached the top of the divide by nightfall and stayed at Sperry Chalet. The next day we found the chalet where we had planned to spend the night partially destroyed by a rampaging grizzly bear, so we went on to the Going-to-the-Sun chalet on Lake St. Mary. On the third day we came out on the east side of the Rockies.

When we tried to see more of Glacier by automobile, the roads were so poor we got stuck. We concluded that while the park's accommodations, built by Great Northern, were fine, its roads and trails were terrible, and that the park badly needed a new headquarters building as well. Mather found that the best site for the headquarters was privately owned and not for sale. So he located a site nearby that was about to be sold at foreclosure, purchased it, and gave it to the park.

Mather returned to Washington more convinced than ever that despite the opposition of some preservationists, the parks desperately needed more roads and tourist facilities so that they could be more widely used. At that time in the development of a national park system, we would not be able to get the necessary support of the American public or of the Congress unless more people were able to visit the parks. Mather and Yard intensified their efforts to publicize the parks.

Gilbert Grosvenor dedicated most of the April 1916 issue of the *National Geographic* to the national parks. A chain of midwest newspapers ran a series of articles on the parks after Mather paid a visit to their owner, a longtime friend from Chicago. And Hough began writing articles on national parks for the *Saturday Evening Post*.

In November, Mark Daniels resigned to return to architectural practice. Instead of hiring a replacement in San Francisco, Mather changed the position to general superintendent of National Parks, to be stationed in Washington. He wanted Bob Marshall for the job, and arranged with the Geological Survey to detail him to the position. (It should be noted that he was not the Robert Marshall who explored the Alaska Arctic and helped found the Wilderness Society.) Mather asked me to become assistant general superintendent, but I declined, reminding him that I still planned to return to California in less than two months to start my law practice. The job went to Joseph J. Cotter, who had been a secretary to Lane.

Later that month, Mather and I had a long talk about our year's efforts. We had made some discernible progress, but his larger objectives still remained to be accomplished. Most important, we had not yet persuaded Congress to pass a law establishing a national park service. He told me he had made the decision to stay on for at least another six months or maybe a year, to see if he could get the job done. I found myself agreeing to remain with him.

I dreaded telling Grace about this rash decision to stay on in Washington for a while. We had been planning to get married around the first of the year, and I had hoped to be finished with my work in Washington and be ready to start my law career in California. Grace said she was willing to wait.

Early in December 1915, Mather asked me to accompany him on a trip to look at Hot Springs Reservation (later named a national park) in Arkansas. "And after you get back, why don't you plan to take a couple of weeks off and get married over the holidays," Mather suggested. "I'll be in Chicago and things will be slow in Washington." So I quickly wrote to Grace, and she set the date for December 23.

On the way back to Washington from Arkansas I spent two days visiting the Chickamauga and Chattanooga battlefield parks, then being run by the Army. As I walked over the ground and relived some of those famous battles, I became convinced that some day these and other historic battlefields really ought to be a part of the national park system.

On December 23, 1915, in the Berkeley First Presbyterian Church, Grace and I were married. She was beautiful in her white satin and lace, and I guess I must have been a vision of nineteenth-century sartorial elegance in the twenty-five-year-old dress suit Professor Miller had given me before going to Washington. It was the first time I'd had occasion to wear it.

Our train trip back to Washington was enthralling to Grace, who had never been outside California. Our honeymoon was a four-day stop at El Tovar Hotel at Grand Canyon. Even then I mixed in some business, talking with L. C. Way, the Forest Service ranger in charge of the Department of Agriculture's Grand Canyon National Monument. We spent one of our days there mushing through the snow to visit with Way and his wife. Grace, like many native Californians, had never seen snow before. She loved the adventure and enjoyed being with the ranger and his wife in their rustic but cozy cabin. Way was indeed a fine man, and I remember thinking that he was the kind of fellow who would make a good national park superintendent.

On the train headed for Washington, I pulled out of my bag a guide book the Geological Survey had published. It had details of all of the geological formations and some history of the entire train route from Chicago to San Francisco. Unfortunately, it had the mile-by-mile trip listed in east-to-west order. So I had a terrible time trying to read the book to Grace backwards! Grace then found out what kind of a man she had married, for during the next two days we sat on the observation platform in the January cold and wind while I read the entire book to her and pointed out the geological formations as we passed.

Wedding of Grace Noble and Horace Albright, December 23, 1915, Berkeley. Albright collection.

3

The Campaign for a Park Service

THE MOST IMPORTANT PIECE OF UNFINISHED BUSINESS FOR MATHER AND ME WAS GETTING CONGRESS TO PASS LEGISLATION to create the National Park Service. Support for a park service had been growing for several years among various organizations and individuals, and with the tireless energy Mather had been putting into promoting it since arriving on the scene a year earlier, the idea was now gathering momentum.

At the beginning of 1916, the need for a park service was greater than ever. The Interior Department had jurisdiction over twelve national parks already established by congressional actions, and bills creating three additional parks were expected to be voted on soon. There were also nineteen national monuments under Interior's jurisdiction, and together with the parks and two reservations they constituted a 4.6 million-acre "national park system" that really was no system at all. The vast domain was being given only the barest custodial care and no coordinated administration. Yellowstone, the largest and most famous, was still under the jurisdiction of the War Department, which only recently had pulled army troops out of Yosemite and Sequoia national parks and turned those parks over to the Secretary of the Interior.

In Washington only two people were officially listed in the budget as working full-time on the national parks and monuments: general superintendent Marshall and editorial assistant Bob Yard. Though

Mather and I devoted almost all of our attention to park issues, we were listed as giving them only three-fourths of our time. Another twenty-six people were listed as devoting varying amounts of time, from departmental assistant attorney W. Bertrand Acker at three-fourths time to Interior Secretary Lane, who was supposed to give parks one-thirtieth of his time, and Amos Hadley, the departmental supply clerk, who was listed as giving the parks one-fortieth of his time, budgeted at $56.25 per year. The total Fiscal 1917 budget request for the Washington administrative work on national parks was only twenty-four thousand dollars. The entire field force for all the national parks and monuments totaled only ninety-nine, to take care of the more than three hundred thousand visitors. There was no trained staff to deal with on-site problems. Most of the small staff of rangers in the parks and monuments were local residents who were employed in the parks only during the summer season.

Members of Congress were more interested than ever in adding national parks, and during the year of 1916, bills were introduced to add sixteen new national parks. Support was strong for Lassen Volcanic, Hawaii, and Mount McKinley national parks, and for Sieur de Monts National Monument (later named Acadia National Park) in Maine.

Herbert Quick, a writer for the *Saturday Evening Post*, wrote in a 1916 issue about a member of Congress who had wanted some information about the national parks. Looking through all the ready reference books about who takes care of what in the government, he found references for the Canadian Commission of Parks, but no mention of a United States Bureau of National Parks or National Park Service. Finally the congressman wrote to the Department of Commerce: "I am in doubt to whom I should apply: but I find no name of Park Service in the Congressional Directory. Will you not help me?" It was from the Commerce Department that he learned that there actually was a general superintendent of national parks and that he was in the Department of the Interior.

Quick also wrote of the dilemma of park superintendents, who got no help from managers of other parks or from Washington when confronted with problems of sanitation, park engineering, landscaping, game preservation, forestry, planting or handling of concessioners. He wrote: "Congress has left the laws in such a state that it is illegal for the superintendents to leave their parks. It has left each park independent of every other park and forbidden the employees of one to venture into any other." *

While things were not quite that outlandish, the situation could well have been as Quick described if we had followed a strict reading of the existing mishmash of rules imposed by various congressional appropriation measures. He concluded his article by noting that friends of the national parks all over the nation wanted Congress to pass the legislation then before it to establish a coordinated National Park Service. "They want this Service embodied in the law," he wrote, "so that it may not be destroyed by the next Secretary of the Interior — as it easily might be." He added that the friends of the parks want the progress already made under Mather ". . . crystalized in law, and made certain of continuance by the unified management which is now so deplorably lacking, and always must be under the present rules."

Foremost among those friends of the national parks were the American Civic Association, which since 1910 had been leading the lobbying for a National Park Service, along with the General Federation of Women's Clubs and the Sierra Club. A number of individuals had devoted time and effort to the cause, including the noted landscape architect Frederick Law Olmsted, Jr., then a member of the federal government's Commission of Fine Arts, whose father had helped set the management philosophy for Yosemite in 1868 when it had still been a state park.

Bills to establish a Bureau of National Parks had been introduced in both the Senate and the House year after year between 1911 and 1915. Senator Reed Smoot of Utah, and Representative John E. Raker of California, had been prominent in the push for legislation. But no bill had ever succeeded in getting out of committee.

In 1911, the bills for a national park bureau had not gone anywhere because the parks had few friends in Congress. Efforts to establish a National Park Service were opposed by the Forest Service, whose officials considered national parks a threat to the national forest domain, and blocked early attempts to pass Park Service legislation. The opposition of Forest Service Chief Gifford Pinchot continued to carry weight even after he was ousted in 1910 following a fierce battle with the Secretary of the Interior of that time, Richard A. Ballinger. Presi-

---

* The *Saturday Evening Post*, June 24, 1916.

dent Taft fired both Pinchot and Ballinger, and when Taft replaced Ballinger with Walter Fisher, many people feared that Fisher would oppose the Park Service bill that had first been introduced in 1911, for he was a close friend of Pinchot. Instead, Fisher turned out to be a strong supporter of the legislation, as did President Taft.

At the end of 1915 and in early 1916 a group of us were meeting fairly regularly for talks on the substance of the new bill to be introduced, and on political strategies for getting it passed. Most of the meetings were at the F Street home of Congressman William "Billy" Kent from California, who in 1908 had given the federal government the land for Muir Woods National Monument. Kent, McFarland of the American Civic Association, Marshall, and Yard were usually at the meetings, and I attended representing Mather. Others at most of the meetings included Olmsted, Grosvenor, Quick, and Hough. Enos Mills also participated in at least one of the meetings.

We felt that although Raker had introduced the bills of 1912 and 1913, it would be better for someone else to introduce the bill we were drafting, because of a sensitive situation involving Raker. Some of his fellow Democrats were advocating including a few undesirable provisions in the bill, and he was having trouble within his party because of it. Also, Raker was bitterly disliked by the House minority leader, James R. Mann, who happened to come from Mather's own district in Illinois. Representative Kent was an Independent, and a good friend of Republican Mann. So although Raker introduced his own bill once again, he gave his blessing to Kent, who agreed to introduce the bill we were drafting.

Some historians incorrectly credit Olmsted with writing the bill. He did not do so. Olmsted was, however, responsible for the wording of the governing sentence, and contributed his ideas on other matters of policy. We particularly wanted the bill to carry a clear definition of what the Park Service should be. We were well aware of the inherent conflicts between use and preservation, but the political reality was that the issue could not be settled in an "organic act" because Congress would never agree to close off enormous chunks of land and exclude them from public use. So we had to find a way to provide for use.

Olmsted had written in November 1915 to the American Civic Association to comment on a draft of the bill they had sent to him. The language Olmsted used in his letter was somewhat stilted, but it articulated the underlying dual purpose of the bill better than anybody else had been able to do. So we agreed to have the Kent bill include Olmsted's language: that the purpose of the proposed National Park Service "is to conserve the scenery and the natural and historic objects and the wild life therein and to provide for the enjoyment of the same in such manner and by such means as will leave them unimpaired for the enjoyment of future generations." †

There was a good deal of discussion over whether to include another idea that Olmsted had put forth in earlier bills, that of establishing an independent commission to actually develop policy for the national parks. Olmsted's idea had been for a small, permanent, independent "board of overseers" that would make systematic inspections of parks, examine the effects of the administration of the parks, and report to the Secretary of the Interior. There was some backing for including in the current bill a less powerful board that would just advise the Secretary on policy. But it turned out that neither of the concepts was included. We wanted to make it as short and uncluttered as possible, while at the same time giving the National Park Service enough general power to establish regulations so it would not be necessary for its director to go back to Congress for new authority every year or so.

We debated long and heatedly over whether grazing should be allowed in parks. Congressman Kent had many ranchers in his California district and had a ranch of his own in Nevada. He also sincerely felt that cattle and sheep grazing would actually benefit the parks by keeping down the fire hazard. Mather was strongly opposed, but tended to take the long view. To him the important thing for the present was to get a National Park Service Act passed; the grazing provision was something we could eventually get rid of.

We also tried to figure out how to provide for visitors' needs such as lodging and food. Although we made no specific provisions for roads and buildings, the draft bill gave the Secretary of the Interior the power to grant leases and permits for the use of park land "for the accommodation of visitors."

By April things began to look promising. The House committee on public lands, chaired by Scott Ferris of Oklahoma, held hearings on Raker's bill and on Kent's bill. Kent and Raker both served on the

† Public Law No. 235, 64th Congress.

committee. After giving a routine defense of his own bill, mostly to keep his constituents happy, Raker put his support behind the Kent bill.

Some committee members questioned Mather on the wording in the bill that could be interpreted as placing all of the national monuments under the Park Service. Chairman Ferris commented that the Department of Agriculture had raised some strenuous objections over giving up the twelve monuments their Forest Service administered, especially the Grand Canyon. Mather assured him that the wording should be changed to refer only to those monuments "now under the jurisdiction of the Department of the Interior." But under questioning by the chairman, Mather admitted that there was talk among some park supporters of wanting Mount Olympus, Grand Canyon, and Lassen national monuments, then under Agriculture, to be made national parks. In fact, a bill was already before Congress to change Lassen's status to a national park.

When the questioning turned to grazing rights in the parks, Mather had to swallow hard and admit that it would be allowed under the proposed bill "in those areas where it would not interfere with the campers' privileges."

When asked about the provisions for charging entry fees for automobiles, Mather said:

> I think the principle of having the parks free is the proper one, and we hope that the time will come when we can make them free to motorists as well as to others. But in the meantime, when Congress has not gotten to the point where it will make as large appropriations as we will need, we have got to depend in a measure on the revenues that we will derive from the parks themselves.

Mather made use of the hearings to let Congress know of the accomplishments that had been achieved in educating the public about the parks, in working to improve and expand the concession activity to accommodate more visitors and to make the national parks become the public laboratories of nature study for the nation.

The ranking Democrat on the committee, Edward T. Taylor of Colorado, quizzed Mather on the issue that was perhaps the biggest obstacle to the bill's passage. He asked: "Can you assure us so that we can say to members of the House that this is not a carte blanche to go on with no limits on these expenditures, but that the force will be held down to a pretty reasonable number?" He reminded Mather of the fight that had taken place in Congress the previous year when the members had forced the Rocky Mountain National Park bill advocates to accept an amendment providing that no more than ten thousand dollars could be spent without a specific authorization from Congress. Mather replied that twenty thousand dollars was all the appropriation the National Park Service would need. This issue continued to worry Taylor, and when Marshall testified, Taylor told him: "The great stumbling block is that the members of Congress fear you are building up another bureau here that will start in a small way and soon get up to a big appropriation."

Representative Irvine L. Lenroot of Wisconsin, a self-appointed watchdog over government spending, shared Taylor's concern and voted against the bill. But most of the committee, including Taylor, who became a supporter after listening to Mather's and Marshall's assurances, favored it. The bill was endorsed by the public land committee by a large margin.

Then the avalanche of publicity Mather and Yard had been generating began to have some results. The April issue of *National Geographic,* devoted mostly to national parks, was placed on the desk of every member of Congress. The *Saturday Evening Post* carried several articles and editorials on national parks and the need for a National Park Service to be authorized by Congress. We released *National Parks Portfolio,* a collection of pamphlets bound in buckram, which Yard had put together to reach a select audience who could travel and support the parks. The Forest Service complained about the book because it included a pamphlet on the Grand Canyon National Monument, which was under Forest Service jurisdiction.

The portfolio had been too expensive to come out of the small national park budget available to Mather. So he contributed the first five thousand of its forty-eight-thousand-dollar cost himself, then got seventeen western railroads to put up the rest. Volunteers from the General Federation of Women's Clubs were solicited to produce a mailing list of 275,000 from the memberships of men's and women's clubs, universities, social registers, business directories, and scientific and professional societies, culling the list for duplicates. Of course, copies were sent to all the members of Congress. The *Portfolio* was a great success, generating newspaper editorials and articles, and letters poured in from those who received it, complimenting the department. It later went into a second edition, paid for by the government, and when it went into a third edition and was sold for one dollar a copy, it became a best-seller.

Despite Mather's intense efforts to rally support, the bill got bogged down in Congress. Representative William Stafford of Wisconsin, who routinely put up vigorous opposition to any attempts to launch new government bureaus, seemed to have the bill stalled in the House. But with the help of Representative Taylor and some lobbying by Mc-Farland and other citizens, an amended Kent bill was passed by the House on July 1. Language was adopted to limit the new National Park Service to administrative expenditures of $19,500 a year, which were to be used to provide a director with a salary of $4,500 a year, an assistant director at $2,500, one chief clerk at $2,000, one drafts-man at $1,800, and a messenger at $600, plus a maximum of $8,100 for other assistants.

With the House bill passed, proceedings began on the Senate floor on the companion bill which Senator Smoot had introduced, and within a short time it too was passed, but it included some variations from the House version. One of the main differences was a provision designed to accommodate Senator Clarence D. Clark of Wyoming, who strongly opposed any grazing being allowed in Yellowstone. So Smoot's bill did not provide for grazing.

Further complicating matters, it was an election year, and many members of Congress were off campaigning in their home states most Fridays through Mondays. When they were in session they had their hands full with priorities other than the national parks bill. It appeared that we would have to wait until the next session of Congress for final action.

Frustrated by the lack of action around Washington, Mather orga-nized a promotional trip to Yellowstone for a group of dignitaries that included Assistant Attorney General and Mrs. Huston Thompson. Mather asked me to go to Denver and arrange for two of the big White touring cars to be sent to meet the party in Thermopolis, Wy-oming for the drive through Cody to the park.

One of Mather's reasons for taking the trip was to address a meet-ing of the Park-to-Park Highway Association. We also wanted to know whether the new road schedules were succeeding in keeping the mechanized stages from interfering with the horse-drawn stages. Al-though the solution was not ideal, the schedules had helped to avoid any major conflict so far.

One morning Mather and I went out behind the Canyon Hotel to check on some bears that had been frequenting the hotel garbage cans. There, sitting on a stump, was a woman about to offer some food to a black bear. We chased off the bear, and I explained to her that feeding bears was extremely dangerous. We introduced ourselves, and the woman said in a heavy Russian accent, "I am Anna Pavlova."

The great ballerina told us she had been enjoying a respite from her company's tour, and had been at Yellowstone for several days. But now she was feeling very sad because she would have to leave. It seemed that she had been forced to vacate her room at Canyon Hotel because it had been reserved by an incoming tour group. The reason for this situation was that in those days most visitors came to the park in tour groups, and the tours were arranged so that a group would spend one night at Old Faithful Inn and see the sights in that vicinity, then move to Lake Yellowstone and the Lake Hotel for one night, and then spend a night at Canyon and a night at Mammoth Hot Springs. This kept all the rooms booked ahead of time. Mather told Madame Pavlova he would see if he couldn't arrange for her to stay at Canyon a few more days, and of course, he did.

During this trip, Mather and I took Huston Thompson and the rest of his party for a drive over the new road that was being built on the twenty-five-mile stretch between Yellowstone and Jackson Lake. The lake had recently been created by a Reclamation Service dam, flooding several thousand acres of national forest. We found that the rising water level was doing considerable damage to the road. At the upper end of the lake we saw hundreds of dead trees jutting out of the water. The Reclamation people had not cleared out the trees before flooding the area, and it made a very ugly sight, especially with the low summertime level of the lake.

These disturbing sights were almost forgotten, however, as we drove on down toward Jackson Hole. It was the first time Mather and I had ever seen the spectacular panorama of the Grand Teton mountain range from the lowlands of the Snake River Valley. I had never beheld such scenery. I knew the Sierra Nevada and had climbed Mount Whitney, but here before us were the Alps of America. Mather and I were both flabbergasted, and we agreed that this whole magnificent area ought to be added to Yellowstone National Park.

We had been back in Washington only a few days when Mather left again for the West. He had arranged to take another party of distinguished guests to the Sierra to look at a proposed John Muir Trail, and to inspect the Kings Canyon area, which he was still hoping to get added to Sequoia National Park.

While Mather was in the West, I had all I could do trying to get appropriations for the existing parks and monuments. We also had bills before Congress to establish Lassen Volcanic and Hawaii national parks, and had to keep things moving on them. As general superintendent, Marshall was in the field much of the time. I kept plugging away on the National Park Service bill, hoping by some quirk of fate or good luck to get the two houses of Congress to work out the differences between their versions of the bill. But with the House and Senate in session only a few days at a time, it was just about impossible to get the conferees together.

On July 8, President Wilson signed a bill establishing Sieur de Monts National Monument. Then Congress established Hawaii National Park on August 1, and Lassen Volcanic National Park on August 9. The Lassen bill included a lot of provisions that we opposed, such as grazing, hunting, and granting leases for summer homes. With such provisions it would be little different from the national forest area which it formerly had been. Mather telegraphed me to get Secretary Lane to recommend a veto of the bill because Lassen did not come up to national park standards. But this was Representative Raker's favorite piece of legislation, and Marshall and I persuaded both Mather and Secretary Lane that a veto would earn us Raker's enmity and ruin any chance we still might have for the National Park Service bill in this session. Besides, we argued, the Lassen bill could be amended later to remove the objectionable provisions.

During most of August I kept going to the Hill, trying to find some way to get a conference set up among the six members from the two houses. It was vital to get their few differences settled so the House and Senate bills could be reconciled and the revised lesgislation be put to a vote in both houses. But the six members were never in town at the same time. So I persuaded the Senate public lands committee chairman, Henry L. Myers of Montana, and the House chairman, Representative Ferris, to come to an agreement on allowing grazing in all parks except Yellowstone, to accept the $19,500 limitation on funding, and to agree to other minor changes. Ferris and Myers finally were able to get all the members of the conference committee in town at the same time so they could convene a conference. I sat in on the conference and answered some of their questions, and they finally agreed to the compromises I had worked out with the two chairmen. The Senate quickly approved the revised bill when it came back from conference.

But we still had one more hurdle — Congressman Stafford. He seemed as adamant as ever about blocking the creation of new bureaus, so some of the prominent park supporters cooked up a scheme to lure Stafford out to the golf course on the day the conference report came up for passage. But this proved to be unnecessary, because Congressman Kent was able to persuade Stafford not to object. The measure went to the floor and was approved by voice vote. Now all that remained was for President Wilson to sign the bill into law.

Mather was deep in the Sierra mountains when the bill passed and there was no way to contact him. He and his party would be emerging from the wilderness at Visalia, California, on August 26, and I knew what a great thrill it would be for him to be greeted with the news that the bill had been signed by the President. That left less than four days to get the official document through the bureaucratic maze, onto the President's desk, and get it signed.

I persuaded congressional staff friends to speed up the process of getting the act printed on parchment, then got it hand carried to the vice president for his signature, and to the speaker of the House, before going to the President. The cabinet officer involved also had to give approval. In this case, of course, it was Secretary Lane, and to save the document from being sent to him, then back to the White House, I arranged for the Secretary to give me a note saying he approved the bill. On August 25, I went to the White House to get acquainted with the legislative clerk, Maurice Latta. I told him how Mather had worked so long and hard for the bill, and asked if he could speed things up. He said he would be glad to help, and even agreed to get me the pen the President used in signing, so I could give it to Mather.

I then went up to the Capitol and saw the enrolling clerk. He said they hadn't had any call for this legislation and the President signed bills only on certain days. As we were talking, the phone rang. I gathered from the conversation at my end that it was the White House calling and that they wanted some bill sent over to be signed. When the enrolling clerk hung up, I asked politely if that was the White House, and the clerk said yes, adding that they wanted the army appropriations bill sent over. I said, "Be a good fellow and stick the

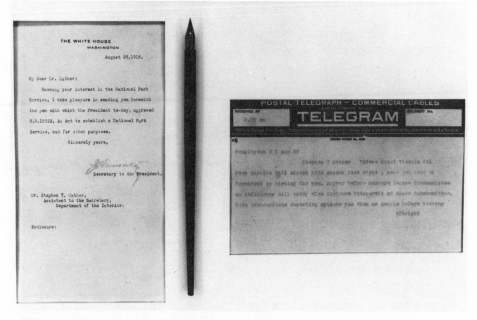

The pen which President Wilson used to sign the legislation creating the National Park
Service, and the telegram sent to Stephen Mather. National Park Service.

Parks Act in the same envelope." He did, and I hopped a street car
and got to Mr. Latta's office before the bill arrived.

Latta said he would see if he could get it to the President some time
during the evening. I was going to be at a friend's house for dinner,
so I gave him the phone number where I could be reached. About
9:00 P.M. the phone rang and it was Latta, who told me: "the President signed the bill." I went right down town to the postal telegraph
office and sent Mather a night letter which he would receive when he
checked in at the Palace Hotel in Visalia: "PARK SERVICE BILL SIGNED
NINE O'CLOCK LAST NIGHT. HAVE PEN USED BY PRESIDENT IN SIGNING
FOR YOU."

UP VERNAL FALLS.

4

Troubles for the Leader

THE TRIUMPHANT MOOD THAT SURROUNDED PASSAGE OF THE PARK
SERVICE ACT FADED QUICKLY as we began the enormous task of trans-
lating that hard-won document into an organization. Historians who
place the beginning of the National Park Service in 1916 are wrong if
they assume that approval of the Act on August 25 magically brought
the Park Service into being. It remained little more than a piece of
paper for almost eight months, because it was April before Congress
appropriated any funds at all to start the Service.

While setting the record straight, I should point out that a search
of the archives will not turn up any such title as "National Park Service Organic Act," as it is commonly known. The Act has no official
short title, its only name being the descriptive heading: "AN ACT to
establish a National Park Service, and for other purposes." *

The entire act occupies only two pages, because no attempt was
made to load all the management rules onto it. The act simply provided for creation of a National Park Service, which it empowered to
promote and regulate the use of national parks and monuments. Con-
sequently, the few amendments made over the past half-century have
not changed the sense of the law. Such elements as the salary limitation of $4,500 per year for the Director of the National Park Service
have since been removed, of course, as has the limitation of $21,500
as the total that could be spent annually for salaries of Park Service
employees in the District of Columbia.

* Public Law No. 235, 64th Congress.

Section 1 of the act created the Park Service, designated salaries, and outlined the fundamental purpose of the Service. Section 2 gave the Director, under the supervision of the Secretary of the Interior, the power to manage and control the parks and other areas that Congress might later create. Section 3 authorized the Secretary to make and publish such rules and regulations as are deemed necessary for the use and management of the parks, and allowed him to grant permits and leases for periods of up to twenty years, provided they do not interfere with free access by the public. This section also allowed grazing in all parks except Yellowstone, the provision it had been necessary for us to accept in order to get Congressman Kent's support. And Section 4 provided that the act would not modify provisions of a 1901 law relating to rights of way through certain parks, reservations and other public lands.

Until we could get an appropriation from Congress, there was no way we could actually organize the new Park Service, and we would have to continue to operate essentially as we had before. Also, the legislation had not put an end to any of the major problems we had been trying to solve, and most of Mather's objectives still remained to be attained.

After receiving the good news about passage of the act, Mather wrote from California asking me to join him in late September at Glacier National Park for a pack trip with a small group from the Sierra Club and the Prairie Club of Chicago. He suggested I bring Grace along and make it the honeymoon we had missed because of my constant work. Grace had never even been on a horse, but she got along splendidly, and was treated like the queen of the pack trip.

When we finished looking things over at Glacier, Mather returned to California, but sent me to Yellowstone to check on the transition from military to civilian control. The army had for several years been increasingly interested in being relieved of the responsibility of taking care of Yellowstone. With the war in Europe heating up, troops were needed for military duty. The army withdrawal had been agreed to, and now a number of details (for instance, the Corps of Engineers wanted to retain control of bridge and road maintenance) needed to be worked out.

So Grace and I went down to Yellowstone and I saw to it that the army turned over to the Park Service not only the barracks and the old fort, but also the hospital and all its equipment. I also made certain that none of the buildings was dismantled. We arranged for Colonel Brett, who had commanded the army detachment in the park and had served as superintendent, to stay on for a while during the transition, and for the army to give discharges to some noncommissioned officers who wanted to remain as park rangers.

After the plan was well under way, Congressman Fitzgerald heard about it and was furious because we had bypassed him. He was so enraged that he announced he would demand the troops be returned to the park. Having Fitzgerald's guns aimed at us was bad enough, but then Mather got into trouble with Montana Senator Thomas J. Walsh and other Montana and Wyoming members of Congress because of his new concession policy.

Mather viewed competition among concessioners as the wrong policy for national parks because he thought it was duplicative and uneconomical and led to inferior standards as operators of concessions tried to reduce costs to beat out competitors. When Mather had taken over the parks, Yellowstone had had one concessioner running the five hotels, two lunch stations, and one stagecoach line, two others running permanent camp systems, another two concessioners running stagecoach lines, and several running traveling camps. Mather's idea was eventually to have only one operator in a national park, who would run all the concessions. He argued that the national park system was an excellent place for regulated monopoly. A monopoly would attract the new capital necessary for increasing the tourist facilities. It was hard enough attracting concessioners who could do the job in the short seasons and put up with the unpredictability of government policy. The concessioner should be able to control prices and not have to fight competition. Mather felt that a strictly regulated monopoly would protect both the public and the concessioner.

In working toward this goal, Mather in the fall of 1916 took away the franchise of one of the three permanent camp operators, the Old Faithful Camp Company, and forced the other two to merge. But the Hefferlin brothers, who operated the Old Faithful Camp Company, had allies in Congress, especially Senator Walsh, who had arranged for them to get a franchise in 1915. The Hefferlins were quick-buck operators who badgered tourists arriving at the railroad station, making outlandish pitches more at home at a carnival than in a national park. They lured visitors to their ramshackle tent camps, which were crammed into the areas assigned to the permanent camps. Their

Superintendent W. B. Lewis, Mrs. Lewis, and author with the first motorcyclist in Yosemite at the old park headquarters, 1917. Albright collection.

facilities were wholly inadequate, and the food and service were unsatisfactory.

While Mather and I were in Yellowstone in 1915, I had inspected the camps, and had told Mather how bad conditions were. The day I had made an inspection visit, twenty cases of ptomaine poisoning were reported at one camp! Mather had immediately asked the army to force the operators to make improvements, but the situation had continued.

After losing their franchise, the Hefferlins appealed to their friends in Congress, and quick-tempered Senator Walsh made a vehement protest to Secretary Lane, directing his criticism at Mather personally. He demanded that all who desired to operate concessions of any kind in Yellowstone should be permitted to do so.

Mather sent Lane a strong report:

> Every national park concessioner has come to recognize me as the administrative officer in charge of the national parks and sees the importance of cooperating with me in my plans for the improvement of the parks. When I denied the Hefferlins a renewal of their license, they appealed to me personally and I stood fast. They saw me again and brought Senator Walsh with them, and again I refused to reverse myself. Then they brought every political pressure they could command to bear upon me. Again I refused. If now my position is reversed by you, every concessioner in the parks will say, very properly: 'never mind what Mather says or does; the Secretary will do what our senators ask.'

If Lane had failed to back him, Mather probably would have resigned, for he had taken the job only on the assurance from Lane that there would be no political interference. Lane defied Walsh and upheld Mather in this situation, so no question of resignation came up. Mather sent me to Yellowstone again to smooth things out with the concessioners. While I was there I made the final arrangements for civilians to take over administration of the park.

Mather had been counting on Marshall to become the first Director of the National Park Service, but his performance caused Mather considerable concern. Marshall knew the parks and was a diligent and dependable worker, but his lack of tact made employees uncomfortable. He also tended toward pomposity in public statements, was heavy-handed in correspondence, and his personal style was in rather jarring contrast to the public image Mather was trying to build for the parks. Some of Marshall's administrative actions had also caused problems. For instance, he had impulsively ordered Yellowstone to be closed two weeks early because of the threat of a railroad strike, which never took place. This upset visitors already on the way to the park, hurt the concessioners' business, and outraged the railroad.

Marshall also got us into a jam at Yosemite. The $150,000 that Mather had obtained with great difficulty from the appropriations committee to build a new power plant at Yosemite ran short of completing the project. The problem was that Marshall had approved some costly changes in the plans that ran the project far over the estimate.

Mather reluctantly concluded that Marshall lacked the qualities required in a first-rate administrator, and in late December told him he was sending him back to the Geological Survey. Marshall did not take the action well, and let it be known among his colleagues that the real problem was that Mather wanted the directorship of the Park Service for himself.

The Marshall episode caused Mather considerable anguish, and Marshall's absence was also felt by the rest of us, who had to take on the work he had been doing. It was especially hard on me, because Marshall and I had been in charge of organizing the five-day conference that was due to start only two weeks later at the National Museum in Washington, D.C. Mather wanted the conference to serve as a showcase for the natural wonders of the parks and their desperate need of attention. He hoped it would inspire members of Congress to make substantial increases in appropriations for the parks, and for that reason he had chosen Washington, rather than one of the parks, as the site of this fourth conference on national parks. The conference would also mark that most important achievement, passage of the act establishing the National Park Service.

Participants came from all over the country, and included many leading conservationists and other supporters of parks. Mather, who was an afficionado of the arts, arranged for the first National Park art exhibition. It was held at the nearby National Gallery of Art, with paintings of national park scenes by twenty-seven artists, including Thomas Moran, Albert Bierstadt, and Thomas Hill.

The conference was much broader in scope than those of 1911, 1912, and 1915, and it was not referred to as a conference of superintendents, as the others had been. Enos Mills talked on the subject of national parks for all the people. Mrs. Sherman of the General Federation of Women's Clubs spoke on the role of women in national parks development. Huston Thompson gave a speech, as did the head curator of the National Gallery of Art, who emphasized the value of the parks to artists. Gilbert Grosvenor of the National Geographic Society spoke on teaching through pictures, and Reverend Charles Gilkey of Chicago talked on the spiritual uplift of scenery in the national parks. Orville Wright's talk included the prediction that people would soon be visiting national parks in airplanes — an idea that most of the crowd, including me, thought was about as far-fetched an idea as we had ever heard.

The conference also served to build our political support. Many senators and members of the House attended, and the opening day featured speeches by Senator Smoot and Representative Lenroot and Congressmen Scott Ferris and Billy Kent, as well as Secretary Lane. Smoot set a wonderful theme by saying: "I do not want to see our national parks robbed of any of their beauty on the ground that it must be done in order to secure money sufficient to pay the expenses of maintaining them. I do not want to see any of the natural resources taken from them that would in any way mar their beauty. I think it would be the best money that Congress could spend, to place the parks in a condition that they can be enjoyed by the people of the United States."

Ferris was chairman of the House public lands committee, and was not to be outdone by Smoot. "I want these parks to be the one green spot in this busy republic where every busy life will feel free at home to lie down in the shelter of the trees," he said. "Let the mission of the parks be to stimulate and promote the higher and better instincts of men."

Lenroot, who had for a while blocked the Park Service Act, tried to put a positive light on his sponsorship of the legislation that limited the appropriation for any park for maintenance and improvement to ten thousand dollars annually, without previous authorization by Congress. Said Lenroot:

In proposing this limitation, I had two purposes in view: First, to make the securing of new national parks less difficult, removing the

objection of immediate, large expenditures upon them, if created; secondly, I do not believe that all of these national parks should be developed simultaneously. To scatter $500,000 annually for improvements over a dozen national parks will not bring as many tourists and visitors to the parks as the expenditure of the same amount of money upon three or four of them.

As the conference organizer I had to be everywhere at once, handling the hundreds of details that needed to be unsnarled. From time to time I would have to scare up Mather and go over some detail with him. He was always quick to work out any problem, and trusted me to carry on without further instruction. We had the most comfortable working relationship imaginable; we had spent a good deal of time traveling together in addition to our day-to-day work, and knew each other so well that a word or two often would suffice for communication of ideas between us. Also, our quite different styles of working seemed to mesh very well. It was not actually a personal friendship, however. The difference in our ages, together with my youthful devotion and tremendous respect for him, kept me from even calling him by his first name, and to this day I always think of him as *Mr.* Mather.

As I came in contact with him during the conference, I sensed that something was troubling him. Instead of his usual highly charged enthusiasm he seemed depressed, and was uncharacteristically expressing doubts about his ability to meet the problems facing us, even though all of the congressional speakers praised his work. But I was far too busy with the conference to stop and think much about it.

Some of his close friends had noticed how depressed he seemed, so at the close of the conference, McCormick, Hough, and a few others threw a dinner party in his honor at the Cosmos Club to cheer him up. They toasted his getting the national park legislation passed, the progress he was making on so many fronts, and the success of the conference. When Mather rose to give his toast, his voice was filled with bitterness and despair. What he was saying lacked coherence, and McCormick became alarmed. He slipped out and phoned me to come over at once.

We got Mather to bed in a guest room there in the Cosmos Club, and I immediately phoned Mrs. Mather in Elizabeth, New Jersey, where she was visiting her mother. She asked us to bring him to Philadelphia next morning, and McCormick and I took him there. Mrs. Mather placed him in a private sanitarium in Devon, Pennsylvania, under the care of Dr. T. A. Weisenburg, a specialist in nervous disorders.

None of us had been aware that in 1903 Mather had suffered a mental collapse from overwork. And we had not recognized the extent to which the stresses of the past two years had been piling up on him. He had been on the road constantly, and with his frenetic style had taken on more than any one man could hope to accomplish. His problems with Marshall, the fight with Fitzgerald over the army troops at Yellowstone, and the battle with Walsh over concession policies all had been pushing him toward collapse.

The doctor prescribed several weeks of complete rest, with no visits, even from his family. Then Dr. Weisenberg called for Mrs. Mather and me to come to Devon. He told us that he believed Mather could make a full recovery if great care was taken to keep him thinking along the lines of his greatest interest, national parks, but without having to make any decisions. That was not good news to Mrs. Mather. She felt that since his illness had been brought on by exhaustion in public service, continuation of national park activity might make his condition even worse.

But the doctor advised that under no circumstances should Mather drop his involvement in the parks. "His life depends upon national parks. It is all he talks about and all he is interested in," Dr. Weisenberg said. "I think I can bring him back through the parks, but without them I don't know what may happen." Mrs. Mather accepted his advice, and said she would do whatever he suggested.

Dr. Weisenberg recommended that I be the one and only visitor other than Mrs. Mather for a while, and asked me to come to Devon once a week, if possible, remaining with Mather a few hours at first, and then gradually extending the length of my visits. The doctor said I could discuss national park affairs, but mainly in answer to his questions rather than taking up matters that might worry him. When a troublesome problem was touched on, I was to treat it in the lightest vein and give cheerful news that things were clearing up nicely.

"Feed him some good news," the doctor advised, "and I think we may be able to bring him out of this thing."

5

Organizing the Park Service

Mather's illness stunned everybody, and his absence cast a pall over our national parks working group. We were all used to being buoyed by his enthusiasm and electric personality. As I had found out early on, Mather had the rare gift of binding men to him with hoops of steel. There were many who were more than willing to help, and I myself stood ready to do anything I could to carry out his plans while he was recovering.

There was no question now of returning to California anytime soon, as Grace and I had counted on doing. Secretary Lane asked me to fill in as acting Director of the National Park Service until Mather's return. That meant I not only had to run all the parks, but, at age twenty-seven, I had to take on the full responsibility of organizing the National Park Service and getting Congress to appropriate enough money so we could staff up.

One morning my secretary, Isabelle F. Story, a highly competent young woman Marshall had brought over from the Geological Survey, said: "Mr. Albright, do you know that as head of the National Park Service you are the youngest person on our staff?"

"That's not possible!" I replied. "I'm surely not younger than you."

"You're a whole year younger."

"What about that boy who is our messenger? I'm not younger than he is."

"He's two years older than you," Miss Story said.

But the nearly four years in Washington had taught me a great deal, especially the two years with Mather. The same problems that had put such pressures on him had forced me to mature beyond my years. Also, unlike my colleagues, I had been in most of the national parks and monuments. I had learned my way around Capitol Hill. Nevertheless, I was well aware that being thrust into the position of acting Director would cause me some difficulties, especially among my senior colleagues on the Interior staff.

The main test came when Bob Yard, who had a long and close personal friendship with Mather, decided that he should be the one in charge until Mather's return. Apparently Yard had written as much to Mrs. Mather, for she immediately wrote to me, telling me to "hold Mr. Yard in," and making it clear that it was her husband's desire that I be in charge. So I had a straightforward talk with Yard, and we reached an understanding that he would consult with me on everything before taking action. We remained on friendly terms during this period, and he was, as always, immeasureably helpful in taking charge of public affairs and insuring a continuous and expanding flow of favorable publicity about the national parks.

The Washington staff for parks consisted of a few people Marshall had borrowed from other Interior agencies. I was also able to draw support from the various department people who had been assigned to spend some fraction of their time on parks matters. Acker, the department lawyer who had been of great help to me since my first days in Washington, was very supportive. He had been handling concession contracts and legal matters for more than twenty years, and loved the parks. Joe Cotter, who had been serving as assistant superintendent of National Parks under Marshall, continued to carry some of the administrative load, though after a few months he decided to return to his previous job in Secretary Lane's office.

Overshadowing all other tasks facing us was the urgent one of persuading Congress to appropriate funds for the National Park Service. Not only did we need to get an appropriation enacted for the 1918 fiscal year (which would begin in July 1917), but we had to have a so-called deficiency appropriation so that we would have operating funds to see us through until the start of the new fiscal year. Without it we could not hire staff or get the new Service started.

To get the appropriations meant tangling with House appropriations committee chairman Fitzgerald, our number one enemy on the

View from Grand Canyon Lodge (North Rim), showing Deva, Brahma, and Zoroaster temples, and Bright Angel Canyon, 1930. George A. Grant photograph. National Park Service.

Hill. And he was still fuming over our removal of the troops from Yellowstone without his permission or knowledge.

I prepared diligently for the hearings. My testimony the first day emphasized that steps were being taken to increase public use, and that we were compelling the camp and hotel concessioners to expand and improve their facilities. Fitzgerald let me have my say. But when I requested funding to hire seven clerks in addition to the five chief officers authorized by the National Parks Act, he let go with both barrels.

"Why does every man who has a job in the government have to have a clerk?" he demanded, and added that every prospective office worker in the National Park Service "ought to be employed by a member of Congress for about six months and they would find out what a day's work is."

I replied: "We are not asking for anything more than we deserve. Every one of us down there has worked overtime for a year or more, and on Sundays and holidays."

I probably should have shown more deference, but I wasn't a typical civil servant worrying about keeping my job — I would not have minded going back to California then and there. It was important not to cross him, though, for the good of the Service.

Fitzgerald started firing questions at me about removal of the troops from Yellowstone, and disputed my assertion that the army had been trying to get rid of the Yellowstone responsibility for several years.

"No!" the chairman cut me off, almost shouting. "I know what happened. The Interior Department started the effort to get the troops out."

Then he shifted to the Yosemite power plant construction that had exceeded funding estimates. He interrupted my explanation and said, "You were given $150,000 to build this power plant, and you proceeded to attempt to build one double the size originally contemplated. The trouble with this service is that it does not imagine it is controlled in any way by either the limitation of law or the appropriation. You come before Congress and ask for a specific appropriation for a definite purpose and after you get the money then you proceed to do as you please, regardless of what you have presented here."

Through three days of that kind of barrage I managed to retain my composure. But I couldn't help thinking how much better Mather could have done. He probably would have been able to stand up to the chairman better than I. But despite Fitzgerald's performance, I did manage to get our case presented.

We proved to have some friends on the committee, especially Congressman Gillett of Massachusetts, who had been a member of Mather's 1915 mountain party. With Gillett's help, the Sundry Civil bill was passed by the House on February 28 with most of our requested funding intact, except the Yosemite power plant. But Fitzgerald got his way on the troop removal, and the measure specified that the army must be sent back into Yellowstone.

The Senate's bill included virtually everything we had asked for, thanks to the help of long-time park supporter Senator Reed Smoot. While a conference committee was deliberating, Bob Yard finished a special national parks road map, and we made copies of it available to all members of Congress for distribution to their constituents. The map was a fine piece of work, and apparently was good for our cause. When the final Sundry Civil Bill was enacted by both the Senate and House in mid-April, it included an additional sixty thousand dollars to complete the Yosemite power plant, and gave us all the other funds we had requested. Chairman Fitzgerald did prevail in the Yellowstone matter, however, and the troops were ordered back in.

Mather had already appointed a civilian acting superintendent for Yellowstone, Chester A. Lindsley, and he was on the job. So we kept him in charge of the park even after the army officers went back in. We also managed to have Lindsley take over the best building in the park for a headquarters, and we kept title to the buildings, horses, and essential utility systems. We kept the issue alive on the hill, finally winning permanent removal of the troops at the end of the 1917–1918 fiscal year. The opposition had lost its power, because Fitzgerald had by then announced his intention to retire from the House.

In mid-April Congress also passed a deficiency bill (today called a supplemental appropriation) to provide funds and authorize hiring of personnel. Now that the National Park Service was officially ready to start, Secretary Lane had to get President Wilson to sign an executive order appointing Mather and me to the Civil Service. Early in May I was sworn in as assistant Director of the National Park Service. And Lane ordered that I would also have the title of "Acting Director" of the Park Service until Mather could return to duty and assume the office. And my $1,600 salary shot up to $2,500 plus the additional $1,000 per year that Mather continued to pay me.

With our appropriation I was able to bring Frank W. Griffith onto the staff officially as chief clerk. He had been on Secretary Lane's staff. Noble J. Wilt, an expert stenographer and accountant, assumed charge of records and bookkeeping. George McClain would be continuing in his position as Mather's secretary. Arthur E. Demaray, a draftsman and expert map maker with experience in the Reclamation Service and the Geological Survey, was officially added to the staff, along with Isabelle Story, some clerks and stenographers, and a messenger. And, of course, Bob Yard continued to head public affairs and publications.

On April 6, 1917, President Wilson signed the congressional resolution declaring war on Germany, and the fact that the nation was now at war affected our prospects and plans in several ways. The national parks still had limited public support and had not gained a position of priority in the nation's affairs. The war would make it harder than ever for us to protect park resources from ranching, timber, and mining interests that sought to use war emergency powers as an excuse to exploit the resources for their own profits. The war effort also made it difficult to recruit the superintendents, rangers, and other workers needed for building the National Park Service. Some of those already at work in the parks wanted to enter the military, and others were subject to the draft. There was even some doubt as to my own status.

I had been a captain in the University of California Cadet Corps, had served two years in the Coast Artillery of the California National Guard, and while a senior in high school I had applied to West Point. Now, like other men my age, I felt an urge to enlist and help my country. When I mentioned to Secretary Lane that I had been giving some thought to joining the army, his reaction was blunt.

"You stay right where you are. You cannot think of going into the military service in any capacity at this time," he said. And he told me he was having me deferred from the draft. "When Mr. Mather gets well and returns, perhaps we can think about it, but for now you must stay on the job."

I had been taking the train up to Devon almost every Friday night to spend the weekend with Mather, who was showing steady improvement. He had been greatly cheered when Congress passed a law late in February establishing Mount McKinley National Park in Alaska, a measure he had been promoting, and which the Boone and Crockett Club had been advocating. The news that we had won most of what we had asked for in our appropriation gave him another boost.

By spring he had improved so much that Dr. Weisenberg let him take his little air-cooled Franklin roadster out for drives, and Mather would drive me around the countryside on some weekends. But when the war started, he expressed concern that Lane might cave in to the pressures to let the resource developers into the national parks. That

was, of course, the very problem I was wrestling with. But in accordance with the doctor's orders, I did not tell Mather how well-founded his concerns were, especially regarding Lane.

Lane was known to favor a utilitarian approach to managing the nation's resources, as his large part in passage of the law to build the Hetch Hetchy dam in Yosemite attested. By his choice of Mather to start the Park Service, and his support of Mather's initiatives for protecting and expanding the parks, Lane had disarmed some of his conservationist critics. But they had never forgiven him for Hetch Hetchy. Now he began to question the policy of keeping the parks completely protected, and suggested to me that Yosemite and other parks be opened to livestock pasturage as a means of helping produce meat for the armed forces.

Benjamin Ide Wheeler, president of the University of California and chairman of California's Council of Defense, urged his old friend Lane to allow fifty thousand sheep to graze in Yosemite. I protested that such an action would spell the ruin of Yosemite. But Lane ordered me to send a telegram to the park saying the grazing was to be allowed, and I was not to tell the Sierra Club.

I prepared the telegram, but could not bring myself to send it. When Lane discovered it had not gone out, he signed and sent it himself. I complied with his order not to tell my friends in the Sierra Club, but the word leaked out, and before long a lot of congressmen were calling the Secretary to demand that the sheep not be allowed in. Lane felt the heat, and we won that battle. However, when the powerful Cattlemen's Association pressed Lane to let stock graze in Yosemite's higher ranges rather than in the Valley, I was forced to let a few cattle graze there.

Then I had to fight a battle with the Washington state commissioner of agriculture, who had the duty of increasing food production in his state. He demanded we let stockmen pasture thirty to fifty thousand sheep in Mount Rainier National Park. I refused, and he got his governor to write to Herbert Hoover, the national food administrator. The governor asked Hoover to intercede and see that the permit was granted.

I decided the way to stop this was to take it up with Hoover to find out whether or not we really needed to open these national parks to utilize their resources. I got an appointment, but Mr. Hoover was too busy to deal with it himself, and after a minute or so he turned me over to one of his associates, Duncan McDuffie, whom I had known in California. Uncertain as to whether McDuffie could do anything, I contacted a former University of California classmate, Ralph P. Merritt, food administrator for the eleven western states, and a close friend of Hoover. Not only did Hoover refuse to grant the permit, but he issued a statement that there was no need to open the national parks to stockmen for the pasturage of their cattle and sheep.

That was another victory. But we continued to tread a delicate line, trying to keep the parks from being violated while not appearing to be inconsiderate of the war effort. For instance, we allowed a small number of cattle to graze in Yosemite, but not in areas used by visitors or where the grazing would permanently harm the park.

As Mather's condition improved, Dr. Weisenburg started encouraging him to consider returning to the Park Service. But Mather continued to argue that his health would not permit it, that he was not the man to be director of the Park Service, that he never had intended to stay in government service anyway, and that he could accomplish nothing during the war. Dr. Weisenburg felt Mather must take the job in order to have an interest that would carry him back to robust health. The doctor asked me to have a talk with Mather and assure him that I would stay on for a year, or until the Park Service was in good shape. In mid-May Mather told Secretary Lane he would come back. His appointment was dated May 16, 1917, but it was almost another year before he actually returned to work.

I continued the job of getting things organized. With the people we had borrowed from the Geological Survey, Bureau of Mines, and the Secretary's office, we had a staff of about twenty at work in Washington by June. And we had been assigned some choice office space in the Interior Department's new quarters. In June 1917, Interior finally moved out of the old Patent Building and other locations where its bureaus were scattered. The new structure on F Street between Eighteenth and Nineteenth Northwest had originally been built to house the Geological Survey, but Secretary Lane arranged to have it called the Interior Building, although he did give the Survey the center wing (the building today houses the General Services Administration, and is one block north of the present Interior building). Both the National Park Service and the Bureau of Indian Affairs put in for space on the fourth floor of the east wing, and Lane awarded it to us. While our furniture was being prepared for transfer, the commissioner of Indian affairs, Cato Sells, moved into the corner office allocated to the Director of the National Park Service. He claimed seniority, which, of course, he had by a good many years. I immediately took the office next door and moved our people to the rooms around Sells.

It was not the kind of thing we wanted to ask Secretary Lane to settle. One day in June, when I found out that Sells was in Texas, I got four burly movers to go in and move all of his furniture out into the hall and spread his rug over it. And I moved Mather's furniture in. When Sells returned, my staff was anticipating a fight. But Sells simply laughed, said I had done just what he himself would have done, and he moved his furniture down to the third floor where the rest of his bureau was. So even though we had only a few rooms, at least they were in a choice location overlooking the Potomac River, the Washington Monument, and the historic Octagon House across the street.

By late June, I felt things were well enough in hand for me to make a long-delayed trip into the field where a lot of matters needed attention. Acker had been too busy with Interior Department legal affairs

Near the Mariposa Grove Museum, Yosemite, 1931. George A. Grant photograph.
National Park Service.

to give much time to concessions work, and much of my time had been taken up with appropriations and getting things organized. Joe Cotter's return to the Secretary's office also had left me with many of his tasks to do, so I had been in the office night and day, and needed to get out to the field. The parks had had little personal attention since Mather had been laid up.

I spent a few days in Denver trying to do Mather-like public relations, assuring the business people that the war would not drastically hinder the stream of summer travel to the parks, and looking into the possibility of adding the Mount Evans area to Rocky Mountain National Park. Then I headed north to meet with Enos Mills and visit the park.

Mills' relations with the Park Service were beginning to sour. He had dedicated his life to establishing the Rocky Mountain park, and now he felt we were not giving it enough attention. Although a great conservationist, he was not an easy person to get along with. He had carried on a life-long feud with the Forest Service, and now accused us of working too closely with them. He complained that we were not fighting to add adjacent Forest Service land south of the park. He also wanted to ban all transportation and lodging concessions while still retaining his own inn and his other property within the park. His adamant attitude seemed to leave no room for reasoning, and we had a difficult, unpleasant meeting.

Yellowstone also had been having problems. When Representative Fitzgerald's actions had forced the army back into Yellowstone in the spring, acting superintendent Lindsley had been forced to lay off the twenty-five rangers he had hired when we had removed the troops. But I was nevertheless able to keep Lindsley in charge of administering the park. He reported an increase in visitors despite the war, primarily because private cars were now being allowed to use the park roads. But he was also getting a barrage of complaints about the bad condition of the roads.

In visits to Mount Rainier, Crater Lake, and Yosemite national parks I found things to be proceeding normally. At Yosemite, I checked on the new hotel being built at Glacier Point by the Desmond Company. But the park's popularity was growing rapidly, and the existing facilities were still not able to take care of all the visitors. There had been considerable pressure from tourists to reinstate the firefall, and we decided to do so.

While in California, I was a guest at the annual Bohemian Grove meeting, where influential national business men and political leaders assemble under the redwoods. One evening a discussion started that really was the beginning of the movement to save the coast redwoods. John C. Merriam, Henry Fairfield Osborn, and Madison Grant, an anthropologist from a wealthy family, led the discussion that night at the Pleasant Isle of Aves camp. They invited me to join them later in the week on a trip to the redwoods area near the California coast where they formed the organization that became known as the Save the Redwoods League. I wish I could have been there, but I had a prior commitment to accompany Douglas White, general passenger agent of the Los Angeles, Salt Lake, and San Pedro Railroad, to Mukuntuweap National Monument in Southern Utah, near where his line ended.

I was so impressed by the red cliffs and wilderness surroundings of Zion Canyon that I determined we should expand Mukuntuweap and have it made a national park. In some ways, it was like a smaller but more colorful Yosemite. It had been described as "Yosemite painted in oils." I telegraphed Mather, who was at Lake Tahoe continuing his recuperation, telling him how beautiful Zion Canyon was and urging that we do something about it. He answered that he had never heard of it. "You must have been taken in by the local chamber of commerce," he wrote me.

By the time I got back to Washington in late September, I had traveled more than ten thousand miles and had visited all the western parks except Alaska's Mount McKinley. The trip gave me a vivid picture of the needs and problems in the national parks, and I was anxious to get at their solutions.

Mather was still not ready to return, but I was able to consult with him frequently on many of the problems and opportunities the new National Park Service presented. One of the most crucial was to find good personnel to staff the parks.

Where were we going to locate the kind of people we could station in the national parks and monuments and entrust with caring for these great natural treasures? In addition to having some idea of how to manage the resources, superintendents and rangers would have to possess a love of the outdoors that would make them willing to live under rugged, somewhat primitive, and often isolated conditions, and do it at very low salaries. And they would have to be able to deal effectively with visitors, get along with the concessioners and the owners of private holdings within park boundaries, and keep peace with political leaders in nearby localities. Training programs would help, but to develop them would take time and funds we did not have.

Some of the superintendents already on the job in 1917 fell short of what we wanted. Many had come into their jobs through the political patronage that had traditionally been practiced in park hiring, and a few of the senators from the western states still guarded that privilege. With a change of administration, some superintendents would be ousted to provide new patronage jobs. In 1913, for instance, when the Democrats had come to power after sixteen years of Republican leadership, Secretary Lane followed the accepted procedure by removing the superintendents of some of the existing parks — Hot Springs, Mount Rainier, Mesa Verde, Platt, and Wind Cave — and appointed deserving Democrats in their place.

At first we were able to borrow and eventually hire some good men from the Geological Survey, mostly topographic engineers and mapmakers whose experience with the public lands fitted them for land management. But except for the few we could find in the Survey and some other bureaus in the Interior Department, we had to look far and wide for people who showed some promise for ranger or superintendent responsibilities and then hope they would learn on the job.

The first priority was to get staff for Yosemite, since it was drawing more visitors than the rest of the parks. In 1913, when the army had moved out, a former army sergeant, Gabriel Souvelewski, had been left in charge of the park. Souvelewski had been assigned to Yosemite when it was first established in 1890, and when Interior took over, he had gotten his army discharge and become a ranger. He was an extremely valuable staff member, and one of the greatest trail builders I've ever known. But he did not have the right qualification for becoming superintendent. Washington B. "Dusty" Lewis, the man we named as superintendent, came out of the Geological Survey. He had a degree from the University of Michigan, had experience in other countries for the Survey and brought to the Yosemite superintendency a lot of skill and breadth of experience. He stayed there eleven years.

Rocky Mountain National Park didn't have enough funding to hire a staff, so we sent out one of the best Interior Department inspectors, Charles R. Trowbridge, and he became its acting superintendent. Later, when we were ready to hire a permanent superintendent, I recommended L. C. Way, the Forest Service ranger at Grand Canyon who had impressed Grace and me so much when we met him during our honeymoon. Way became the first regular superintendent at Rocky Mountain National Park.

The head ranger at Sequoia and General Grant national parks, Walter Fry, had received high marks from Mather for his participation in the 1915 conference. Fry had worked in the parks for years and had demonstrated good leadership qualities, so we promoted him to superintendent.

Crater Lake's superintendent, William F. Arent, was a politician who had begun his patronage job in 1902, and now needed to be replaced. We hired Will Steel, who had virtually founded the park. Steel had fallen in love with Crater Lake at his first sight of it in 1885 as a visitor from Kansas, had moved to the area, and stayed to fight a seventeen-year battle to have it declared a national park. What Steel lacked in administrative know-how he made up for with his love of the land and his ability to work with the concessioners and the people in the area.

For years, Mount Rainier National Park had given us special problems because of the feuding factions in Tacoma and Seattle which vied for its control. We found another good Geological Survey man, Dewitt Raeburn, for the superintendent's job. He had experience in Wyoming and Alaska and had built railroads in South America before joining the Survey.

By one means or another we managed to place capable people in key field positions so that we could begin to bring some coordination and management to the national parks.

Before I knew it the time had come to start preparing the first annual report of the National Park Service to the Secretary of the Interior. How could all the frenetic activities of that formative first year be boiled down to a few pages? From the battle for an adequate appropriation from Congress; the efforts to hire staff both at headquarters and in the field; the continuing campaign to build public interest in the parks and thus generate support; to the drawing up of policies, it had been quite a year. With Mather's approval I decided to center the report on the seven most urgent needs facing the Park Service.

First was to remove the legal inhibition that limited funding for Rocky Mountain National Park to ten thousand dollars, thus preventing improvements. Second was to get the War Department out of Yellowstone, and the Army Corps of Engineers out of Crater Lake National Park (where they were in charge of construction and improvement of roads). Third, Sequoia National Park should be enlarged to include the Kings and Kern River gorges and the crest of the Sierra Nevada, including Mount Whitney. Fourth, part of the Teton Mountains, Jackson Lake, and the headwaters of the Yellowstone

Mt. Rockwell and the lagoon near Two Medicine Campground, Glacier, 1932. George A. Grant photograph. National Park Service.

River should be added to Yellowstone National Park. Fifth, Grand Canyon National Monument, then under the jurisdiction of the Forest Service, should be raised to national park status and added to the national park system. Sixth, Congress needed to pass appropriations for road and trail improvements and the preservation of national monuments. Seventh, funds must be appropriated to enable the National Park Service to assume administrative control of and provide protection for Mount McKinley, Hawaii, and Lassen Volcanic national parks.

As 1918 opened, I was still in charge, and continued as acting Director until late spring. My own Park Service colleagues accepted my temporary leadership cordially. But I sometimes got the impression that some of the other Department of Interior officials wondered what a twenty-eight-year-old was doing in their midst. However, one day early in the year, there was an incident that caused my stock to soar.

I was returning to the department at noontime after a meeting with congressional staff when an elderly man stopped me on the street and asked where he could find a place to eat nearby. I started to give directions to the nearest restaurants, about five blocks away, but had trouble communicating because he was a little hard of hearing. He was somewhat shabbily dressed and looked like he needed a meal, so I invited him to be my guest at the Interior Department dining room. He protested that he did not want to impose, but I insisted, and he finally accepted. On the way into the building I introduced myself, and he identified himself as Tom Edison, from New Jersey.

"Not *the* Thomas Edison!" I exclaimed. Yes, he admitted, he was Thomas Alva Edison, and had come to Washington for a meeting connected with the war effort.

When we entered the executive dining room I introduced my colleagues to Mr. Thomas Edison. You can imagine their reaction. About two months later, as luck would have it, I again encountered Edison on the street near the department at the noon hour, and he again accepted my invitation to lunch. From then on my colleagues refused to accept my explanation that it was just a coincidence. I became known as a close friend of the great inventor — which, of course, was not really true. I'm sorry to say that I never saw Mr. Edison again.

6

A Creed for the Parks

TOWARD THE END OF 1917 AND EARLY IN THE NEW YEAR I HAD BEEN WORKING UP A SET OF POLICY OBJECTIVES for the National Park Service, using many of Mather's ideas. I wrote a first draft based on ideas, suggestions, conversations, and much reading in 1915, 1916, and 1917. I had my draft copied on paper with large margins, and with a space or two between lines for typing in comments, and I sent it out with a covering letter asking for comments, advice, and suggested revisions. I sent copies to Will Colby, Francis Farquhar, W. F. Bade, and Joseph LeConte, Jr., all active in Sierra Club affairs and all destined to be presidents of the club. I also sent the request to J. Horace McFarland, president, and Harlean James, executive secretary, of the American Civic Association, George F. Kunz of the American Scenic and Historic Preservation Society, Gilbert Grosvenor of the National Geographic Society, and even Robert B. Marshall, who had remained friendly to me after Mather had sent him back to the Geological Survey.

Most of these people returned my draft with worthwhile suggestions, and heartily approved the draft. Bob Yard was most helpful not only in making some suggestions that improved the content, but also lending me the benefit of his more than thirty years of writing experience. When I had the final draft in a form that satisfied Yard and me, I sent it to Mather. He promptly returned it with his full approval. Inasmuch as the changes from my original draft were few, I felt justified in considering it one of the best things I ever did. I sent the policy objectives up to Secretary Lane, suggesting he issue them as a letter to Mather.

The Lane letter, dated May 13, 1918, was a landmark for those early years, and became our basic creed. "For the information of the public, an outline of the administrative policy to which the new Service will adhere may now be announced," the letter stated. It added that "This policy is based on three broad management principles: First, that the national parks must be maintained in absolutely unimpaired form for the use of future generations as well as those of our time; second, that they are set aside for the use, observation, health, and pleasure of the people; and third, that the national interest must dictate all decisions affecting public or private enterprise in the parks."

After stating the management principles, the policy directive listed twenty-three specific points, some of them especially significant in fighting the battles for the national parks. The statement directed that the national park system should not be lowered in standard, dignity, and prestige. Roads, trails, buildings, and other improvements should always be constructed in a manner that pays attention to the harmonizing of the improvements with the landscape. All of the private holdings in the national parks should be eliminated as far as practicable in the course of time either through congressional appropriation or by donations. Educational, as well as recreational, uses should be encouraged. And adjacent areas should be added when they would complete a park's scenic purpose or would facilitate its administration.

The twenty-three items in that historic letter are as follows:

> Every activity of the Service is subordinate to the duties imposed upon it to faithfully preserve the parks for posterity in essentially their natural state. The commercial use of these reservations, except as specially authorized by law, or such as may be incidental to the accommodation and entertainment of visitors, will not be permitted under any circumstances.
>
> In all of the national parks except Yellowstone you may permit the grazing of cattle in isolated regions not frequented by visitors, and where no injury to the natural features of the parks may result from such use. The grazing of sheep, however, must not be permitted in any national park.
>
> In leasing lands for the operation of hotels, camps, transportation facilities, or other public service under strict Government control, concessioners should be confined to tracts no larger than absolutely necessary for the purposes of their business enterprises.
>
> You should not permit the leasing of park lands for summer

homes. It is conceivable, and even exceedingly probable, that within a few years under a policy of permitting the establishment of summer homes in national parks, these reservations might become so generally settled as to exclude the public from convenient access to their streams, lakes, and other natural features, and thus destroy the very basis upon which this national playground system is being constructed.

You should not permit the cutting of trees except where timber is needed in the construction of buildings or other improvements within the park and can be removed without injury to the forests or disfigurement of the landscape, where the thinning of forests or cutting of vistas will improve the scenic features of the parks, or where their destruction is necessary to eliminate insect infestations or diseases common to forests and shrubs.

In the construction of roads, trails, buildings, and other improvements, particular attention must be devoted always to the harmonizing of these improvements within the landscape. This is a most important item in our program of development and requires the employment of trained engineers who either possess a knowledge of landscape architecture or have a proper appreciation of the esthetic value of park lands. All improvements will be carried out in accordance with a preconceived plan developed with special reference to the preservation of the landscape, and comprehensive plans for future development of the national parks on an adequate scale will be prepared as funds are available for this purpose.

Wherever the Federal Government has exclusive jurisdiction over national parks it is clear that more effective measures for the protection of the parks can be taken. The Federal Government has exclusive jurisdiction over the national parks in the States of Arkansas, Oklahoma, Wyoming, Montana, Washington, and Oregon, and also in the Territories of Hawaii and Alaska. We should urge the cession of exclusive jurisdiction over the parks in the other States, and particularly in California and Colorado.

There are many private holdings in the national parks, and many of these seriously hamper the administration of these reservations. All of them should be eliminated as far as it is practicable to accomplish this purpose in the course of time, either through congressional appropriation or by acceptance of donations of these lands. Isolated tracts in important scenic areas should be given first consideration, of course, in the purchase of private property.

Every opportunity should be afforded the public, wherever possible, to enjoy the national parks in the manner that best satisfies the individual taste. Automobiles and motorcycles will be permitted in all of the national parks; in fact, the parks will be kept accessible by any means practicable.

All outdoor sports which may be maintained consistently with the observation of the safeguards thrown around the national parks by law will be heartily indorsed and aided wherever possible. Mountain climbing, horseback riding, walking, motoring, swimming, boating, and fishing will ever be the favorite sports. Winter sports will be developed in the parks that are accessible throughout the year. Hunting will not be permitted in any national park.

The educational, as well as the recreational, use of the national parks should be encouraged in every practicable way. University and high-school classes in science will find special facilities for their vacation-period studies. Museums containing specimens of wild flowers, shrubs, and trees, and mounted animals, birds, and fish native to the parks and other exhibits of this character will be established as authorized.

Low-priced camps operated by concessioners should be maintained, as well as comfortable and even luxurious hotels wherever the volume of travel warrants the establishment of these classes of accommodations. In each reservation, as funds are available, a system of free camp sites will be cleared, and these grounds will be equipped with adequate water and sanitation facilities.

As concessions in the national parks represent in most instances a large investment, and as the obligation to render service satisfactory to the department at carefully regulated rates is imposed, these enterprises must be given a large measure of protection, and generally speaking, competitive business should not be authorized where a concession is meeting our requirements, which, of course, will as nearly as possible coincide with the needs of the traveling public.

All concessions should yield revenue to the Federal Government, but the development of the revenues of the parks should not impose a burden upon the visitor.

Automobile fees in the parks should be reduced as the volume of motor travel increases.

For assistance in the solution of administrative problems in the parks relating both to their protection and use, the scientific bureaus of the Government offer facilities of the highest worth and authority. In the protection of the public health, for instance, the destruction of insect pests in the forests, the care of wild animals, and the propagation and distribution of fish, you should utilize their hearty cooperation to the utmost.

You should utilize to the fullest extent the opportunity afforded by the Railroad Administration in appointing a committee of western railroads to inform the traveling public how to comfortably reach the national parks; you should diligently extend and use the splendid cooperation developed during the last three years among chambers of commerce, tourist bureaus, and automobile highway associations for the purpose of spreading information about our national parks and facilitating their use and enjoyment; you should keep informed of park movements and park progress, municipal, county, and State, both at home and abroad, for the purpose of adapting whenever practicable, the world's best thought to the needs of the national parks. You should encourage all movements looking to outdoor living. In particular, you should maintain close working relationships with the Dominion parks branch of the Canadian department of the interior and assist in the solution of park problems of an international character.

The department is often requested for reports on pending legislation proposing the establishment of new national parks or the addition of lands to existing parks. Complete data on such park projects should be obtained by the National Park Service and submitted to the department in tentative form of report to Congress.

In studying new park projects you should seek to find scenery of supreme and distinctive quality or some natural feature so extraordinary or unique as to be of national interest and importance. You should seek distinguished examples of typical forms of world architecture, such, for instance, as the Grand Canyon, as exemplifying the highest accomplishment of stream erosion, and the high, rugged portion of Mount Desert Island as exemplifying the oldest rock forms in America and the luxuriance of deciduous forests.

The national park system as now constituted should not be lowered in standard, dignity, and prestige by the inclusion of areas which express in less than the highest terms the particular class or kind of exhibit which they represent.

It is not necessary that a national park should have a large area. The element of size is of no importance as long as the park is susceptible of effective administration and control.

You should study existing national parks with the idea of improving them by the addition of adjacent areas which will complete their scenic purposes or facilitate administration. The addition of the Teton Mountains to the Yellowstone National Park, for instance, will supply Yellowstone's greatest need, which is an uplift of glacier-bearing peaks; and the addition to the Sequoia National Park of the Sierra summits and slopes to the north and east, as contemplated by pending legislation, will create a reservation unique in the world, because of its combination of gigantic trees, extraordinary canyons, and mountain masses.

In considering projects involving the establishment of new national parks or the extension of existing park areas by delimitation of national forests, you should observe what effect such delimitation would have on the administration of adjacent forest lands, and wherever practicable, you should engage in an investigation of such park projects jointly with officers of the Forest Service, in order that questions of national park and national forest policy as they affect the lands involved may be thoroughly understood.*

The war continued to serve as an excuse for those who advocated sheep and cattle grazing and timber cutting in the national parks. We had to fight off proposals from food processors to slaughter buffalo and elk herds in Yellowstone — they maintained that the meat was needed for the war effort. Fortunately, the Food Administration run by Herbert Hoover turned down the proposals, as they had earlier ones.

Glacier and Mount Rainier were particular targets of sheepmen. When Mount Rainier came under fire we got help from the Mountaineers Club, a Pacific Northwest outdoor organization. Its members called the bluff of the sheepmen by volunteering to let sheep graze on their front lawns rather than have them ruin the park. Their offer got attention in the newspapers, public opinion was aroused, and the Secretary refused to let sheep graze in Mount Rainier National Park.

Meantime, the Penfold Sheep Company was applying pressure for use of Glacier National Park for grazing, and Senator Walsh of Montana was pulling strings for Penfold in Washington, even though he was an investor in the company. Secretary Lane felt it would be unwise to defy Walsh, and told me to make arrangements for the grazing permit.

I headed for Montana to try to persuade the Penfold Company not to use the park, but they would not budge. When I was ready to return home, and was sitting by the fireplace in the Glacier Park Hotel, waiting gloomily for the train, two men came over and sat with me. I recognized one of them as Bruce Kremer, the chairman of the Montana State Democratic Party, and he introduced me to his companion, Walter Hansen, who ran a meat packing business in Butte.

They remarked about the beauty of the park and how much they had enjoyed their visit, and especially the wildflowers. "Well," I said, "you gentlemen aren't going to have the same kind of park anymore, because we're under terrible pressure to open the park for sheep grazing. You'd better go back and take a last look — the sheep will have the wildflowers by next season." And I told them how Senator Walsh had pressured the Secretary to allow the grazing.

Both men reacted with disgust, and Kremer used some unprintable

* Annual Report, National Park Service, 1918.

language to describe what he thought of Walsh, who he said was crazy to try this kind of thing, because he had an obvious conflict of interest. Then Hansen suddenly came up with a suggestion: "Why not lease the grazing rights to me? If you can get the permit for my company, I'll only turn loose a token herd of cattle, just a carload or two. Then all other applications could be denied. I certainly won't do any damage to the park." I told him I would have to talk to Secretary Lane about it, but that I would surely do it if I could. Secretary Lane readily agreed — he was delighted to have a chance to take a crack at Walsh.

Earlier in the year we had at last won the battle over troops in Yellowstone that Fitzgerald and Walsh had waged with us for so long. We had testified at congressional hearings and presented data showing the cost of maintaining a military force in this isolated post where there was no opportunity for troop drill or other army work.

Congress passed legislation giving the National Park Service complete control of the administration, protection, and improvement of the park, and mandated removal of the army troops and the Corps of Engineers. We then established a permanent ranger force of thirty, many of them mountain men skilled in forestry and woodcraft.

My efforts to get the Jackson Hole area and the Teton Mountains added to Yellowstone took Arthur Demaray and me to Wyoming in July. We made some good contacts in Jackson and in early fall we drew up a bill for Wyoming Congressman Frank Mondell to submit to Congress. The bill called for adding the Teton Range, Jackson Lake, and the upper Yellowstone River — eight hundred thousand acres — to Yellowstone National Park.

Foreign travel was of course restricted during the war years, so we promoted a "See America First" campaign. Mather and I had met Howard Hays in 1915 when he worked for Wylie's camps in Yellowstone. He was now manager of a tourist bureau sponsored by the Union Pacific and Chicago and Northwestern railroads. Hayes cooperated with us in the campaign. The idea was to get people, who might ordinarily be going to Europe for vacations, to try the national parks instead. Hays' tourist bureau published a series of attractive booklets promoting various parks.

We did not have much hope of adding new areas to the national park system during the year, yet in 1918 we managed to bring into the system the largest area to date. After the great 1913 volcanic eruption of Mount Katmai in Alaska the National Geographic Society had sent

Mt. Moran from upper Jackson Hole, 1919. Author at far right. Albright collection.

an expedition led by Robert Griggs to explore the site. The Society was concerned about preserving the area and preventing mineral development, and they published several articles on it in 1917 and 1918.

Early in 1917, Gilbert Grosvenor had asked me to meet him at the Cosmos Club to discuss ways of getting Katmai's fourteen-mile-long crater, the Valley of Ten Thousand Smokes, and the numerous nearby lakes and wildlife habitat set aside as a national park. I told Dr. Grosvenor that if he would present his data I thought we might be able to get it declared a national monument.

I went to see Secretary Lane, who readily gave his approval. Then we gave the proposed boundaries to the General Land Office and the Geological Survey for checking. With their help I wrote up a proclamation and gave it to Secretary Lane, he took it over to the White House, and on September 24, 1918 President Wilson issued the proclamation setting aside 2 million acres in Alaska as Katmai National Monument. The new area was larger than Yellowstone! But we had not a penny from Congress to provide any protection or develop any visitor facilities.

About this time, two situations complicated things for us. First, Congress passed a law, effective July 1, 1919, prohibiting the support of any government work by private funds. This meant that Mather no longer could personally supplement the salaries of Bob Yard and myself, and that of a clerk in Yard's office, as he had been doing from the start. Mather's supplement to my salary was only one thousand dollars a year, and although I would feel the difference, its loss would not hit me as hard as it would Yard. His six thousand dollar salary depended almost entirely on the money Mather contributed in order to match what the veteran newspaper man had been receiving in private life. This meant that Mather would soon lose Yard's services, and would have to find some other position for Yard outside of government, because he felt an obligation to him.

The other situation was one Mather got us into in a rash moment in the fall of 1918. He was having lunch one day with Hough, who had written many articles in support of the parks. Feeling grateful for Hough's staunch help, and without thinking of the consequences, or even thinking that Hough would accept, Mather offered Hough the job of superintendent of Yellowstone! To Mather's amazement, Hough felt flattered and accepted the job. Mather knew instantly that he had gotten himself and all of us in hot water. Hough really had no qualifications for the job other than a love for Yellowstone. He had never had any administrative experience, was very difficult and unpleasant to work with, and was then in his sixties, really too old for the job. He was also strongly disliked in Jackson Hole, a factor that would complicate our efforts to add the Teton area to Yellowstone. It was also generally known that Congressman Mondell, who was introducing our bill to expand Yellowstone, had no use for him.

As it happened, Hough was staying at my apartment with me temporarily, while Grace was back in Berkeley with her parents, awaiting the birth of our first child. So it became my uncomfortable task to try to talk Hough out of accepting the position. I reminded him of some of the drawbacks of the job — that he would have to stay in the park most of the time, could not do any writing, and would get only thirty-six hundred dollars a year, far below his accustomed earnings. As it turned out, Hough decided not to accept the job. But the part I had been obligated to play in getting Mather out of this hole would become a complicating factor in my future in the Park Service.

With Mather now firmly at the helm I found myself making repeated trips out west to handle various problems in the parks. I had been putting quite a bit of time into trying to get the Mount Evans area near Denver added to Rocky Mountain National Park. But Enos Mills felt things weren't going fast enough, and wrote a blistering letter to Secretary Lane attacking me personally as a menace to the entire cause of the national parks. I drafted an indignant letter to Mills, but then thought better of it and decided not to dignify his attack by replying. So I tore up my letter. But Mather did write to Mills, strongly defending me. I remember gratefully what he wrote: "in and out of season he has given of himself without stint to the exacting duties of his office, carrying a particularly heavy burden during the period when my own illness threw everything on his shoulders. Your charges are not even worth discussing, but I simply will not stand by in silence and have slanderous statements go by without a protest." When I went to the Rocky Mountains in October to inspect the Mount Evans area again, I made no contact at all with Mills.

In October, at Mather's suggestion, I went to San Francisco to set up an office as a base for working on the extension of Sequoia, getting California to build an all-year road into Yosemite, and lobbying the California legislature to allow the national parks in California to enforce laws and regulations within their borders. It would also allow me to be near Grace the last few months before our child was to be born.

I had been in San Francisco only a few days when I received a wire from Secretary Lane directing me to return to Washington at once; and on the way, I should stop over in Chicago and see Jack Hill, manager of the Stock Yards Inn. I was not to tell Mather that Lane had ordered me back.

Puzzled and concerned, I caught the first train east. Meeting with John A. Hill in Chicago, I found out what had happened in the two weeks since I had left Washington. Harry Child's son, Huntley, who had taken over the Yellowstone hotels and stores concession from his ailing father, had been fighting Mather over removal of the troops and the resulting loss of business. Young Child was a ruthless, unscrupulous fellow. He had come to Washington to see Mather and made a number of strong demands, and Mather had ordered him out of the office and said he would take over operations in Yellowstone. When Child defiantly replied, "Oh, I don't think you will do that," Mather instantly called in a stenographer and dictated a telegram to the acting superintendent, ordering rangers to take possession of the Yellowstone

Park buses and the hotel, and called Hill and told him to assume management of the Child concessions.

Hill assured me he himself had not taken any action on it, realizing that there was something peculiar about the whole matter. I agreed — these actions violated Mather's firmly held principle that concessions should be owned and run by private interests, not the government.

As soon as I got back to Washington, I went to see Secretary Lane, who told me that Mather was acting so wildly that it appeared that he was suffering a recurrence of his illness, although this time it was

Author, Mr. and Mrs. John Sherman, and Enos Mills (kneeling), Rocky Mountain National Park. Albright collection.

manifesting itself in extreme aggressiveness instead of the deep depression he had sunk into previously. Lane said Mather's latest brainstorm was to become a kind of one-man political action committee, with Mather sending fat checks to help re-elect those congressmen who were supportive of the Park Service.

From Chicago I had wired Mather that I was returning home to consult with him. So when I walked into his office, we talked for a while about Sequoia and Yosemite issues, then I gently brought up the Child affair and asked what was going on. In a totally uncharacteristic manner, he snapped, "You are not going to monkey in this. Go to your own office. I will see you tomorrow."

When I got to the department next morning I was told to be in Mather's office at 9:15 to attend the training classes he had been holding to teach principles of government to all the Washington officials of the Park Service and chiefs or officers of other Interior bureaus. It was embarrassing and ludicrous to see him conducting his class like a kindergarten teacher — even shushing me when I whispered to a colleague.

I went to him afterward, and asked, "Look, Mr. Mather, what is all this you are doing?"

"Don't you like it?" he replied.

"Well, it's just that we can't . . ."

"You're fired!" Mather shouted. "You have no business interfering with anything I'm doing. I am back here now and either you do what I say or get out."

Even though it was obvious he was not himself, I was stunned to hear him talk that way. I got on the telephone and called Mrs. Mather and his attorney in Chicago, and they persuaded Mather to spend some time in Chicago on the pretext that he could use it as the base for his election campaign activities. I accompanied him on the train trip, and once in Chicago we managed to get him home, where he could rest and receive treatment. Within a few weeks he was well enough to go to Henry Fairfield Osborn's secluded estate on the Hudson River, and from there went down to Hot Springs Reservation, where various friends spent time with him while he completed his recuperation.

At first, Secretary Lane talked privately of replacing Mather as Director of the Park Service with someone from outside. But he finally decided against it, and asked me to resume my role as acting Director.

While Mather was at Hot Springs, Harry Child came to Washington to talk to me about the confrontation between his son and Mather. Child wanted to know what he could do to get his properties back from the government.

"Go down and see Mr. Mather at Hot Springs," I told Child. "It's your son Mather had the dispute with, not you — maybe he'll give them back to you."

Child did so, and after a couple of days at Hot Springs he remarked to Mather: "The hotels were always a trouble to me. I'm really tickled to death to get rid of them. I hope you'll do better with them than I did."

Mather said, "Well, Harry, I'd rather see what you can do with them. I'm going to give them back to you."

7

A Turning Point

As 1919 BEGAN, I WAS BACK IN THE LITTLE OFFICE I HAD SET UP IN
SAN FRANCISCO (really just a desk the U.S. Public Health Service let
me use in its offices there). Mather was back on the job full time and
very much his old self, and I was able to put much of my time into the
role he had given me as his chief troubleshooter in the field. All the
national parks and most of the monuments were in the West. The
myriad of problems that cropped up could not be resolved with a phone
call (in those days we were very restricted in our use of long distance
telephone), telegraph was costly and did not permit discussion, and
travel from Washington to the West Coast meant a five-day train trip.
I had my hands full, juggling the several assignments Mather and the
Secretary had given me.

California still had law enforcement authority over the national
parks in the state — Yosemite, Sequoia, Lassen, and General Grant.
The situation proved increasingly cumbersome for the Park Service,
but to change it would require action by the California Legislature. I
spent a good deal of time in Sacramento explaining to legislators that
administration of the national parks in California was severely handi-
capped by lack of a federal tribunal, and that we needed the power to
punish people who violated regulations governing protection of fish
and wildlife or committed other misdemeanors. The Park Service
needed to have a federal commissioner appointed who could try cases
and assess penalties immediately, rather than having arrests made by
police or deputy sheriffs and cases tried outside the parks. One of my

colleagues from the University of California, Charles Kasch, was now a member of the state assembly. He proved to be a big help in persuading the legislature to pass a bill early in April that gave the National Park Service law enforcement jurisdiction within our park boundaries.

The managers of the Yosemite Company wanted a contract to expand their lodge development and I had to negotiate with them. Secretary Lane had a theory that companies operating concessions should pay the government top dollar for the privilege. So I had the difficult task of trying to get them to pay the government a higher percentage of the profits than they were accustomed to paying. They would have none of it. They needed to sell bonds to raise the needed capital, and being bound to a contract that cut that deeply into their profits would render the bonds unattractive to investors. They warned that the whole project would have to be scrapped. I talked and argued, even threatened, but they refused to budge. In the end we settled on their terms because Yosemite National Park sorely needed the additional visitor accommodations the new camp would provide. The fruitless negotiations ate up about a month of my time and caused a year's delay in getting the camp built.

Mather's highest priority as we entered 1919 was to get the expanded Sequoia park he so long had sought, taking in the canyons of the Kern and Kings rivers, the Mineral King region, and the high country around Mount Whitney. Conservation organizations, especially the Sierra Club, supported the expansion. But opposition was strong in several quarters. The U.S. Forest Service opposed giving up the timbered area they controlled; cattle and sheep grazers claimed they would lose valuable summer range lands and launched a strong protest. The city of Los Angeles had plans for eventually developing water resources in the area, and didn't want a national park. Most of the sportsmen's organizations opposed the expansion on grounds that it would put some of their favorite hunting places off limits.

When Theodore Roosevelt died early in January, Mather, always ready to seize a good opportunity, decided to change the name of the proposed Sequoia enlargement to the Roosevelt National Park, as a memorial to the great conservation-minded President. Actually, it was not a very logical idea. T. R. had never been to the area, and his normal inclinations would probably have led him to favor the side of the Forest Service, if the proposal had come up while he was President.

James D. Phelan, U.S. Senator from California, sponsored legislation to create the new Roosevelt Park, and quickly got it passed by the Senate by a unanimous vote. But when the measure was introduced in the House, the opposition was led by the congressman from the area, Denver S. Church.

Mather made a trip out to Fresno, the heart of Church's district, and made an emotional speech before the Commercial Club. He emphasized that Fresno would become a major tourist gateway, because the expanded park would attract more visitors than Yosemite. I concentrated on selling the idea in Visalia, and spoke to a gathering of business leaders from the area. I emphasized that Secretary Lane, Mather, and I were all native Californians, and were thinking of what was best for California when we proposed the new Roosevelt National Park. The influential Visalia *Delta* editorialized the next day: "We wish that every citizen opposed to the enlargement of Sequoia National Park could have heard Horace M. Albright. We are firmly of the opinion that nine out of ten would have come out of the encounter boosting for the larger park, for Mr. Albright has a vision, is armed with facts, and as a native of Inyo County has an unbounded enthusiasm for California's mountain wonderlands." Those were flattering words, but they didn't keep us from taking a beating. Back in Washington, Congressman Church, taking advantage of a shortened congressional session that adjourned on March 4, succeeded in bottling up the bill in the public lands committee, and the legislation was dead.

So much was going on that we hardly had time to stop and worry about the Sequoia defeat. Some of the previous year's work adding to the system was paying off, and before the end of 1919 the nation had three new national parks.

Legislation to transfer Grand Canyon National Monument from the Forest Service to the National Park Service had been passed by both houses of Congress in 1918, but final agreement had not been reached to resolve the differences between the House and Senate bills. Mining interests were opposing the legislation, and the Forest Service was still dragging its feet over some boundary questions. I was assigned to negotiate with the Forest Service, and worked out a compromise regarding the amount of its land south of the canyon rim that would be included in the park. Mather got support from enough members of Congress, especially Senator Henry Ashurst and Representeative Carl Hayden of Arizona, to pave the way for final passage, and the legislation creating Grand Canyon National Park was signed by President Wilson on February 26, 1919.

The Zion area in Utah had been one of my pet projects since the day I first saw it two years earlier. With the help of Utah Senator Reed Smoot, President Wilson had been persuaded to use his executive power to enlarge the existing Mukuntuweap National Monument in 1918 and rename it Zion National Monument. But I was determined that the magnificent site should have full protection as a national park. In November, during my brief stint as acting Director,

The Great White Throne, Zion, 1929. George A. Grant photograph. National Park Service.

I had gone to visit Smoot in his Senate office. I mentioned how good it would be for his state and for the Park Service to have a national park in Utah, and said: "Why not introduce legislation to make Zion a national park?" He went right to work on the idea, and early in 1919 introduced a bill. Zion National Park was thus created by act of Congress in November 1919.

In February, Congress had established Lafayette National Park on the coast of Maine, the very first national park east of the Mississippi River. In my opinion, it could have been named George B. Dorr National Park, for if ever a park was achieved by the inspiration and determination of one man, it was this one.

Dorr was an affluent Bostonian, sole heir of a textile company fortune. Like a number of wealthy people at the turn of the century, he had a home on Mount Desert Island, the largest rock island on the Atlantic coastline of the United States. In 1901, a small band of these home owners had become so disturbed by the growing development of Bar Harbor and other towns on the island that they formed a non-profit public corporation "for the purpose of acquiring and preserving for the perpetual use of the public key scenic areas and points of interest."

Head of the corporation was the president of Harvard, Charles W. Eliot. Dorr became its executive director and driving force. By 1913, Dorr had acquired several areas for the corporation, including Sieur de Monts Springs and the summit of Cadillac Mountain. But the Maine legislature nearly succeeded in passing a law to take away the corporation's charter. The measure was defeated only through Dorr's last-minute lobbying. To prevent further threats to the area, Dorr decided that the land already acquired must be given a more permanent form of protection. He convinced Eliot and the other trustees that an all-out effort should be made to get the federal government to make Mount Desert Island a national park.

I first encountered Dorr in 1913, soon after my arrival at the Department of the Interior. He had made several trips to Washington, and had been sent on one wild goose chase after another, for in those days few bureaucrats had any idea who was in charge of national parks. From Interior, where he had first sought help, he was sent to the Coast and Geodetic Survey, to the Smithsonian Institution, and finally back to Interior, where he had not been able to drum up any particular interest in his cause. He impressed me as a well-educated and obviously dedicated man, and when he told me his mission I did what little I could to help him. Up to that time, national parks had been created only out of land already owned by the federal government, and there was thus no precedent for Congress establishing a national park on privately donated land. But I told him it might be possible for him to get President Wilson to accept the land and declare it a national monument, as had been done in 1908 with Muir Woods in California. Secretary Lane pledged his support of such an effort.

Dorr worked for more than two years to secure clear deeds and prepare other documents. Finally, accompanied by a strong letter of support from Lane, the proposal for a national monument went to President Wilson in April 1916. The package even included a drafted proclamation for the President to issue when creating what Dorr wanted to call Sieur de Monts National Monument (after the French explorer whose expedition had led French colonists to settle on the island in 1613).

Several weeks went by with no response from the White House, so Dorr came to Washington to find out what was holding up the proposal. He enlisted help from Federal Reserve Board Chairman Charles Hamlin, an old friend of his from Boston, and Hamlin arranged a meeting at the White House—not with the President, but with the first lady. Dorr told Mrs. Wilson that he had come to extend to her and the President an invitation to spend a vacation at Mount Desert Island and see the proposed national monument. Mrs. Wilson told him that the President had indeed spoken to her about the area, but that he doubted that legal justification could be found for signing the proclamation.

Dorr rushed over to my office with this new piece of intelligence. I told him I suspected that the Forest Service was behind the President's misgivings, but Dorr assured me that the Director of the Forest Service, Henry Graves, supported it. Dorr turned to Maine Senator Charles F. Johnson for help. He gave Johnson documents confirming the legality of the proclamation, and persuaded him to go see the President the next day. Johnson emerged from the White House feeling assured that the President would now sign. But still nothing happened.

Dorr took his appeal to the President's son-in-law, Secretary of the Treasury William G. McAdoo, and asked him to find out what the problem was. McAdoo soon tracked down the source of the trouble: Secretary of Agriculture David F. Houston, who had great influence with the President, had sent him a memorandum pointing out that the National Monuments Act did not empower a President to accept private land for a monument. Dorr's friend Hamlin happened to be a neighbor of Secretary Houston. At Dorr's request, Hamlin contacted Houston and reminded him that President Roosevelt had proclaimed Muir Woods National Monument in 1908 under exactly the same circumstances when he accepted private lands from Representative William (Billy) Kent.

Then Dorr played his trump card. He got Harvard President Eliot to send a letter to Houston, who had been a Harvard professor. It said: "I know this does not come within your province, but I cannot but feel that you will be interested to cooperate with Mr. Dorr and myself in what we believe to be so much for the public good." After receiving the letter, Houston wrote to the President: "I have changed my view in regard to the proposed reservation on the coast of Maine and now think it highly desirable that you accept." Three days later, on July 8, 1916, President Wilson signed the proclamation, and much of Mount Desert Island became Sieur de Monts National Monument.

Dorr agreed to become superintendent of the monument at a salary of one dollar per year. Although sixty-three years of age, he was vigorous and enthusiastic, and there was no one who could have been a better choice for the job. But Dorr would not be satisfied until the area could be made a national park. And with dogged single-mindedness, he gathered support from every possible quarter and got legislation introduced in Congress. When Dorr learned that the House appropriations committee was holding it up late in 1918, he prevailed on ex-President Roosevelt, who wrote a letter to the committee. John

D. Rockefeller, Jr., whose gifts of land had created a large portion of the proposed park, also let it be known that he favored the legislation. Dorr proposed that the new park be named Lafayette after the historic French friend of America, because Sieur de Monts proved to be too obscure a name. Thus, as a result of George Dorr's almost superhuman efforts the legislation creating Lafayette National Park was signed by the President on February 26, 1919. (Ten years later it would be enlarged and renamed Acadia National Park.)

Mather put a good deal of time and effort into getting the ball rolling toward acquisition of the land for a redwood national park, specifically to preserve large stands of *sequoia sempervirens*. These tall, stately trees, native to coastal areas of northern California and southern Oregon, were being rapidly depleted for timber. Mather had been one of the key organizers in 1918 of the Save the Redwoods League. Early in 1919 he encouraged *Saturday Evening Post* editor George Horace Lorimer to tour a number of national parks, and to include a visit to the redwood groves we were considering for a national park. Lorimer must have been impressed, for he wrote an editorial deploring what was happening to the great trees, entitling it "Selling Scenery," and calling the saving of the redwoods as much a national matter as if Independence Hall or the Capitol in Washington needed saving from destruction.

In February 1919 our son, Robert Mather Albright, was born in Berkeley, and I was more grateful than I can say to be based in California and thus be near Grace during that important time in our lives. My work had kept us apart far too much the past several years. Grace did not like the oppressive summer heat and humidity of Washington, so she had been spending the months of June, July, and August in California with her parents. After little Robert was born, we talked long and seriously about our future. Now that the war was over and Mather was well and working at full strength, I no longer felt there were any factors obligating me to stay. I had already put off starting my law career for six years, and was now twenty-nine. I had had two excellent offers from San Francisco law firms, and Grace and I came to the conclusion that the time had come for me to submit my resignation.

It was a wrenching decision. The national parks and their mission had become central in my life. But my prospects in the Park Service seemed limited. Although I knew that Mather wanted me to succeed him at such time as he might decide to leave, I knew that Secretary Lane did not share his view. When I had been filling in as Acting Director during Mather's second illness and Lane had been contemplating a replacement for Mather, Lane had made it clear that I would not be among those considered. The one job that might keep me in the service would be that of superintendent of Yellowstone. That appealed to me as a tremendous challenge. It also would be field work, which would free me from the bureaucratic desk work of the Capital. The job paid thirty-six hundred dollars a year plus a comfortable home and use of an automobile, a lot better than my present twenty-five-hundred-dollar salary. Best of all, Grace would enjoy Yellowstone's delightful summer climate. But I saw no possibility of getting the job, since I had been the one stuck with the task of talking Hough into declining the job when Mather had unthinkingly offered it to him in the fall of 1918. How could I now seek it for myself?

In mid-March I put most of this soul-searching into a nine-page letter to Mather and submitting my resignation effective July 1, or as soon thereafter as he could find someone to take my place. "All that has already been accomplished is in greatest measure due to your broad vision, energetic and enthusiastic work, your financial backing and your wonderful personality," I wrote. "What I accomplished looks big to you, but I did everything easily because I was associated with you, and because I drew my inspiration from you. It will not be difficult now for you to work without me, and it seems that now is the time for me to form new connections in the West if I am ever to take this step."

I added in the letter that for several years, I had hoped that circumstances might make the superintendency of the Yellowstone available to me.

> Back in 1916, when Colonel Brett left, I wanted the place, but I felt that I could help you more in Washington then; I have thought longingly of the Yellowstone ever since. Your offer of this place to Emerson Hough last fall seems to make it impossible for you to consider any other person for it now. I was put in a position where I had to condemn the Yellowstone job in order to get Mr. Hough out of the idea of taking it, because I know it would be ruinous to our administration to have him in charge of this great reservation. I could not say that I was a candidate for the place, because I could not with propriety compete with Mr. Hough for it. In view of all that I have said, my appointment to the place would

doubtless alienate Mr. Hough's friendship for you as well as for me, and neither of us can afford to lose his friendship.

It is hardly necessary for me to say that I shall never get into any line of work that will interest me as much as national park work. I have been with you so long, and have really grown up with you in the national park development work, hence I have a deeper interest in this activity than I could ever form in any other. You and I know more about the parks than any other men on Earth; the National Park Service is our child; we have felt the thrill of achievement in public service through our activities. These things alone have bound me closer to the National Park Service than I can well express. If I could have my wife and my baby and my home, and at the same time continue in my beloved National Park Service, I should ask for little more in this world. Wealth I have never craved, but home life is as dear to me as anything can be, and this I do crave, this I must have.

Mather immediately wired me to reconsider my decision and return to Washington as a favor to him, to again take over as Acting Director while he and Secretary Lane were in Hawaii. They had planned a six-week trip to inspect Hawaii National Park and settle some difficult land acquisition problems. Because of my affection for Mather, I agreed to come to Washington for two months, but did not withdraw my resignation.

When I arrived early in April, Mather again tried to persuade me to stay in the Park Service, and as his ultimate lure, he offered me the superintendency of Yellowstone. "Think it over while I'm away," Mather said. "The job is yours if you will take it." While Mather was on his Hawaii trip, Grace and I reached our decision. I would tell him I had decided to cast my lot with the Park Service, and I would give up the idea of going into the practice of law.

It was a busy six weeks filling in while Mather was away, and I had to resist the temptation to let my thoughts dwell on the exciting challenges that lay ahead at Yellowstone. Throughout the growing national park system there were issues demanding attention. I still had to deal with Mills and the other impatient people in Denver who felt we were not trying hard enough to extend Rocky Mountain National Park to include the Mount Evans area. We had to start developing Grand Canyon as a national park, and decide how to expand the concessions to accommodate visitors. We were still trying to get good people to fill field positions, so I had to spend some of my time interviewing applicants.

Men were coming back from the war, and one day a full-fledged army colonel came in and asked for a job. In a slight English accent, he introduced himself as Colonel John White. He was tall, red-haired, and had quite a history. He had run away from England at the age of sixteen, looking for a war to get into. The only war he could find was between the Turks and the Greeks, so he joined the Greek army and got shot two days later. In the hospital recovering from the wound, he read about this war and concluded he had been fighting on the wrong side. Being English and only sixteen, he had no trouble being released from the Greek army. He came to America, arriving just in time to head for Alaska and the Klondike gold rush. He never found any gold, and wound up sweeping out a saloon. When he got back to the States, he had just missed the Spanish-American War, but joined the Minnesota Regiment, which was passing through Seattle on its way to the Philippines and needed some more men. When the U.S. troops were withdrawn, he joined the Philippine constabulary, fought in some of the bloodiest battles, and advanced to the rank of colonel. He then developed tuberculosis, and was retired. He came back to the States, took a cure, then spent his time knocking around in the mountains of the West, particularly in the national parks in California.

When World War I broke out he had become a U.S. citizen and tried to enlist. But he was rejected because of his health record. He wangled a desk job as an officer in the Signal Corps in Washington, and on Sundays he learned to fly. There was a severe shortage of pilots, so he managed to get sent to France, but the war ended before he got into the fight. He had known General John J. Pershing in the Philippines, and when Pershing heard he was in France, he made White one of the provosts in Paris during the peace negotiations. Now here he was applying for a job in the national parks.

"We just haven't any jobs for a man of your experience, Colonel," I said.

"Never mind the 'colonel,' " he replied. "What do you have? I don't care how menial it is, I want a job in the parks."

I couldn't offer a superintendent's job without checking with Mather. So I opened my desk to see what personnel possibilities we had. I found that we had several openings at the new Grand Canyon National Park.

"We've got a job open for a ranger in Grand Canyon," I said. "But you'd have to pay all your expenses getting down there, buy your

Superintendents' meeting, Denver, 1919. Stephen Mather and the Albrights second, third, and fourth from right in second row. Albright collection.

own uniform, and pay your own board and room. You may even have to buy a horse. And it pays only one hundred dollars a month."

Without hesitation, Colonel White replied: "I'll take it."

The next year, French Field Marshal Ferdinand Foch, the commander in chief of the Allied armies who had accepted the German surrender, visited the Grand Canyon. Ranger John White had the job of arranging his itinerary. Inasmuch as White spoke French, we had him meet Foch, show him the canyon, and tell him about the national parks. White took Foch out to Hermit's Rest and found a spectacular viewpoint. He thought that if Foch should make some quotable remark about the Grand Canyon, it would reverberate around the world. So he took along a little notebook, and asked Foch what his thoughts were on looking at this magnificent sight with the canyon floor five thousand feet below. Hands in his pockets, Foch walked to the edge of the canyon and looked down.

"Ah," Marshal Foch said. "What a place to bring a mother-in-law!"

White remained at Grand Canyon for two years, then went on to become superintendent of Sequoia National Park.

During Mather's trip we also brought aboard another former army officer. During the war, a very personable young major who was stationed in Washington, Roger Toll, had come around the Interior Department to talk about national parks. He was one of three mountaineering sons of a pioneer Colorado family that had been active in creating Rocky Mountain National Park. I had kept in touch with Toll after he had left the army and moved to Hawaii, so I suggested to Mather that he contact him while in the Islands as a possible candidate for the superintendent's position at Mount Rainier National Park, which was then vacant. Mather was quite impressed with young Toll, and hired him for the job.

When Mather returned at the end of May, he told me he had talked over my situation with Lane on the boat on the way back, and that Lane also very much desired me to take the Yellowstone superintendency. Mather said he wanted me also to act as his field assistant, and to come back to Washington during the winter months when Yellowstone was closed, help with preparation of the budget, and work with congressional committees. As one last assignment, I was to help find my replacement as assistant Director in Washington.

I had been thinking about the matter, and had decided to recommend Arno B. Cammerer for the position. Cammerer had worked his way up from a Treasury Department clerk to become private secretary to the assistant secretary of the Treasury, and then had become assistant secretary to the national Commission of Fine Arts, where he prepared the annual budget, appeared before committees of Congress, handled the Commission accounts, and at the same time was secretary of the Public Buildings Commission of Congress. He was about ten years older than I, and had been in federal service since 1904. I had worked with Cammerer on a number of park matters and had found him exceedingly competent. Mather also knew him from contacts with the Fine Arts Commission. After interviewing Cammerer, Mather hired him and announced the changes early in June.

I still had to stay on in Washington a few weeks. I had been dealing with the congressional appropriation committees on the 1920 Park Service funding in Mather's absence, and had to stay until the Congress finished its work on our appropriation. Finally, early in July, I made the move to Yellowstone.

8

The Yellowstone Era Begins

MY ARRIVAL AT YELLOWSTONE NATIONAL PARK ON JULY 10, 1919, opened an entirely new chapter in my life, and was nearly as big a change as going to Washington six years earlier. Not yet thirty, I was now to have full responsibility for the management and protection of one of America's greatest natural treasures, the world's first national park and our country's largest, covering more than two million acres.

Since its establishment in 1872, Yellowstone had never known the benefit of any real planning. Its first superintendent, Nathaniel P. Langford, was one of those early explorers who had fostered creation of the park. He had no funds or personnel, nor was there any formal plan for park management. There was little to guide him except the general wording of the 1872 Yellowstone Act, which allowed the Secretary of the Interior to provide rules and regulations to preserve the natural resources "in their natural condition."

In the first fourteen years of its existence as a park, Yellowstone had virtually no protection: sportsmen and commercial hunters shot bison, ranchers let their cattle graze within the boundaries, and visitors threw objects of all kinds into geysers and fumaroles to see what would happen — some even poured in soap flakes, hoping to trigger eruptions. On one occasion tourists traveling to the park by stagecoach were attacked by Nez Perce Indians fleeing the army.

The military presence shielded the park from poaching and prevented vandalism, but it didn't do the natural resources much good. The army had been sent in to provide protection and run the park in 1886, and the officers who served as superintendents over the years had no real understanding of wildlife management. Mountain lions, wolves, and coyotes were killed in large numbers; non-native fish such as rainbow, brown, brook, and lake trout and perch and bass were introduced without regard for the effects on native trout.

At the time the National Park Service was authorized in 1916, only one Interior Department employee was on the Yellowstone staff, chief clerk Chester Lindsley. When the army departed, he had taken over in a caretaker capacity as acting superintendent, and had been holding things together during the unsettled period when the army had been sent back in and then out again.

When I arrived, the permanent staff consisted of Lindsley, twenty-five rangers (five of them former army scouts), and a few engineers and maintenance people. But counting the temporary personnel hired for the summer, there were actually 258 employees in the park, including one blacksmith, a few mechanics, a buffalo keeper and a buffalo herder, and summer rangers.

As superintendent, I was of course responsible for all of them, plus the concessioners and their numerous employees, and I also had to see that the transportation system and primitive telephone line were properly run and maintained.

Concession management had improved only slightly since Stephen Mather had started knocking heads together back in 1916, and the four hotels, four permanent camps, several stores, and the transportation system were in need of attention. The government's own facilities, which had been adequate through the war years, were now being sorely stressed. Growing numbers of tourists were coming to Yellowstone by automobile. Although we had three hundred miles of roads, most were narrow, one-way roads built for stages, and every one was in urgent need of improvement. The campgrounds lacked running water and were extremely primitive, and the concessioners' camps had inadequate sanitation facilities.

I plunged into the work at hand, meeting the staff and coping with the dozens of situations that presented themselves at the height of the park's busy season. I left it to Grace to settle our little family into the fine house provided for the superintendent. For her, of course, my assignment to Yellowstone meant far more than simply a move to a new community. After four years as a fairly typical young Washington housewife, she was now the wife of the superintendent, and quickly found that a whole set of responsibilities and protocols went with the position. She took them on with her usual sensitivity and humor.

To get acquainted with the wives of park service employees, Grace held several receptions. It became apparent that many of the women had never before seen the inside of the superintendent's house. The get-togethers were a good source of information on the issues that affect morale. After one group was in for morning coffee, Grace reported to me that one of the most urgent and deeply felt problems in the park was the unfair pattern of employee housing. She had learned that an unmarried white-collar clerk was living in one of the well-built, four-bedroom houses, while a mechanic and his wife and four children were living in a one-bedroom house. "I don't care how many other things you're doing that seem more important," she pleaded. "You've just got to do something about this situation, and right away." She added that it would also be an awfully nice way to establish a good relationship with our official park "family."

I knew the problem. The employee housing complex, including the superintendent's house, had been built ten years earlier by the

THE FAN GEYSER.

army, which had assigned quarters strictly on the basis of rank. The large, sturdy houses, some with four or five bedrooms, went to officers. On the perimeter of the fort area were very small houses built for what the army called the "dirtynecks" — the enlisted men who did the manual labor. The size of a man's family was not a factor. When the army left and civilian staff had come in, Lindsley had been influenced by his wife in assigning quarters. As the sister of one of the army officers, Mrs. Lindsley had lived in the park for many years, even longer than her husband, and to her it seemed natural to continue the rigid military system.

Grace and I worked out a plan, and to launch it I called in the master mechanic, Bert Stinnett, who had the four children.

"Bert," I said, "your house is way too small for your family, isn't it? You know, that big house across the street from mine is vacant, why don't you and your family move in there?" Well, he just couldn't believe it, and neither could any of the other employees. The family moved in, and then we went on and shifted all the staff around into the housing that best fitted their need. Naturally, some who lost the choice houses weren't very happy, but they accepted the action on its fairness.

I soon found out that one of the superintendent's more pleasant responsibilities was to show distinguished visitors around the park, and Yellowstone had more than its share of them. I got to be a pretty good tour guide, because I had been reading the history and geology of Yellowstone for several years and could give the VIPs some background about the park. It gave me a welcome break from administrative work, and more than incidentally, made some good friends for the national parks.

About three weeks after I started as superintendent, 150 New Yorkers arrived on a tour arranged by the Brooklyn *Eagle*. The group was led by H. V. Kaltenborn, who was then associate editor of the *Eagle* and later became a famous radio broadcaster and commentator. I met the group in Denver and escorted them to Rocky Mountain National Park before showing them around Yellowstone. I also escorted them up to Glacier National Park, where Kaltenborn planned to present to the Blackfeet Indians a contribution raised by the paper.

The Indians met the special train and put on a series of dances, and Chief Two Guns White Calf and his colleague Fish Wolf Robe made Kaltenborn an honorary member of the tribe and bestowed on him the name "Mountain Chief." Kaltenborn was so moved that he wanted to respond with a personal gift, and gave the only thing he had available, his valuable Swiss watch that chimed. Later, at dinner, Kaltenborn was feeling blue about parting with his watch, so the next morning I arranged to buy it back from Fish Wolf Robe for fifteen dollars. Kaltenborn was elated, and so was Fish Wolf Robe.

The *Eagle* group was full of enthusiasm and esprit de corps, and soon were calling themselves "Eaglets," a name that stuck. Kaltenborn took them on to Mount Rainier, and later led other Eaglet tours to Grand Canyon, Mount McKinley, and Hawaii national parks. The tours won us many friends among easterners who might not otherwise have learned to appreciate the parks. Kaltenborn remained a close friend of mine and of the national parks the rest of his life.

Right after the Eaglets' departure I gave the "royal tour" to U.S. Assistant Attorney General Thompson and his family. Later in August I went down to Salt Lake City, where a governors conference was being held, and extended the governors an invitation to make a visit to Yellowstone afterwards. Not only did fourteen of them accept, but Delaware's Governor John Townsend recommended that I be made an honorary "governor" for that part of the 1919 conference.

One of those who came on the Yellowstone tour was Governor Robert Carey of Wyoming. I had stopped off in Cheyenne on my way out to the park from Washington, to talk with him about developing tourism in the Teton region and getting the area added to Yellowstone. He seemed to think it was a good idea, and while on the tour with the other governors, he mentioned that he was going to be addressing a public meeting in Jackson Hole a few days later. He suggested I attend too.

Remembering the warm reception the people of Visalia, California, had given my talk a few months back, I gave a similar talk to the citizens at Jackson Hole, describing the tourist growth that would be assured if their area was included in the national park. What a mistake! There was hardly a person in the meeting who favored the park. They let me know in no uncertain terms that they were vehemently opposed to hordes of tourists cluttering up their area.

Things got worse when someone held up a map showing a proposed road over Two Ocean Pass and around the eastern side of Yellowstone Lake. The pass straddles the point on the Continental Divide where water flows to both the Pacific Ocean and to the Atlantic.

Howard Eaton, originator of the "dude ranch," had brought the proposal to us in Washington, and we had given it some consideration. Eaton had a ranch near the Bighorn Mountains near Sheridan. He saw the road as a way for dude ranchers to move chuck wagons and other supplies for guests taking horseback trips into the backcountry area near Lake Yellowstone. But the idea was a red flag to the rest of the ranchers and dude ranchers, who saw it as a forerunner of federal interference and as the opening wedge in bringing unwanted development.

I had made a serious tactical mistake in not carefully checking the attitudes of the citizens before going to the meeting. I had assumed that these rugged Wyoming individualists were like other westerners we had encountered, most of whom welcomed national parks nearby because of the tourism and related economic development generated. Of course, tourism was by no means the main reason for wanting to get the Teton area included under national park protection, but since I had blundered into mentioning it, I would now have to bide my time and eventually find ways to win the group's support.

For me one of the greatest features of Yellowstone was its abundance of animals. Since boyhood I had been interested in wildlife, and in 1916 I had represented the Department of the Interior at a conference on wildlife protection held in the old Waldorf Hotel in New York. It was a source of satisfaction now to be superintendent of the park that was the country's largest wildlife preserve.

We had a very dry year in 1919, and had to fight a great many forest fires all summer. Then with the first snow storms in September, the elk started coming down from the high country, and finding no food, wandered into the valleys of the park. One day Chief Ranger Jim McBride, who had been an army scout at Yellowstone for many years, came to my office.

"Mr. Albright," he said, "there are hundreds of elk out on Blacktail Meadows. I wish you'd come and see them. It's a great sight." So we saddled our horses and rode out to a high point where we could look down into this great open valley. Elk were all over the place, as far as the eye could see. Jim said there were more than three thousand. Looking through my high powered glasses, however, and counting as best I could, I estimated that it was probably more like fifteen hundred.

It was a magnificent sight, but also foreshadowed a tragic situation. The valleys couldn't provide enough forage for so many animals, and as the storms drove more elk down from the high country, many strayed outside the park and were shot by hunters. We had never made a practice of feeding the elk, but now we tried to as a means of keeping them inside the park. William C. Gregg, a wealthy man in Hackensack, New Jersey, who had visited the park that year, heard about the situation and donated eight thousand dollars to buy hay. In Washington Mather went to work on Congress to get a small supplemental appropriation for the purpose.

Grace used her camera to record the sad scene of emaciated and dead elk, their carcasses being hauled away. When I went back to Washington I took the pictures along to help impress upon the appropriations committee the urgent need. Many newspapers published the photographs along with feature stories about the plight of the elk.

The extended 1919–1920 drought also provided a handy excuse for renewed efforts by Idaho, Wyoming, and Montana interests to raid Yellowstone National Park and divert some of its waters with huge reclamation projects.

As long as there had been any national parks, there had been attempts by reclamation interests to bend or change the laws so dams could be built to tap the water resources in the parks. Except for Hetch Hetchy in Yosemite, none had ever been built. The efforts continued, however. Mather and I kept an eye on the Federal Water Power Act being drafted this summer of 1919, for there was a move afoot to include in it a provision that would make all national parks and monuments subject to water-power projects.

At Yellowstone we were fighting not one but four separate proposals for huge water projects. The one posing the most immediate danger was a scheme by Idaho irrigation interests to build dams at the confluence of the Fall and Bechler Rivers in the southwestern corner of the park. The dams would form reservoirs within the park to supply irrigation water to eastern Idaho. Farmers in the area were claiming that the draught would cause them losses of $10 million in 1919. They argued that the desired site was a worthless, swampy part of the park, and the only water storage site available to them. Of course, plenty of other sites were available outside the park, but in none of them could water be supplied as cheaply as at the Bechler River site; the cheapness lay in the fact that it was government land, which they hoped to use without fee. It looked to me like this Fall River-Bechler project showed promise of being Yellowstone's Hetch Hetchy!

The area the dam proponents were referring to as a "worthless swamp" had been described in the 1878 Hayden Survey report as beautiful falls "which succeed one another at short intervals, have heights, respectively, of 12, 6, 12, 40, 20, and 30 feet and a short distance downstream, two falls of 20 feet and a third of 47 feet, also close together." A U.S. Bureau of Fisheries expert who visited the so-called worthless swamp in 1919 described it as follows:

> We found one of the most beautiful, if not the most beautiful valleys in all the park — flat as a floor, abounding in wild and domesticated grasses, and meandered by fine, clear streams in which native trout of large size may be taken in large numbers. At the head of the valley, within an area of not more than three miles, not less than eight streams fall from the timbered plateau, over falls and cascades which rival any in the park save the Great Falls of the Yellowstone.*

The Idaho irrigation advocates, with Senator Frank Nugent pushing their cause, appealed to Secretary Lane to allow a survey of the area, to pave the way for legislation to authorize a Reclamation Service dam and irrigation project. I protested to Lane, as did Mather, urging him to deny the permit. We told Lane that if he allowed the survey, the dam interests would then have a foot in the door, making it very difficult for us to prevent the project. However, the philosophy that had guided Lane years earlier as the chief government advocate for building Hetch Hetchy evidently still influenced him. Anxious to assist the Idaho sponsors, he wrote to Idaho Congressman Addison T. Smith: ". . . I thoroughly sympathize with the desire of the Idaho people to secure use of the waters within the park for the irrigation of their lands where such use would improve the park instead of injuring it, as would appear to be the case here." † Secretary Lane gave permission for a survey to be made.

I had no intention of doing anything to aid the survey, and when I received a letter from the Idaho people in late August informing me that they were ready to start the survey, I had all the horses taken out of the park for the winter. Yellowstone Lake was also to be included in the survey, so I had all the boats put up for the winter. It was at

* Annual Report, National Park Service, 1920.

† Hearing before the committee on rules, "Rule for H.R. 12466," 66th Congress, 2d session (May 25, 1920).

least some satisfaction to know that I had prevented any progress on the survey until spring.

Idaho was sponsoring another even larger scheme called the Bruneau Project. The desire was to dam Yellowstone Lake near the site of the now-famous Fishing Bridge. The project would tunnel under the Continental Divide from the Flat Mountain Arm of Yellowstone Lake to Beaver Creek. Such a scheme would seriously damage one of the park's most beautiful areas, including Heart and Lewis lakes. The project also included dams that would flood the Fall River valley.

Some Idaho politicians and farmers felt nature had conspired against them. The waters of Lake Yellowstone flow north into Montana through the intrusion of the Continental Divide between the lake and the irrigated areas of Wyoming. They also knew that Montana did not use all of the flood waters each year. So they advocated a project that would include a dam at the outlet of Lake Yellowstone, raising the water level twenty-nine feet, sending the stored water west through a tunnel into the Snake River watershed. According to our estimates, the project would ruin several thousand acres of feeding grounds for elk, deer, and other game, destroy 18 million board feet of lodgepole pine and spruce, and obliterate many picturesque islands in Yellowstone Lake.

When Montana politicians heard of Idaho's plans, they reacted quickly. If any state was to have the benefits of a reservoir in the park, they felt it should be Montana. So ten Montana counties mounted an effort to raise forty thousand dollars for preliminary surveys that could lead to major surveys by the U.S. Reclamation Service. They also proposed bonding the state of Montana to raise $20 million for construction costs.

These four projects, plus the dangerous provision in the Federal Water Power bill, would demand careful attention in the coming months.

In late September it was time to close the park for the winter. It had been quite a season, with a record number of more than sixty-two thousand visitors. The number of automobiles had increased from 4,700 (in 1918) to 10,700. All over the system, in fact, the national parks and monuments saw the number of visitors almost double, from 451,000 in 1918 to 755,000 in 1919, and the number of private automobile visits rose from 54,000 to 98,000.

Superintendent of Yellowstone, 1919. J. E. Haynes photo. Albright collection.

I left Yellowstone after closing the park for the winter, and headed back to Washington to help Mather and Cammerer in dealing with Congress. Mather had been building up the organization, and now had formed two new divisions — general engineering and landscape engineering.

While visiting Crater Lake in 1915, Mather and I had encountered a top-notch road builder, George E. Goodwin, who was working for the U.S. Army Corps of Engineers, planning and constructing roads at Crater Lake National Park. Mather hired him away from the Corps and made him our chief engineer, and later, director of a new general engineering department for the National Park Service. It was headquartered in Portland, Oregon.

Except for whatever overseeing Mather and I had been able to do, there had been no integrated planning in the construction of new buildings, camps, villages, entrances, roads, and trails. The situation called for someone who could give central direction and assure that whatever was built in the national parks and monuments was designed to have minimum impact on scenic values and harmonize with the natural surroundings. So Mather formed a division of landscape engineering, and hired as its director Charles P. Punchard, then working for the Office of Public Buildings and Parks of the District of Columbia. Punchard had accompanied Mather on several of his park visits since joining the staff, and helped out both at Yosemite and Yellowstone in planning and location of new permanent camps as well as rehabilitation of older ones.

Meantime, Mather continued to get expert advice from old friends. Yosemite and Sequoia benefitted from a 1919 visit by Charles Moore, chairman of the Commission of Fine Arts. And Frederick Law Olmsted advised on the planning at the new Lafayette National Park in Maine.

Mather was also continuing his efforts to get states to improve highways leading to the national parks, and to cooperate in establishing a national park-to-park highway. He made an auto trip through Washington, Oregon, and California, talking to state officials, and came to Yellowstone to speak to a conference of the National Parks Touring Association. The organization's stated purpose was "to secure the cooperation and coordination of all state and national highway

Author with elk calf in Yellowstone, ca. 1922. Albright collection.

associations with a view to a composite road system leading to and connecting the national parks."

Mather also drove through the coastal redwood grove area of California, still pursuing his long-range goal of getting a Redwood National Park established. He was accompanied on that part of the tour by Madison Grant, president of the New York Zoological Society, who had been one of the principal organizers of the Save the Redwoods League. Mather and Grant stopped in most of the towns along the way, urging community leaders to back the concept of preserving the best of the redwood groves and especially the big trees along the highways.

In Washington during the autumn, Mather and I decided we must oppose Secretary Lane on the various irrigation and power projects coming before Congress. But if at all possible, we wanted to handle it in such a way that we wouldn't be put in a position of having to resign over the matter. In the 1919 annual report to the Secretary of the Interior, which was a public document, Mather made a very bold statement on the subject:

> I contend that there can be no utilization of the lakes of the park, or of the Falls River Basin, for irrigation that will not bring with it desecration of the people's playground for the benefit of a few individuals or corporations. All of the lakes of the park are in heavily timbered districts. Great forests reach down to the water's edge. In some parts of the park, level tracts of land embracing thousands of acres lie at an elevation of only a few feet above these lake shores. Raising these lakes would kill millions of feet of timber, wipe out miles of roads and trails, and create a scene of chaos and destruction that would be an eyesore for a thousand years.
>
> Is there not some place in this great nation of ours where lakes can be preserved in their natural state; where we and all generations to follow us can enjoy the beauty and charm of mountain waters in the midst of primeval forests? The country is large enough to spare a few such lakes and beauty spots. The nation has wisely set apart a few national parks where a state of nature is to be preserved. If the lakes and forests of these parks cannot be spared from the hand of commercialization, what hope can there be for the preservation of any scenic features of the mountains in the interest of posterity?
>
> Yellowstone Park has been established for nearly half a century. Every plan to exploit it for private gain has failed to receive the consideration of Congress. Mighty railroad projects have even gone down to everlasting defeat. Must all the victories of the past

now become hollow memories by the granting of reservoir rights that will desecrate its biggest and most beautiful lakes, and form the precedent for commercial exploitation of all of its scenic resources — its waterfalls, its forests, its herds of wild animals, its mineral waters? It is to be hoped that the projects now being developed will meet the fate of the others that have come before Congress in the past.

I centered some of my anti-dam efforts on working with the American Civic Association, the Sierra Club, the Boone and Crockett Club, and the National Parks Association. They lobbied Secretary Lane as well as members of Congress, seeking to defeat the Yellowstone water projects.

One of our best allies was our old colleague Bob Yard, who was now executive director of the recently formed National Parks Association (later to become the National Parks and Conservation Association). Yard had been obliged to quit the Park Service after the new federal law prohibiting use of private funds to pay for federal work had forced Mather to stop paying the bulk of Yard's salary. Mather had then helped to fund the startup of the National Parks Association in mid-1919, and had arranged for Yard to be its executive director. It was organized along the lines of the American Civic Association, with several distinguished national leaders on its board. Its president was J. Horace McFarland of the American Civic Association, and vice presidents were Nicholas Murray Butler, president of Columbia University, Congressman Billy Kent of California, Henry Suzzallo, president of the University of Washington, and John Mason Clarke, chairman of the geology and paleontology section of the National Academy of Sciences. The stated purpose of the National Parks Association was "to defend the National Parks and National Monuments fearlessly against the assaults of private interests and aggressive commercialism."

The Fall River-Bechler water project bills had been introduced in the Senate by Frank Nugent and in the House by Addison Smith. In February 1920, the House committee on public lands requested a report from the Interior Department giving its position on the Smith legislation. Mather and I were in a quandary. Secretary Lane demanded that Mather prepare a favorable report on the bill, and Mather shifted the task to me.

I dragged my feet and delayed getting at the report, but finally came to the point where Lane was pressing me so hard that I would have to start on it. The night I sat down and faced the task, I realized I simply could not write favorably about it, and in a moment of total frustration I just pushed the whole file into the wastebasket, and then took the position the next morning that the charwoman must have mistaken the file for trash and thrown it away.

We gained a few more days' time while the department sent to the House public lands committee for a new copy of their request for the report. When the new request came I was really on the spot. I had no choice now but to write the report or else resign. I had a long talk with Mather about how to approach it. We even discussed whether both of us should resign over the issue and then fight it from the outside. We were still undecided on the approach when we had another stroke of what we were beginning to call "Park Service luck." Lane resigned! He had been in poor health for quite a while, and decided to quit for health reasons.

The new Secretary, John Barton Payne, who had been director general of the Railroad Administration during World War I, was an old Chicago friend of Mather. When Payne took over as Secretary of the Interior in mid-March, Mather immediately brought the Fall River irrigation scheme and the other water projects to his attention.

"I don't want to see Yellowstone invaded under any circumstances," Payne told Mather. "We'll kill those bills." It was just one of many indications that the new Secretary was going to be a great friend of the national park cause.

9

Defending the Parks

SHORTLY AFTER THE NEW YEAR BEGAN, MATHER PUT THROUGH PAPERWORK OFFICIALLY DESIGNATING ME AS HIS FIELD ASSISTANT, formalizing the work I had been doing for a long time. He felt the title would remind other park officials that although I was now superintendent of Yellowstone, I was also acting for Mather in general supervision of field operations in all of the national parks and monuments west of the Mississippi. Between those two jobs and trips to headquarters in Washington, I felt like a juggler trying to keep three objects in the air at once. But I enjoyed the challenge.

Early in 1920 I went to Washington to help Cammerer prepare the new budget and to take up the fight against the Yellowstone water project bills and the Federal Water Power Act. Although Secretary Payne had pledged to help us defeat them, there was still a danger they might become law.

In March, Mather gave me a wonderful assignment. I was to inspect Hawaii National Park, which had been created by Congress in 1916. I was to report on improvements that should be made, study possibilities for attracting visitors, and suggest possible additions to the park itself. Most important, I was to work out the details of land exchanges and remove the various obstructions that had been preventing actual establishment of the park.

It was a trip I would not have wanted to make without Grace. We figured that our family budget could afford the cost of her expenses, so she arranged for her parents to care for little Robert, and we sailed in mid-March to Honolulu. We were accorded a royal welcome and everyone made our stay delightful, but I could not help being acutely aware that a great deal was riding on the negotiations that were to occupy my days there.

The legislation creating the park contained two major stumbling blocks that had prevented us from doing anything at all to protect the area, staff it, or plan for visitor use. First was the usual restriction of that time, that no more than ten thousand dollars could be appropriated for any new park in a given year without a special authorization by Congress. The other problem was that no money at all could be appropriated for the park until the United States acquired perpetual easements and rights of way over such private lands in the park as were necessary to make it "reasonably accessible in all its parts." For this reason, Congress had provided only seven hundred fifty dollars for the park in 1918, the same in 1919, and one thousand in 1920.

The negative attitude of some congressmen toward the park is illustrated by a comment by one from Oregon, who said during the 1916 House debate on the bill: "It should not cost anything to run a volcano." Yet if we were to have a park, it was essential that we acquire the land and protect the resources. Vandals were pulling up and selling rare silversword plants. Among other problems requiring attention, feral pigs and goats also were overgrazing, causing serious erosion.

The park was divided into three large sections: Kilauea and Mauna Loa volcanoes on the island of Hawaii, and Haleakala Volcano on the island of Maui. More than half of the land within the designated park boundary was privately owned, and the rest, which was federal land, could not legally be maintained or improved until we could settle the problems of access to the privately owned portion.

When Mather and Secretary Lane visited Hawaii in 1919, they had tried to resolve the land acquisition issue. They had succeeded in working out an exchange plan in which other lands owned by the territory of Hawaii could be traded for private holdings in the park, but the individual exchanges remained to be worked out. Soon after creation of the park, the Parker and Bishop estates had given the territory some lands within the park boundaries and had promised to cooperate in exchanges for their other lands inside the park. However, the agreement was contingent on Congress passing legislation to give the governor of Hawaii the authority to make these exchanges. Such legislation had been enacted by the Senate in 1919, but not by the House. Finally, it passed both houses of Congress and was signed into law by President Wilson on February 27, 1920.

In Honolulu I worked on the land exchanges with Territorial Governor C. J. McCarthy, his staff, and with Land Commissioner C. T. Bailey and trustees of the Bishop estate. The Bishop trustees took a highly patriotic view of all problems affecting estate lands within the national park boundaries. In 1916 the trustees had offered to sell or exchange 11,837 acres of their land near and inside Kilauea crater and including part of Halemaumau, the active fire pit. The land also included some of the best forests in the park. Although by 1920 the value of this sector of land had risen to more than $125,000, the Bishop trustees held to the 1916 valuation of $52,800. While I was there an exchange was worked out with the territory of Hawaii. Nine hundred acres of sugar fields the territory owned on the island of Hawaii (valued at fifty thousand dollars) were traded for the 11,837 acres of Bishop land. The territory then turned over the Kilauea land to the federal government for the national park.

I also used the time in Honolulu to promote Hawaii National Park and its potential for tourism. In that connection, Grace and I were entertained one Sunday morning by the venerable Judge Sanford B. Dole, the first president of the republic of Hawaii and the first governor of the territory. I also met with officials of the Hawaii Tourist Bureau, the Hawaii Publicity Commission, and the Trail and Mountain Club of Hawaii. Lorrin A. Thurston, a prominent Hawaiian editor and publisher, who was a friend of Mather and had attended our 1919 park conference in Denver, was also trying to help boost tourism, and was helpful to me.

The interest in tourism was very great. There were only three large first-class resort hotels in Honolulu at that time, and all had lost money during the war years. Their proprietors were now counting on Hawaii National Park to attract more visitors to the islands.

Grace and I sailed from Honolulu to the island of Hawaii, landing at Hilo. Charles S. Judd, the territorial forester, accompanied me on my extensive field inspections. He was a most valuable source of information on many issues the park would have to deal with.

The Kilauea section of the park was a veritable treasure store of wonders — steaming and dead craters, with forests of great primeval tree ferns, many of which had fronds thirty feet long. There were tree molds — perfect casts of great trees that had been buried by torrents of lava and then burned up, leaving behind in the ground perfect impressions of their form. Birds were abundant and beautiful, but I learned that several species were near extinction.

The central feature of Kilauea was Halemaumau, the large, live "lake of fire," a sight that impressed me so much that I wrote in my report to the Secretary that it was

> the most wonderful feature of the National Park Service, surpassing the geysers of the Yellowstone, the waterfalls of the Yosemite, and even the big trees of Sequoia National Park. It is the most awe-inspiring thing that I have ever observed, and I have no hesitation predicting that when once the people of the United States realize what a remarkable thing this volcano is it will become the objective of thousands of visitors.

During my tour, there was a spectacular but temporary phenomenon to be seen about six miles from the crater. A lava flow had burst forth a few months earlier (December 1919), sending rivers of molten lava down valleys to the sea, and at one area forming a 150-foot-high hill that was still growing when I saw it. This so-called Kau Flow was not inside the park boundary, so I recommended that it be added. It had significant scientific value, and even after the flow stopped and the lava hardened, it would give visitors an idea of the overwhelming size and power of a lava flow.

At the rim of Kilauea's crater the U.S. Weather Bureau maintained the Hawaiian Volcano Observatory, and I met with its director, the distinguished volcanologist, Dr. T. A. Jagger, Jr. Just outside the park, I inspected a 650-acre tract that included Volcano House, a small inn and guest house, located on the road that was the main approach to the park. This was the logical site for a hotel and campgrounds, but the Bishop trustees had been considering subdividing the property. The status of the inn was also now in doubt because its owner had recently died. I recommended to Mather that we try to get Congress to extend the boundary to include these 650 acres, and advised him that the Bishop trustees seemed likely to be amenable to a land exchange, and that is what later was worked out.

At the Mauna Loa section of the park there were no acquisition problems because the Bishop estate had already given its holdings there to the territory. However, there was an urgent need for management and protection of the park land. Cattle grazing needed to be elimi-

The Albrights return from Hawaii trip, 1920. Albright collection.

nated and the number of feral pigs reduced because of the erosion they were causing.

On the way to Kona on the other side of the island, we visited Honaunau, the City of Refuge. In the seventeenth and eighteenth centuries it had been a walled temple area that provided haven to fugitives and victims of religious persecution. The enormous temple of stone, though partly in ruins, is still considered the best preserved of all the ancient buildings of the islands. I felt Honaunau was of great historical value, both as an ancient refuge and place of religious rites, and as an example of the feats of strength achieved in a time when there was only manual labor available to lift huge rocks to build the temple walls. Although it was in private hands, I found out that its owners would consider donating it to the government if they could be assured that the ancient temple would be cared for properly. I recommended that the ruin be given consideration as a national monument. It finally became a national historical park in 1955.

On the island of Maui I inspected Hawaii National Park's second-largest section, the 10,032-foot-high Haleakala peak and its vast, beautiful crater. With a twenty-mile circumference, the crater is one of the largest in the world. Judd and I spent most of two days walking the sixteen miles down into and across the crater, camping overnight near the far rim. The crater floor was like another world, its cinder cones and lava a colorful mix of reds, browns, yellows, and blacks. Although hardly any vegetation was visible, we saw large, spiked, gray-green silversword plants in groups of a dozen or more at various points, growing out of the stark ground pumice and cinder that covered the crater's surface. The silversword is unique to Hawaii, growing only in this crater and on some high mountain slopes of the island of Hawaii.

Two large meadows just outside the crater were owned by the Haleakala Ranch Company, and I recommended in my report that the park boundary be extended to include them. I had learned from officials of the company that they would agree to a land exchange.

Our final stop was on Kauai, the Garden Isle. Although none of the park was located on Kauai, there was some thought of including its Waimea Canyon, and my mission was to assess whether it ought to be given further consideration. I found it to be a beautiful miniature of the Grand Canyon of the Colorado, though its abundant vegetation made its walls greener. I reported that I believed it would not be advisable to push at this time for its addition to the park. Waimea appeared to be in no danger, and Kauai was not then in any position to handle the influx of tourists that would result from Waimea being added to the national park.

I spent much of the three-day voyage back to the States on the Matson Line's flagship *Matsonia*, writing my report. Returning to Yellowstone, I learned that the dam situation had been heating up in Congress. In April Senator Nugent's legislation, S. 3895, "A bill authorizing the granting of certain irrigation easements in the Yellowstone National Park," was passed by the Senate. Representative Smith's similar bill (H.R. 12466) was reported on by committee. Smith tried twice to get it passed on the unanimous consent calendar, but in each case we were able to get a supportive member to object, thus preventing a vote. Then Smith introduced a resolution calling for special immediate consideration after one hour of debate. Several conservation organizations launched a protest and demanded a hearing by the House rules committee on the merits of the Smith resolution. The protests, together with Mather's testimony at the hearing, resulted in a favorable response from the rules committee. So the Smith bill failed to reach the House floor for a vote.

The dangerous federal water power bill still hung over us. Lane had supported it without even consulting Mather. When Payne became Secretary, Mather had explained how the legislation would allow construction of dams and power projects within national parks and monuments, and that we must try to get it amended to delete that possibility. Payne went right to work on it and had a meeting with President Wilson. The President then called the bill's sponsors to the White House. They were Wesley L. Jones of Washington and our perennial enemy, Walsh of Montana. President Wilson told them he would veto the legislation unless he received their promise that they would amend the bill during the next session of Congress to eliminate national parks and monuments from provisions of the act. Nor would he allow any permits for projects within Yellowstone in the interim.

They gave him their word, and President Wilson signed the Federal Power Act into law in June 1920. The newly-created Federal Power Commission almost immediately received several applications for water-power rights in Sequoia and Yosemite National Parks. Secretary Payne quickly intervened, and the Commission adopted a resolution to the effect that no applications for water rights in national parks and monuments would be considered until after Congress had had an opportunity to amend the power act.

Many of Yellowstone's elk had failed to make it in the devastating winter, but the major part of the northern herd survived. On my early winter trip to Washington, I had lobbied with Mather and Cammerer to persuade Congress to make a general deficiency appropriation, and we obtained thirty-eight thousand dollars to buy feed. Even that had not been enough, however, when additional heavy storms had swept the park in March and early April. Concerned citizens and the American Red Star Animal Relief had then come to the rescue with an additional forty-seven hundred dollars in donations to buy more hay, enabling hundreds more of the elk to survive.

The heavy snows followed by a cold spring made it seem almost impossible to get the park ready for visitors by June 20, the scheduled opening date. By May 10 there were still huge drifts in the passes, and there was no way anything could move more than four miles south of the park headquarters at Mammoth Hot Springs. Neither horses nor men could possibly remove all that snow and open all the roads in a month, even if we had had the personnel and the funds, which we did

**Muir Woods National Monument, 1936. George A. Grant photograph.
National Park Service.**

not. Then our master mechanic had an idea. He set to work and constructed a huge plow in his shop, and secured it to the front of a
seventy-five-horsepower Caterpillar tractor, with the idea of using it to
push the snow from the road. He endured a lot of sarcasm about his
outlandish contraption, but the remarks turned to cheers when he succeeded in clearing a roadway eleven feet wide from Mammoth to Old
Faithful, to the Grand Canyon of the Yellowstone, and to Yellowstone
Lake by June 1. And he cleared the passes shortly thereafter, with
time left for repairing the roads and enabling us to open the park on
schedule.

Just before the park opened, I had to deal with a situation that infuriated me. The previous December, the Museum of the California Academy of Sciences had applied for a permit to collect a family of four grizzly bears as specimens, claiming that Yellowstone National Park was the only place where they could be secured, and that the mounted group of grizzlies would be of great scientific value. Knowing that we had only an estimated forty grizzlies in the entire park, I had flatly refused the permit. However, Secretary Lane overruled me.

On June 1, the representatives of the California Academy arrived and set up headquarters at the Grand Canyon of the Yellowstone. The scientists, who were experts with bow and arrow, told me they would use arrows to shoot the grizzlies. I insisted for their safety that they take an experienced bear hunter, Ned Frost, with them. They quickly killed three grizzlies. When I reminded them that their permit allowed them to take only one more, they told me they had not been able to find another suitable specimen, and asked permission to kill a particularly large grizzly that had been seen near the canyon garbage dump. I refused permission, not wanting them hunting in an area frequented by visitors. Nevertheless, they stationed themselves beside the trail used by the grizzlies to get the garbage, and there they killed *four more* bears! After this killing, no bears, either black or grizzly, appeared in the area for nearly ten days. Not only did this incident destroy seven bears, it left four young cubs motherless. I sent Mather a full report on these killings, with a strong recommendation that in the future no more permits of this kind be issued.

When the park opened, record numbers of visitors arrived, and among them a record number of Very Important Persons. Secretary of the Interior Payne came in July accompanied by Secretary of the Navy Josephus Daniels. When it had become known that Payne was planning to make a personal survey of the proposed Yellowstone Lake irrigation projects, Senator Walsh had joined the party to argue his position. Payne, with his good sense of humor, goaded Walsh with questions about why he was so eager to sacrifice Yellowstone National Park. But Walsh remained determined to push ahead on the dam projects and also on the federal water power bill.

While in Washington, I had invited Congressman James W. Good of Iowa, chairman of the House appropriations committee, to visit Yellowstone. Right after Payne and his party left, Good arrived with seven members of the committee, along with N. J. Sinnott, chairman of the House public lands committee, J. B. Beadle of the U.S. Reclamation Service, and the wives and friends of several of the members. I personally accompanied them for the five days of their visit, which they considered to be an "official fact-finding mission." Louis Cramton of Michigan, a great friend of the National Park Service, was in the party, and I made certain that he and all the others got to Yellowstone Lake and heard our story of how proposed dams and irrigation projects would ruin the park. But dam proponents also made sure their side was heard. U.S. Reclamation Service Director A. P. Davis and his construction engineer met with the congressional party at the Lake Hotel to press their case.

I managed to take several congressmen on a side trip to Jackson Lake so they could see the advantages of expanding Yellowstone to include that area and part of the Teton Range. In fact, I saw to it that all our influential visitors visited Jackson Lake and heard why the Teton area should be added to Yellowstone. When I took *Saturday Evening Post* editor Lorimer and his family there he remarked, "The best part of Yellowstone Park is not yet in the park," and he volunteered to work for the addition of the Teton Range and the Jackson Hole area through a series of editorials in the *Post*.

I also realized that to make progress on protecting the Teton-Jackson Hole area I was going to have to win the trust of the group there. I must demonstrate to them that I wanted protection of the area just as much as they did. In the summer of 1920, an issue came along that I thought might give me a chance to do so.

The U.S. Reclamation Service, the state of Wyoming, and some development-minded cattlemen and business people in Jackson Hole were pushing Congress to approve construction of dams on Leigh, Two Ocean, Emma Matilda, and Jenny lakes. Under the Carey Irrigation Act of 1894, the Department of the Interior was allowed to approve some dam building projects without congressional approval, and private interests were seeking to use political pressure to get the dams built. All of them would have been within the area that I hoped someday to bring into a national park. The dam proposal for Jenny Lake was the worst, since it would raise the water level several feet, ruining what is surely one of the scenic jewels of the nation. I let writer-dude rancher Struthers Burt and the others in the Jackson Hole group know that I was siding with them in fighting the dams. In my opposition, I made an enemy of the state of Wyoming's chief engineer,

Frank Emerson. He later became governor and caused the Park Service trouble.

There was a legal technicality that I thought might help us. In 1918, when we had thought the Yellowstone extension bill would pass, President Wilson had issued an executive order withdrawing from all forms of entry or disposal about six hundred thousand acres within the Teton National Forest. This was done to prevent development interests from claiming mineral, grazing, or other rights before we could acquire the land for a park. That executive order had remained in effect, even though the Yellowstone extension bill had failed, and it still gave the National Park Service veto power over the Forest Service in certain management decisions relating to the Teton National Forest, where the proposed new dams would be built. The Forest Service quickly tried to get the presidential executive order revoked, but Mather and Cammerer were able to block the move, and our opposition resulted in the Jenny Lake and Leigh Lake proposals being withdrawn.

The state of Wyoming meantime continued to push for damming the other two lakes, which were in a different area, some distance from the Tetons. They admittedly were not as scenically important as Jenny and Leigh Lakes, but to dam them would go against all that I was working for in the area. The Forest Service favored the dams, however. Our opposition brought those two dams down to defeat as well, and the folks in Jackson Hole began to form a better opinion of me and the Park Service. Burt and the other Jackson Hole protectors still were not ready to back addition of the area to Yellowstone National Park, because that would involve a ban on hunting and some of the other activities they wanted to continue. However, they did begin to think in terms of some sort of federal recreation area, perhaps under the jurisdiction of the National Park Service. They had found they could not trust the cattlemen, the state, the Forest Service, or the Reclamation Service. So they all were beginning to look at the Park Service as perhaps their best ally.

The parade of VIP visitors to Yellowstone continued all summer, including two more U.S. senators, four other representatives, officials of five railroad companies who were interested in bringing tourists to the park, a tour group from the National Park-to-Park Highway Association, and twenty-seven members of the Massachusetts Forestry Association making their annual tour of parks and monuments. Bob Yard of the National Parks Association came, and Emerson Hough and his wife spent six weeks in our home (working on a novel, "The Covered Wagon," which became a best-seller). Hal Evarts of the *Saturday Evening Post* came to do research for a magazine article on Yellowstone. No conventions were held in the park that summer, but many groups arranged their trips to or from the Democratic National Convention in San Francisco to include a visit to the park, as did people attending other conventions in the western states, such as the Shriners' in Portland, Oregon, and the National Education Association's in Salt Lake City.

Most visitors' enjoyment of the park seemed to be enhanced if they listened to talks or lectures explaining and interpreting the geological phenomena, the wildlife, the trees, and the flowers. I was taking steps to make more such talks available. For many years the hotel and camp concessioners had offered occasional talks, some of them quite good, some not. When the army was administering Yellowstone, soldiers had at times given "cone talks" for visitors at Upper Geyser Basin, although an 1888 report indicates that their accuracy may have left something to be desired. In 1904, a Lieutenant Henry F. Pipes had established an arboretum and botanical garden and labeled its trees and plants. As early as 1911, Jack Haynes, operator of the photographic concession in Yellowstone, had given lectures to visitors at Old Faithful, and the Wylie Camping Company had been presenting campfire programs at their camps.

Shortly after assuming my duties as superintendent, I had heard a lecture by naturalist Milton P. Skinner, who had been employed by the hotel concessioner, Harry Child, to give talks to guests. He had

NOON AT THE CAMP.

been studying Yellowstone's wildflowers, mammals, and birds for many years and had good ideas about presenting programs to the public. I felt he could accomplish more by becoming a member of the Park Service staff, and I arranged to hire him as a ranger. The next year I was able to create an entirely new position of park naturalist, and Skinner expanded the educational program. He organized additional natural history lectures, guided field trips to points of interest, prepared natural history bulletins that were given to visitors or posted around the park, and started developing a park museum in the former bachelor officers' quarters at park headquarters. I also hired two seasonal rangers to help him with lectures and guided trips. One was Frank Reedy of Southern Methodist University, who had been visiting the park each summer. The other was Isobel Bassett Wasson, whom I had discovered the previous year with Kaltenborn's Brooklyn *Eagle* party.

The *Eagle* tour group from New York was visiting the park, and I was walking through the lobby of the Mammoth Hotel one evening after dinner just in time to overhear a young member of the party giving a talk on Yellowstone. She was doing an outstanding job of it. So I returned the next evening to hear her talk on the geysers and geological features of the park. She really knew her subject, and even included comparisons with geysers in New Zealand and Iceland. Complimenting her afterwards, I learned that her name was Isobel Bassett, she was a geology major just out of college, and she was on the *Eagle* tour with her parents (her father was a city planner and former congressman). I told her that if she would come back next year I would be glad to hire her as a seasonal ranger. She was married in the meantime, but still came to work for us in the summer of 1920 as Yellowstone's first woman ranger, one of the first in the National Park Service.

Other interpretive activities had been going on here and there in the national parks and monuments as well. In 1905, Frank Pinkley, custodian of Casa Grande ruins in Arizona (which was then a reservation and later became a national monument), had built an exhibit of archeological artifacts found in the ruins. Long before Rocky Mountain had become a national park, Enos Mills had guided people who were staying at his own Longs Peak Inn and conducted training courses for nature guides. The Glacier National Park Hotel Company had offered guided nature walks in 1919, and had employed Gertrude Norton, who came to be known as the "flower lady."

Mt. Hillman (Glacier Peak), the Devil's Backbone, Llao Rock, and Wizard Island, Crater Lake National Park, 1933. George A. Grant photograph. National Park Service.

Mather, of course, had been "educating" people about the national parks by every means he could think of ever since joining the Department of the Interior. He had encouraged various nature interpretation activities at Yosemite, and in 1919 had arranged with the University of California extension division to put on a series of twelve lectures in June and July. They were called the Le Conte Memorial Lectures, in honor of University of California professor Joseph Le Conte's contributions to science and to the park. One of the lecturers, Dr. Francois Emile Matthes, a geologist with the U.S. Geological Survey, stayed on in Yosemite after the series to give talks at the public camps and at the evening campfires of the Sierra Club hiking groups.

That same summer, Mather heard about an interpretive program at Lake Tahoe and went there to investigate. A Sacramento couple, Dr. and Mrs. C. M. Goethe, had become interested in nature education during a trip to Europe. With resort owners in the area, the Goethes hired Dr. Harold C. Bryant, education director of the California Fish and Game Commission, and Dr. Loye Holmes Miller, a professor at the University of California at Los Angeles, to work during their vacations giving nature talks and guided tours at Fallen Leaf

Lake near Lake Tahoe. Mather talked the Goethes into letting Bryant and Miller bring their educational program to Yosemite, where it could serve a larger audience, and he hired the team for Yosemite's 1920 summer season. Mather got the California Fish and Game Commission to contribute Bryant's salary, and raised the rest of the necessary funds through contributions.

With Bryant directing and Miller assisting, the Yosemite Free Nature Guide Service was launched. Park ranger Ansel F. Hall was assigned to work with them. A graduate forester from the University of California, Hall had spent a year as a park ranger at Sequoia National Park before going to France during World War I with the Army 10th Engineers. He rejoined the Park Service in 1919. Guided nature walks, evening lectures at hotels and campgrounds in Yosemite Valley, "nature play" activities, and games for children were offered on a regular schedule in various parts of the park. It was usually possible, in a ninety-minute guided excursion, for visitors to see fifteen to twenty varieties of birds, about twenty kinds of wildflowers, some ten or twelve species of trees and shrubs, and even a few bird nests. More than twenty-seven thousand visitors participated in the programs that first season, and many of them also attended the Le Conte lecture series, which was continued at Yosemite in 1920.

Mather spent many summer days at Yosemite, and closely followed this experiment in natural history interpretation. Eager to extend interpretation activities, he financed a lecture series which Bryant and Miller gave in the fall in the midwest and east. He also featured them at the National Conference on State Parks.

By the time we closed Yellowstone for the winter, the park had recorded more than eighty thousand visitors, an increase of 28 percent over 1919. We added twenty-eight miles of trails to accommodate the growing popularity of hiking, and by the end of the year had a 620-mile trail system. About two-thirds of our visitors came by car and we estimated that 60 percent of them carried their own tents and equipment and camped out. We put in new campgrounds at Mammoth Hot Springs, Upper Geyser Basin, Grand Canyon of the Yellowstone, and the Yellowstone Lake outlet, and piped drinking water to them. But toilet and sewage treatment facilities were and would continue to be far from adequate.

In late September, after the last of the visitors had left, I took a two-hundred-mile pack trip through the southwestern wilderness of the park, accompanied by Joe Douglas, an assistant chief ranger. No superintendent had been through this wilderness for twenty-five years, and I wanted to see for myself the areas that would be affected by the proposed irrigation projects. It was easy to see why Thoreau had written, "In wildness is the preservation of the world." Those days were among the most thrilling of my life. We were totally on our own in some of the most beautiful, wild, and rugged country in the United States. There were wonderful opportunities to see quantities of wildlife — buffalo, elk, deer, bear, and some of the park's largest moose. When we reached the Fall River Basin, it was clear that the Reclamation Service topographer who had described it as "swampy" had been dead wrong. I later got the Geological Survey to do a new survey, which corrected the maps.

I returned to Washington in late September to find presidential election year politics filling the air. The Republican challenger was Warren G. Harding, and there were signs that he might win. Although our jobs were not political appointments, we were uncertain that we would be able to keep them if there was a change of administration. Mather had strong friendships with many Republican leaders, but there were others who might not feel too charitable toward us — Harry Child, for instance.

Child had gotten his hotels back after his son's fracas with Mather, but he was still upset with us over various matters concerning his Yellowstone interests. He was also an influential Republican and boasted of his friendships with Harding and Theodore Roosevelt. When Harding won the presidential nomination, Child had been heard to make remarks to the effect that changes would take place in the National Park Service. He was annoyed that superintendents had authority to oversee his concession operation. But I had found, when I arrived as superintendent, that Child's hotel and restaurant facilities were not kept up as they should have been. He also had been encouraging his hotel managers to catch fish for the dinner meals. As soon as I was made aware of the situation I prohibited the commercial marketing of fish, and tried to get Child to improve his hotel facilities. At the same time I restricted the areas where he could cut dead and down timber for fuel, and I put the hotel's woodcutting under the supervision of the chief ranger. Child was indignant and threatened to get me fired.

Toward the end of the 1920 season I wrote a report to Mather listing violations of Park Service regulations by Child and owners of other concessions. I noted, "My idea in writing this report is that should, by any chance, I not be in charge of the park after this year, my observations and findings of the operation of these companies may be useful to the Service in perhaps more than one connection."

Mather stayed out of the election campaign, but when Harding won our trepidation increased. We certainly would have a new Secretary of the Interior, who might well want to pick his own Park Service Director. This was the first time the administration had changed hands since the establishment of the Service, so there was no precedent.

When Congress began its lame duck session in December 1920, we renewed our efforts to get the Federal Water Power Act amended. Senators Walsh and Jones had reneged on their promise to President Wilson that in the next session they would push through an amendment to protect national parks from water-power projects. But we had powerful allies. Secretary Payne worked on members of Congress, and most of the major newspapers supported protecting the parks.

The amendment that finally passed exempted national parks and national monuments from provisions allowing permits for water power projects to be granted. But the amendment applied only to parks and monuments already in existence. So any time a new area was established, we would have to ensure that special protection was written into the legislation creating the area. President Wilson signed the legislation as one of his last official acts before leaving office on March 4, 1921.

We had one other major fight in Congress during the lame duck session. Senator Walsh introduced a bill to erect a dam across the Yellowstone River, alleging that it was needed to prevent spring flooding, which he said did great damage each year to crops in Montana. At the first hearing on the bill, the Park Service was not asked to testify, but we and our friends made such a protest that two days were set aside for additional hearings.

The Senate committee on irrigation and reclamation of arid lands was stacked against us. Among its twelve members were Jones, Walsh, Albert B. Fall of New Mexico, and Frank R. Gooding of Idaho. I testified about the effect of the proposed dam upon the park, and the

Park Service chief engineer, George Goodwin, gave persuasive testimony on the engineering reasons against building the dam. Secretary Payne's strong statement enraged Senator Gooding, who accused Payne of endangering the food supply of the entire nation.

"What do you say to *that*, Mr. Secretary?" Gooding asked sarcastically.

"Well, Senator," replied Secretary Payne pleasantly, "there's a heap more in this world than three meals a day."

Our lobbying was successful. Despite the efforts of those western senators, the legislation was defeated.

We then had to await President-elect Harding's nomination of a new Secretary of the Interior. When he announced as his nominee his old Senate crony Albert Fall, gloom settled over all of us in the National Park Service. Not only was Fall one of the committee members who had opposed us on the dam issue, he was known to have personal interests in mining, stock-raising, and ranching and, as far as we knew, had no leanings toward protection of national parks. It looked like very bad news indeed.

10

A Grotesque Scheme

ALBERT FALL, THE SELF-STYLED, ROUGH-AND-TOUGH WESTERNER AND
ADVOCATE OF RESOURCE DEVELOPMENT, HANDED US A PLEASANT SUR-
PRISE. Several of our influential friends knew how worried Mather
and I were that Fall would replace us with people who might ruin all
that we had worked for. But when they went to visit the Secretary-
designate after Harding's inauguration, Fall told them he had no
intention of replacing Mather or me, or of disturbing the National
Park Service in any way. We got another nice surprise when Harry
Child, despite all his veiled threats, actually influenced the Montana
state legislature to pass a joint resolution recommending that President Harding retain Mather and me!

Mather felt it would be a good idea, however, to "educate" the
new Secretary, and he persuaded Fall to take two trips with him to
visit national parks during 1921. In early summer they spent several
days at Yosemite, and at the end of the summer they came to Yellowstone for ten days. There they were joined by Mrs. Fall and their
young grandson, and by Idaho Governor D. W. Davis and the director
of the U.S. Reclamation Service, A. P. Davis.

I gave them the full treatment, including a carefully planned stop
to view the potential damage that would be done to the Fall River-
Bechler area if a dam were to be built there. I made sure the party —
including Reclamation Director Davis — saw the mess in Jackson
Lake caused by his bureau's failure to cut and haul out trees before
flooding the area when they built the Jackson Lake dam in 1911.

I showed them the Grand Tetons and gave my usual sales talk about the importance of protecting the Teton-Jackson Hole country by adding it to Yellowstone National Park. Mrs. Fall won everyone's heart by pitching in to help with the cooking when the party stopped for a meal at a ranger station. She and their grandson stayed behind with Grace when the men took a rugged wilderness pack trip into the Absaroka Mountains in the southeastern part of the park.

Mather missed no opportunities to impress on Secretary Fall the importance of preserving all of the park areas. On the pack trip he repeated my argument that most of Yellowstone should be left in its original natural state, untouched by the hand of man. I don't know how much the Secretary knew about conservation when the tour started, but by the time he headed back to Washington, he had become a parks enthusiast. Mather told me that Fall had assured him that we were free to select rangers and any other employees without regard to their political affiliation, and that he would give us his support in stopping the irrigation and reclamation projects in Yellowstone.

Secretary Fall must have felt he was among friends, for over the campfire one night he poured out his troubles to us. He told how his long public service had kept him from his ranch operation, and he was deeply in debt. He said he had to get back to the ranch, and probably would not stay long at Interior. He also talked about the problem of the oil reserves that had been put under the jurisdiction of the Navy Department. He believed they belonged under Interior, and he was going to try to get them back and open some of them to exploration and development.

I summoned the courage to argue that even if the oil reserves were turned back to the Interior Department, they should be kept "locked up." Secretary Fall replied: "Albright, I'm surprised at you taking that position. You are a western man; you know how important oil is. We must be sure we have enough of it going into production to prevent any slowing up in our industrial growth."

I couldn't let that pass. "Oh, but you see, I'm a confirmed conservationist," I said, "and I want to see our resources protected for the future."

In September, Hough and his wife came to the park again, but this time they borrowed a house from Child. Grace was expecting our second child, and we were both relieved not to have the writer and his wife staying with us. It seemed like Hough was just naturally grouchy, and he was downright unpleasant to have around. To make things worse, his wife was as disagreeable as he was, and she made life miserable for him as well as for us. Hough had taken to arguing with me, particularly over my efforts to build up visitor use of the park. Then in mid-September he stirred up a tempest.

It seemed that at the Canyon Lodge, a luncheon of trout had been served to a group of two hundred railroad men. Hough heard about it and accused me of not enforcing the regulation about commercial fishing. I looked into the situation right away, and found out that although some lodge employees had indeed caught the fish and served them to the guests, no one of the workers had exceeded the legal limit of ten trout each. It was therefore not a legal infraction, but I told the concessioner in no uncertain terms that it violated the spirit of the regulation. He assured me it would not happen again. When I told Hough about the conversation, he ranted that I had double-crossed him, that I was just protecting the concessioner and that I should have thrown the book at him. I figured it was just another of Hough's grouches, and considered the matter closed. But it was not.

When Hough went home, he wrote an editorial for the *Saturday Evening Post* about the desecration of an unnamed national park.* The editorial said in part that "the violator of the law who escapes punishment in a national park goes home ripe for further contempt of all game laws. His offense runs on, it grows. So also does the offense of any official who winks at violations of his own regulations."

He hadn't mentioned my name, but I thought it was perfectly obvious who he was writing about, and I felt it also cast aspersions on the management of national parks generally. I was furious, and complained to Mather, saying he ought to do something about it. I also wrote to *Post* editor Lorimer, and when I went east for the winter, I visited him in Philadelphia and had dinner at his home. Lorimer admitted that the editorial had somehow gotten past him, and agreed that it was unfair. In the future, Lorimer told me, Hough would write nothing but fiction for the magazine. "Mr. Lorimer," I replied, "if you asked me, I'd say he hasn't written anything but fiction for years, including a lot of your editorials."

Once I cooled down, I recognized that there had been no need to react quite so strongly. Hough was, after all, a valued friend of the

* "Shall Our Game Join the Dodo?", January 21, 1922, p. 22.

Secretary of the Interior Albert Fall's party at Yellowstone Lake, 1921. Fall in front standing second from left, Stephen Mather second from right, author fourth from right. National Park Service.

parks, and despite his unpleasant personality, a good friend of mine. As it turned out, no one paid much attention to the editorial.

It had been even more difficult than usual to part with my little family and undertake my field work and a trip to Washington, for Grace had given birth to a beautiful little girl, Marian, just four days before Christmas. My yearning for home was at least partially pushed aside by the intensity of the work. I found the headquarters staff in the throes of an exceedingly embarrassing situation created by Secretary Fall. Shortly after he had returned from his 1921 tour of the national parks, he had sprung on Mather an elaborate scheme for an all-year national park in New Mexico. He said he was acting in response to the urgings of the chambers of commerce of El Paso, Texas, and several towns in southwest New Mexico — Tularosa, Las Cruces, Alamogordo, and others — which had organized an association to secure enactment of a bill to establish such a park. Some proponents referred to it as the Mescalero Park Bill or the Mescalero Park and Indian Bill, for it not only would establish a national park, but it contained several provisions that would provide benefits for the Indians on their reservations. Fall called his idea the All-Year National Park, and the group of chambers of commerce called their organization the All-Year Park Association.

After the association had drafted the bill, Fall redrafted it, explaining that he wanted to make sure that the members of the Mescalero Apache tribe, who were his friends and supporters of the bill, would be fully protected. The park was to be composed of about five areas unconnected with each other. One area of about two thousand acres was on the Indian reservation. Another area was to be the Malapais, an extensive region of lava beds forty miles northwest of the center of the reservation. Another proposed sector was the White Sands area, sometimes called the Gypsum Hills. The plan called for the inclusion of Elephant Butte Reservoir, which was administered by the Reclamation Service, and was ninety miles west of the center of the proposed park and some fifty miles from either Malapais or the White Sands.

So the park, made up of these various unconnected units, would look like a kind of strung-out horseshoe. In the midst of it all, but outside the park boundaries, sat Fall's ranch, in the Three Rivers area adjacent to the Mescalaro Reservation. In describing it, Fall was fond of saying that this would be a different kind of national park. Indeed it would be, allowing hunting, grazing, timber cutting, irrigation projects, and mining, thus introducing into a national park nearly every possible form of commercial exploitation. To arguments that what he was proposing bore little resemblance to a national park, Fall offered the answer that Hot Springs and Platt weren't really national parks, either. So why not have something like this all-year park?

The proposal put Mather in a very difficult position, for it was exactly what he did not want national parks to be. He had been working to establish higher — not lower — standards. In addition to the bad precedents that were involved, there would surely be criticism of Fall for trying to establish a national park surrounding his own ranch. During the winter of 1921–22, Mather was able to devise ways to delay action on the scheme, but in the spring, Fall renewed his efforts. In May 1922, Mather found himself unable to continue putting off the Secretary, who wanted him to visit the ranch and look over the sites for the proposed park. Still dragging his feet, Mather went first to Rocky Mountain National Park and took a snowshoe trip with Superintendent Toll, then went to Denver with the park transportation concessioner, Roe Emery. Then he and Emery went on down to New Mexico by car, arriving at Tularosa near the Mescalero

Apache Reservation on May 1. They spent several days traveling over the area before Mather went home to Chicago, where he wrote me a long letter in which he tried to sort out his thoughts on the situation.

"The Elephant Butte dam and reservoir is an interesting body of water but not adapted to national park use as we know it," Mather wrote. "Everybody is quite enthusiastic in that section for the park idea but it is because they must have some place to get out of the heat of the desert and so the mountains and the lake mean so much to them." He concluded, "I don't see how the thing is workable at all; certainly not as a real national park, but only as an adjunct of the Indian Reservation."

I had barely received the letter when I got a wire from Mather to meet him in Denver. When I arrived, he had been trying to draft a report for the Secretary to transmit to congressional committees endorsing the All-Year National Park, and the more he wrote the more disgusted he had become.

Mather, in a gloomy mood, poured out his feelings about how grotesque Fall's park scheme was, and showed me a penciled draft of the memorandum he had been writing to the Secretary, reporting negatively on the project. But he had been agonizing over whether to send it. He had spent many months trying to educate Fall on the national park concept, and had carefully built a good relationship that had benefited the parks despite this one crazy scheme. Now, if he sent the negative report, he would put all that in jeopardy. Yet he could not let this travesty of a national park go unchallenged.

I felt useless, not being able to offer any solutions, but he didn't expect any. He seemed only to want to talk out his problems with me, as he had done so often over the years. After I went back to Yellowstone, I found out that Mather had not returned to Washington. Evidently seeing himself heading into another breakdown, he had gone to a sanitarium in Stamford, Connecticut, and remained out of action for six months. Later, he joked about his disappearance, when his friends applauded the "fortuitous" illness that helped him avoid getting himself fired over the all-year park issue. Having talked to him that night, however, I believe the danger of another serious breakdown had been real.

During Mather's absence, Cammerer took over as acting Director. Fall asked him to visit the all-year park area so he could write the report which would have to go to Congress as the Interior Depart-

Superintendent of Yellowstone, 1922. Albright collection.

ment's position on the proposed national park. Cammerer told Fall: "I have to stay here and run the parks while Mather is out. And besides, I don't have the background for judging something like this. After all, I came here from the Fine Arts Commission." Fall answered, "Well, then, let Albright go down and look at it." Cammerer replied that I was busy opening Yellowstone, but he would ask me.

I knew that anyone would be in trouble with that report, so I said it would be difficult to leave Yellowstone at the time, which was true. Not only were we having the busiest season ever, but we were deeply involved in preparations for celebrating the fiftieth anniversary of the founding of Yellowstone National Park.

I had always been intrigued by the story of how the whole idea of a national park had been born near the confluence of the Gibbon and Firehole Rivers on the night of September 19, 1870. Cornelius Hedges and others in the Washburn-Langford expedition had been sitting around a campfire that night, talking about the geological phenomena and scenic wonders they had discovered in this uncharted area. As the story goes, Hedges remarked to his colleagues and then wrote in his diary that "God made this region for all the people and all the world to see and enjoy forever. It is impossible that any individual should think he can own any of this country for his own in fee. This great wilderness does not belong to us. It belongs to the nation. Let us make a public park of it and set it aside . . . never to be changed, but to be kept sacred always."

Whatever influence this incident may have had, Yellowstone became the world's first national park by act of Congress on March 1, 1872. To celebrate the golden anniversary, we lined up a host of dignitaries to participate in a ceremony in the park on July 14.

So I had a legitimate excuse for not going to New Mexico and then writing the All-Year Park report. Not to be deterred, Fall decided to write a report himself. He then persuaded New Mexico Senator Holm O. Bursum, who had taken over the Senate seat left vacant when Fall had become Secretary, to introduce and push the legislation in the Senate.

With no official report from the National Park Service, but with a strong recommendation from Secretary Fall in favor of the bill, Bursum held hearings and quickly got the Bursum Mescalero Bill (its official title then) to the Senate floor, where it passed unanimously with only a few senators present. When Fall tried to get the bill through the House, however, he ran into trouble. The rules committee sent the bill to the committee on Indian affairs rather than to the public lands committee, which usually considered park measures. Fall did not have much influence on the Indian affairs committee, and the bill languished there until the 1922 session adjourned.

When the new session of Congress started early in January 1923, we were still having difficulty with Secretary Fall over his idea for Mescalaro National Park, or All-Year National Park, as Fall chose to call it. The House committee on Indian affairs scheduled a hearing on January 11, even though it still had not received a report on the proposed park from the National Park Service. No representative of the Park Service was present, although a coterie of conservationists appeared to testify against it. Mather was by this time in Chicago, completely recovered and ready to return to work, but I had advised him to stay out of Washington until after the hearings. We did not want him to come back and face the choice of resigning or writing the report on the all-year park. We also believed that Fall's days as Secretary were numbered. There were indications that his rumored participation in the Teapot Dome and Elk Hills oil leases, being investigated by Senator Tom Walsh, was about to explode into a scandal.

The hearings opened with the big guns of the conservation movement loaded for action. They included J. Horace McFarland of the American Civic Association, Bob Yard of the National Park Association, and George Bird Grinnell, president of the Boone and Crockett Club. They opposed the bill on several counts. The park would be made up of too many widely separated sites, none of which had features that would qualify them for national park status, and the proposed park lacked the protections given other national parks. McFarland made the point that National Park Service Director Mather had not made a report on the bill, and that the committee should not act until it had an authoritative report on the national park quality of the scenery from Mr. Mather, who had inspected it. McFarland also commented that instead of making a national park, Congress was in danger of making a national joke, and referred to a *Saturday Evening Post* editorial which called the proposed park "Mexican Freckles," because it was made up of so many discontiguous areas.

Senator Bursum spoke in support but was obviously unfamiliar with the bill's provisions and expressed vague and sometimes contradictory views as to how the park would be managed. Others speaking in favor of the bill were representatives of the chambers of commerce in the area, the Office of Indian Affairs, and a citizen from Las Cruces.

After lunch, Secretary Fall arrived to testify, having been summoned hastily by a despairing park advocate who perceived that the entire committee appeared to be against it. The Secretary gave his reasons for having started the idea: since the National Park Service provides ranger service, sanitary camp sites, hotel and transportation facilities for the people who visit the national parks, he said, there was no reason why the people in the southwest should not have this service extended to them, too. He thought that the Indians would be benefited by having park areas within the reservation, because they could make a profit guiding tourists, renting horses, and selling crafts. He saw no difficulties in administration. But he was unable to designate the particular areas which would be in the park because the surveys had not yet been completed.

All of the committee members asked Fall tough questions, and he was driven during three hours of testimony to abandon point after point in the bill, including the reservoir, the badlands, and the gypsum desert, until little was left except New Mexico gaining the status of having a national park. The committee seemed ready to compromise by making it a recreational area under the Indian Bureau, but Secretary Fall stuck to his original concept, and would not accept anything less than a national park.

The opposition by conservationists and the lack of a report by the National Park Service kept the bill from being reported out by the committee so it could come to a vote in the House. Then, in late February Fall suddenly resigned, and the all-year park disappeared from the scene and was not heard of again.

Fall was, of course, later convicted of accepting a bribe from the wealthy oil man, Harry Sinclair. I have always had the feeling that Fall was the victim of circumstances. The leases he sold to Sinclair and Edward L. Doheny were correct. The trouble was a conflict of interest — Fall borrowed money from the oil men and then lied about it. But he shouldn't have gone to prison. I never could understand why, if Sinclair was acquitted of giving a bribe, how they could convict Fall of accepting one. Secretary Fall had always been fair with the National Park Service, never insisting that we promote or testify in favor of his pet scheme. I continued to remain friendly with him, even visited him many years later when he was in a veteran's hospital and almost penniless.

11

Building the Ranger Mystique

By 1923 THE NATIONAL PARK SERVICE WAS FIRMLY ESTABLISHED. With rapidly increasing numbers of visitors coming to the national parks, we concentrated on building a strong internal structure for the Service. Dr. Hubert Work, the Secretary of the Interior who took over after Albert Fall resigned in 1923, was supportive, and left Mather alone in running the parks.

From 1923 to 1928 I continued my multiple duties, spending most of the time at Yellowstone, but also getting into the field a great deal in the winters and spending a few weeks in Washington, especially around budget time. Improving Yellowstone and its services to visitors as the flagship of the National Park Service and securing protection for the Tetons and the Jackson Hole country, however, were the projects on which I placed my highest priority.

Those years of the mid-twenties did not see the addition of much land for parks, although we achieved a milestone in 1926 when Congress authorized three major new national parks in the East — Great Smoky Mountains in North Carolina and Tennessee, Shenandoah in Virginia, and Mammoth Cave in Kentucky. Important as that was, the funds had to be raised to acquire the private lands comprising most of the three parks. The laws authorizing the parks stated that all the private land had to be acquired for each park before it could be established and opened for visitor use, which took many years. In 1923 Carlsbad Caverns in New Mexico was declared a national monument by presidential executive order and Alaska's Glacier Bay National Monument was established in 1925.

The most important achievement during those years was the progress we made on building a national park *system*. When we had organized the Park Service in 1917, each of the fifteen existing national parks was an independent entity. Gradually we had hired new superintendents, enunciated our policies for managing the parks, added to the field staffs, and begun to make them feel they were part of a National Park Service rather than just employees at an individual park.

In 1923 the parks had almost ten times the 356,000 visitors they'd had in 1916, and as the crowds increased, Mather came to realize that his idea of looking to other agencies to supply the expertise for specialized work was impractical. So we were beginning to build up within the Park Service the capability to provide services and maintenance and to improve the quality of the experience a visitor could have in a park. A key element in the latter was the national park ranger.

Mather had a special vision of what the rangers should be. He felt they must bring to the Service not only knowledge and skill, but an ability to relate to the public and a considerable measure of dedication.

The seeds of a national park ranger tradition had already been sown before Mather and I arrived on the scene. Some of the qualities that still characterize park rangers today are derived from the distinctive backgrounds, skills, and experience of those early park protectors.

It is said that the first national park ranger was one Harry Yount, who was appointed "game-keeper" of Yellowstone in 1880, even before the army was sent in to give protection to the park. He had been in the Union army during the Civil War and had worked as a bull whacker and buffalo hunter in the Yellowstone area before the park was established. The superintendent of Yellowstone at the time was Philetus W. Norris, the park's second superintendent. Yount's job was to see that hunting limits were observed (hunting was not prohibited in those days) and to keep the geological features from being vandalized. The one-thousand-dollar salary he received for his yearly work represented a substantial part of the fifteen thousand dollars appropriated by Congress for Yellowstone in 1880. He acted as guide for visiting officials, and escorted Secretary of the Interior Carl Schurz on an 1880 tour of the southwestern part of Yellowstone.

Yount resigned at the end of 1881, telling Superintendent Norris that the large area covered by the park made it impossible for a game-keeper to protect the game properly. He recommended that "the game and natural curiosities of the park be protected by officers stationed at different points of the park with authority to enforce observance of laws of the park maintenance and trails."

When army cavalry troops were sent to Yellowstone in 1886 to protect and administer the park, regulations allowed the hiring of a few civilian scouts. These scouts were picked for their skill in woodsmanship and wilderness survival, and their lore and ways of life rubbed off on some of the soldiers. Among them were Jim McBride, Harry Trischman, and Raymond Little, who became park rangers and remained at Yellowstone for many years.

In another branch of the rangers' "ancestry" were the old forest rangers hired temporarily by national parks in California in 1898. Army troops were then administering and protecting Yosemite, Sequoia, and General Grant national parks, but in that year the troops were withdrawn for a few months to fight in the Philippines.

The Department of the Interior's General Land Office (which was then in charge of national forest reserves) hired these "forest rangers" to take the place of the troops. They were to prevent poaching, remove sheep that were grazing in the parks, fight fires, and even plant fish. When the troops returned, the army kept two of the forest rangers in Yosemite over the winter for protection, and then hired them as regular all-year employees. In 1905, when Congress transferred the forest reserves from Interior to the Department of Agriculture, four of the forest rangers who had been working in national parks in California elected to remain with the parks. At first they continued to call themselves "forest rangers," even though their pay vouchers identified them as "park rangers."

In 1906 the Interior Department appointed Gabriel Souvelewski as supervisor in charge of the park rangers and other employees who remained in Yosemite over the winters. He was also in charge of the two regular park rangers in the park during the summer season. Souvelewski brought some special experience to the ranger tradition. He had joined the army in 1888 and advanced from private to quartermaster sergeant, and served with an army troop in Sequoia National Park in 1891 and then with a troop in Yosemite from 1895 to 1897. He had gone off to the Philippines with the soldiers, and when they returned, he had served as a packer and guide. When the supervisor of rangers post was offered him, he left the army and spent the rest of his career with the national parks. He served as superintendent of Yosemite for a brief period in 1916 (although the post was then called park supervisor), and when Washington B. "Dusty" Lewis was appointed superintendent later that year Souvelewski became supervisor of maintenance and trails.

Walter Fry, who became a ranger at Sequoia in 1905, had a degree from Kansas State Normal College. He was selected to be in charge of both Sequoia and General Grant national parks during the winter seasons, when the army troops were not present. In 1912, Fry was named chief ranger and, during the winters, acting superintendent. When the army pulled out permanently in 1914, Fry became the first civilian superintendent of Sequoia.

A man who contributed both skills and force of character that became recognized as desirable in rangers was Forest Townsley. He was a patrolman on the Sulphur Springs Reservation in Oklahoma Territory, and became a park ranger when Platt National Park was created out of Sulphur Springs Reservation in 1906. He applied for a job as a park ranger at Yosemite in 1913. No transfers were allowed in those days, so he had to resign from his job at Platt to take the job at Yosemite. Within three years he became chief ranger at Yosemite, a post he held for twenty-seven years except for brief periods when he was sent to organize a ranger force at Grand Canyon National Park and to serve as acting superintendent at Lassen Volcanic National Park.

A rather loose national park ranger service had been formed in 1914 during the brief time Mark Daniels had served in San Francisco as general superintendent of the national parks. We had rangers in nine national parks at that time, and Daniels was supposed to bring uniformity to the ranger activity. He was not able to do much along those lines, however, because each park pretty much set up its own procedures for its rangers. Daniels did manage to draft a set of regulations governing rangers in the national parks, and they were signed by Secretary Lane in January 1915, just before Mather took over administration of the parks as Lane's assistant.

Mather liked the regulations and had them distributed to all the parks. They provided for a standard uniform (which Daniels had designed), and for rangers to write monthly reports showing the duties performed each day, their travels, conditions of the game animals, any unlawful trespass, and other activities. Applicants for ranger positions had to be between twenty-one and forty years of age, of good character, sound physique, and tactful in handling people. They were required to possess a common-school education, be able to ride and care for horses, have experience in outdoor life, be a good shot with rifle and pistol, and have some knowledge of trail construction and fighting forest fires.

With the uncoordinated state of ranger activities in the various parks, however, the regulations caused a good deal of confusion. By the time Daniels left his post, little progress had been made toward establishing anything resembling a coordinated ranger service. After the organic act was passed in 1917, there was no longer any need for the separate ranger service Daniels had set up, and it was merged with the new National Park Service.

Mather had a number of ideas for the national park ranger mystique that he wanted to create, and he implemented them over the years as funds and circumstances allowed. For one thing, he wanted to be able to transfer rangers from park to park. He thought higher educational standards should be required. He also wanted rangers to take entrance examinations and meet qualifications similar to those required by the Civil Service (at that time Park Service field employees were not technically under the Civil Service). He was thinking in terms of careers for Park Service personnel.

In his 1916 annual report, Mather wrote,

> The longer a man is in the service the more valuable he is, and, therefore, I think a ranger should enter the service with the desire of making it his life's work, and after the service is once fully organized, promotion to higher positions should be made in the corps, so that each man would have the fullest incentive to give his best service, knowing that advancement would be based solely on character and general efficiency.

It was a long time before these aspirations could be realized, however, and Mather had to exercise patience while putting through the bureaucratic changes that would make them possible. Meantime, he was attracting good people to the service through something less tangible. He called it *esprit de corps* and he used every means at his disposal to build it. One of his earliest tools was *National Park Service News*, a six- to eight-page monthly newsletter that he started in 1919. In launching it, Mather wrote that it was important for the personnel in the individual parks to be brought into closer contact with each other and also to know what was going on in the Washington office, "and to realize some of the broad purposes which we are trying to carry out."

Each year Mather visited as many parks as humanly possible, spreading his Park Service gospel, that those entrusted with the care of our nation's great national parks are members of an elite corps. And he believed it sincerely. He proudly made it a point to wear a ranger uniform when he was in the parks and monuments.

One day at Yellowstone in the summer of 1923, I got word that visitors were upset with a ranger directing traffic at Tower Falls. It seems he was throwing his weight around, lecturing people about little infractions of the rules and generally making the visitors very unhappy. I couldn't imagine which ranger might be doing that, so I went out to see what was going on. Mather at the time was in the park, taking a few days rest at Camp Roosevelt, and I particularly didn't want him to find out. When I got to Tower Falls, I couldn't believe my eyes when I saw who the "ranger" was. It was Mather in his park uniform, directing the bus drivers how to park their vehicles, shouting at the drivers because he didn't like what they were doing and forcing them to repark. When I told him about the complaints he said he didn't see what the people were so upset about. "I'm just enforcing the rules," he insisted.

"Mr. Mather, the visitors think you're splitting hairs and making a fuss about things that don't matter that much."

"Nonsense," he said. "The trouble is you're too soft. You don't enforce the rules strictly enough."

When I said firmly that he must stop it, he got quite huffy and said I had no right to tell the Director what he could and could not do.

"Maybe not, Mr. Mather. But I do have authority over my rangers, and if you're going to play ranger here at Yellowstone, you're going to have to do what I tell you."

Well, that did it. "All right," Mather replied. "I'll be Director and quit being your ranger."

He got over his pique quickly, and we had many a laugh over the incident later. But it said a lot about the intensity of his regard for the job of the national park ranger.

His visits to the various parks were always eagerly anticipated by the rangers for they were always times of good fellowship. Through these frequent visits his distinctive vision of the national parks and the uniqueness of their personnel permeated the outlook of the whole Service.

There is no question that Yosemite was his favorite of all the parks, and he spent time there every year. It was the place where he launched his newest programs, tried out his ideas, and worked to enlarge and improve the concessions. One innovation was the Rangers Club House he erected in Yosemite in 1920, financed out of his own pocket. Rangers can seldom walk about a park or go into public places without being "on duty," answering questions of visitors. The club house gave them a place to relax together out of the public eye and in a place exclusively theirs. Once it was built, Mather himself usually stayed at the club house rather than at one of the hotels.

Through my combination of duties as field assistant and superintendent of Yellowstone, I was able to do a great deal to help Mather spread this Park Service spirit. I took a special interest also in helping build the ranger force into the competent and dedicated unit that it was to become. Spending time in the various parks as field assistant gave me wide contact with the rangers. Even at Yellowstone I was constantly on the road (averaging ten thousand miles a year, mostly by car), visiting the ranger stations, consulting with the men about their various problems and ideas, and keeping in close touch with the other staff. I also made yearly pack trips deep into the back country, and the rangers seemed to appreciate having a superintendent who wanted to know every part of the vast wilderness area within the boundaries.

One of my priorities was to raise the standards for the recruiting and training of rangers. The practice of employing well-educated seasonal rangers had started at Yosemite in 1914, where ten University of California people, mostly senior students, had been hired. At Yellowstone I continued the practice, hiring college people as seasonals — we called them "ninety-day wonders" because that was about the length of the summer season. As some of the older rangers retired, or as other new positions opened up, we were able to draw from the college-trained seasonals as permanent replacements. They handled much of the educational work, giving programs for the visitors and guiding them on nature walks.

There was a natural resistance on the part of the traditional rangers when the college-trained people began to come in on a permanent

Stephen Mather at right, with Harold "Doc" Bryant at Glacier Point, Yosemite, 1926. National Park Service.

basis, but the old-timers soon learned that a college education didn't make this "new breed" so different after all. They got the same starting salaries as other rangers, and "put their pants on one leg at a time," just like the others.

The starting pay for rangers in 1923 was only one thousand dollars a year, and they could eventually work their way up to $1,320. Out of their small salary they had to buy their own uniforms and pay for their own food. Despite the low pay, I was swamped with applications every year at Yellowstone, especially for seasonal ranger jobs. Thousands of college youths wrote in wanting to be rangers. So I developed a form letter in 1923 to answer them. Designed to discourage the casual applicant, it laid out the unvarnished facts about what a ranger's job was like at that time. It said:

> It has been our experience that young men often apply for a place on the park ranger force with the impression or understanding that the ranger is a sort of sinecure with nothing resembling hard work to perform, and that a ranger's position offers an opportunity to pass a pleasant vacation amid the beauties and wonders of Yellowstone Park, and with very frequent trips about the park and innumerable dances and other diversions to occupy one's leisure hours.
>
> Again, young men very often apply for ranger positions with the feeling that the duties of the place require no special training or experience and that any man with a reasonably good education can perform these duties regardless of whether he has a good or bad personality or whether he has or has not had experience in outdoor activities.
>
> Also, many young men apply for ranger positions in the hope of making and saving considerable money to aid them in continuing their college work.
>
> The conceptions of the duties of the ranger as just mentioned are just as untrue as it is possible for them to be, and unfortunately the pay is so small that boys earning their way through college, and who live at a distance from the Park cannot afford to become a ranger if tendered a place.

The letter went on to outline the pay as being one hundred dollars a month, with the applicant having to pay his own expenses to and from the park, furnish his own subsistence and clothes, including a uniform costing about forty-five dollars, bring his own bedding, and do his own cooking. No transportation around the park would be provided, except possibly at the end of the season if facilities were available. The minimum age in the application was twenty-one but, the letter said, men twenty-five to thirty years of age were preferred. Big men were preferred to small men inasmuch as the ranger is primarily a policeman. The ranger would be required to rise at 6:00 A.M., retire by 11:00 P.M., and be subject to duty for more than eight hours a day, but would not be paid overtime. He could be called from his bed for emergency service, would have to obey every order of the station chief who would be a permanent ranger, and would be expected to observe semi-military discipline. The letter concluded:

The duties are exacting and require the utmost patience and tact at all times. A ranger's job is no place for a nervous, quick-tempered man, nor for the laggard, nor for one who is unaccustomed to hard work. If you cannot work hard ten or twelve hours a day, and always with patience and a smile on your face, don't fill out the attached blank. You have perhaps believed Government jobs to be "soft" and "easy." Most of them are not, and certainly there are no such jobs in the National Park Service. The ranger's job is especially hard. There will not be more than twenty vacancies in next year's force of rangers, and there is really very little chance of your being considered unless you possess *all* of the qualifications mentioned herein. . . . If you want to come for pleasure you will be disappointed. If you want a summer in the Park as an experience in outdoor activity amid forests and a fine invigorating atmosphere, apply if you are qualified. Otherwise please plan to visit the Yellowstone National Park as a tourist.

While the seasonal rangers played an increasingly important role, the permanent rangers remained the core of the park management, and in the various parks we had some wonderful old timers who went on serving year-round for many years. Some were great characters, real men of the mountains. One of the finest was Ranger Billy Nelson at Yosemite.

In 1919, King Albert of Belgium, his queen, and the crown prince visited Yosemite, and Nelson was selected to guide them on a horseback trip along a four-mile trail to Glacier Point. Billy had been coached by the superintendent on how to address the king and queen as "Your Majesty," and he thought he had it down pat. He was a very intelligent fellow, but he felt stampeded by the responsibility of guiding a king and a queen.

As they were riding along, Nelson saw something he wanted to call King Albert's attention to, so he rode up to him, but he couldn't remember how to address him. So he looked up at the king and said, "I forgot what to call you, but I want to show you something. Suppose I just call you King and you call me Billy." "All right," said the King, "I'll call you Billy. And you can call me King."

They became fast friends during the king's stay in Yosemite. Nelson was one of the best camp cooks in the whole ranger service, and the king made him "Camp Cook by Special Appointment of His Majesty." One night while he was preparing dinner, the members of the royal party were horrified to hear Billy call out: "Say, King, shoot me that side of bacon, will you?"

In 1926, President Calvin Coolidge issued an order revoking the practice of appointing park rangers without examination and directed the Civil Service Commission to prepare qualifications and a written entrance examination for rangers. An oral examination was also required for those passing the written test. The existing permanent rangers were blanketed into the Civil Service without having to take the examination. With salaries that now started at $1,680 a year, the ranger positions required one year's experience in outdoor vocations, and the jobs were open to men and women aged twenty-one to forty-five. The announcement described the duties of a park ranger:

> Under general supervision, to be in responsible charge of a ranger district in a National Park, or of specific units of work on a Ranger District, or to act as an assistant to a park ranger in responsible charge. Such duties involve knowledge of methods of fighting forest and prairie fires; packing of horses and mules; habits of animals; ability to ride and handle horses; construction of fire lines and trails; reading of topographic maps and compass; tact in handling people; cooking; use of firearms; driving motor cars and motorcycles; and in those parks where needed, skill on snow shoes and skis; incidental clerical and information work.

From the beginning, of course, the individual superintendents had set the tone for their parks, for better or worse. The annual conferences of superintendents were the forums for spreading the best ideas and tackling the biggest problems throughout the system. After Mather began to build up the organization, the conferences included key personnel from the major parks and headquarters, as well as the superintendents.

Mather continually urged superintendents to expand their horizons, so he tried something a little different in the way of transportation to the 1925 conference, which was held at Mesa Verde National Park. Instead of taking the train, the superintendents were to form motor caravans and visit various national parks along the way and get a good look at the country. I led a caravan for those in my part of the country, and Mather joined the caravan that Dusty Lewis led from Yosemite. It was a huge success, and everybody not only learned a lot from seeing the other parks, but enjoyed getting better acquainted with each other.

Cammerer announced at the conference that a superintendents' manual was near completion. It wouldn't be a perfect document, he warned, but should help to standardize many practices. Mather interjected that while the manual would be very helpful in many ways, he didn't want it to rob the parks of the individuality he thought each should maintain. "We don't want to get down to a common, routine manner of handling our work. We don't have to feel that we have to have the same sort of trail sign in each park. I think people will enjoy the parks more if they feel each has a certain individuality."

Ranger-naturalists were being hired in some of the parks, and Ansel Hall had been named chief naturalist of the National Park Service. There had been quite a bit of misunderstanding over these positions. Hall told the conference that the confusion came from the fact that since there was no Civil Service classification for naturalists, they had to be hired as rangers. But there was a distinction: they were people with four or five years of college behind them, and while they were just as much a part of the ranger force as any of the others, they were given special duties, and should be called naturalist or ranger-naturalist.

Mather emphasized the basic element of service to the public.

"We are merely servants of the people," he said, "and are out to serve them. What we have tried to inculcate into the Park Service is that we are merely serving the public as a whole. We are not owners of the areas, but are merely custodians." The morale and sense of professionalism got a boost when Mather told the superintendents: "I believe the chief rangers should get together; they are doing important work, and a conference would help develop them very much. It would also make them realize that they are thought much more of." So in January 1926 the first conference of chief rangers was held in Sequoia National Park under the chairmanship of Yellowstone Chief Ranger Sam T. Woodring.*

They met for three days, and discussed problems such as private holdings within the parks, increased visitor use (the biggest source of concern), fighting forest fires, and eliminating grazing of cattle. They left the conference with an accumulation of shared information and a greatly enhanced feeling of the significance of their work.

In May, I held a similar conference at Yellowstone for all of the Yellowstone ranger force. That early in the season the park was still

---

* Minutes of the Eighth National Park Conference, Mesa Verde National Park, Colorado, October 1–5, 1925. Harpers Ferry, West Virginia: National Park Service History Collection.

snowbound, so for many of the thirty-three people who attended, it was quite a trek. Park Ranger Lee Cotrell, stationed at Snake River Station, made his way on foot and on snowshoes by way of Thumb Station to Old Faithful, where a car picked him up for the trip to the Headquarters Station where the conference was held. Roby Roy Wisdom, stationed at the East Entrance, had to walk and snowshoe through Sylvan Pass to Lake Station where we picked him up by car.

The evening before the formal beginning of the conference, I showed our new lantern slides and motion pictures and explained how they were being used to create a national park education program. In opening the conference the next morning, I emphasized the keen interest Mather had in the park and its rangers and the high value he put on the ranger force. And I told them never to forget that as the people who had the most contact with the public, they were the key to the success of the National Park Service.

At the conclusion of the conference, I reminded the rangers of the important position our National Park Service occupied as a bureau of the Department of the Interior, again emphasizing that the general public's impression of the entire Department is made largely by the rangers of the National Park Service.

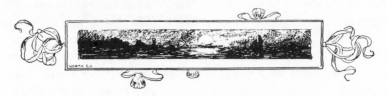

12

Of Parks and Politics

WHETHER I HAD IT IN ME FROM THE START OR PICKED IT UP FROM MY YEARS WITH MATHER, I DON'T KNOW, BUT A LOT of what we both accomplished for the national parks happened because we knew how to take advantage of opportunities when they came along. Often we had to "create" these opportunities. In the summer of 1923, that is just what Mather did. He somehow learned that President Warren G. Harding was planning a vacation to California and Alaska. So Mather got his White House contacts to talk the President into scheduling stops at three national parks along the way. No president had been in Yellowstone since Teddy Roosevelt in 1903. Harding, however, had been in Yellowstone as a young man. As President, he had not expressed much interest in national parks, although he had been helpful to us on several matters.

Early in 1923 Harding had signed presidential proclamations setting aside or expanding a number of national monuments. In January his executive order had created Aztec Ruins National Monument, protecting the excavated and stabilized community of Pueblo Indian civilization in New Mexico. In March he had created Hovenweep National Monument, consisting of six groups of pre-Columbian towers, pueblos, and cliff dwellings in Utah and Colorado (a gift from the Mormon church). And in May Pipe Spring National Monument, a historic fort built by Mormon pioneers in northwestern Arizona, was added to the Service. The 2,080-acre Pinnacles National Monument in central California was also greatly expanded.

There was a flurry of preparation at Yellowstone for the visit of President Harding. Colonel Edmund "Bill" Starling of the Secret Service came ahead to oversee arrangements for appropriate security during the two-day whirlwind tour we had laid out for the President. I worked overtime to make sure the trip would gain the best possible publicity for the park.

President and Mrs. Harding stopped first at Zion National Park in southern Utah. On June 27 the President inaugurated service on the Union Pacific branch line to Cedar City, from where people might be bussed to Zion, Bryce, and the North Rim of the Grand Canyon.

After a stopover in Salt Lake City, the President's train proceeded to Gardiner, Montana, near the north entrance of Yellowstone. Secretary of the Interior Hubert Work (his first visit to Yellowstone), Secretary of Agriculture Henry C. Wallace, Secretary of Commerce Herbert Hoover, Speaker of the House Frederick Gillett, and Mather completed the central group of the seventy-two-member party. A coterie of reporters and plenty of newsreel cameras recorded every event.

When the presidential train pulled into the Gardiner railway station at 6:00 A.M. on June 30, I was there to meet it. After breakfast I escorted the President to the large, open touring car we had prepared for him, and the motorcade proceeded the short distance to the north entrance of the park. The newsreel cameras whirred and shutters clicked, recording the event for the world to see. Eleven mounted park rangers formed an honor guard as the President's motorcade passed under the historic forty-foot stone arch, its message from the original 1872 Yellowstone Act carved into the stone: "FOR THE BENEFIT AND ENJOYMENT OF THE PEOPLE."

We made our first stop at Mammoth Hot Springs. The President climbed out of the big touring car and walked up to watch the clouds of steam shooting up all around the travertine deposits. A large crowd had gathered at park headquarters, and the President waved to the people. All during the tour I sat in the jump seat facing him so I could answer his questions. As we started south on the Grand Loop Road toward Old Faithful, Harding asked me: "When do we meet the next crowd?"

"We aren't going to meet any crowds for a while, Mr. President," I answered, and added that we would encounter no cars. "We are keeping the roads clear and have prevented cars from coming through because we want you to be able to see elk and deer and possibly some

President and Mrs. Harding at Upper Geyser Basin, Yellowstone, 1923. Author at right. J. E. Haynes photograph. Albright collection.

moose. If we let people get ahead of us and chase the wildlife with their cameras, you wouldn't see the animals."

"Now, are you sure we are not going to see anyone?" the President repeated.

"I'm absolutely sure, sir," I answered. "It will be twenty miles before we see another soul."

Well, the President stuck his hand in his pocket and pulled out a package of tobacco, bit off a piece, and started to chew. He spat the juice over his shoulder, neatly clearing the side of the car. He continued enjoying his tobacco until we got near Norris Geyser Basin, where we saw that some people were gathered, and he hastily got rid of his cheekful.

Old Faithful performed magnificently for the President in late afternoon, and the ranger in charge, Eivind Scoyen, told Harding that there was a geyser nearby whose eruption was longer than Old Faithful's — nearly fifteen minutes at a time, shooting higher and higher, up to 180 feet in height. The President wanted to see it, so we made the short walk and stood under a tree to wait for Grand Geyser to go off. Scoyen thought he had the geyser's schedule figured out pretty well —

although the Grand's eruptions were quite irregular. Sometimes eight hours or more could elapse between eruptions, but Scoyen figured it was due to blow very soon. We waited and waited. After about an hour I was feeling increasingly embarrassed and was afraid that Scoyen had miscalculated. I suggested to the President that we return to the Old Faithful Hotel, where we were scheduled to have dinner. He insisted on waiting, however. When the Grand finally erupted, it was an exceptionally good display, and the President declared that it was well worth the wait. Then we went back to Old Faithful where he shook hands with about five hundred people before dinner.

The party spent the night at Old Faithful Inn, and the next morning the motor tour continued south along the Grand Loop Road. This route enabled the president to see the park's finest features. I had arranged for an early morning stop at Shoshone Point, where with clear weather, there is a good view of the Grand Tetons to the south. As we rode along I told the President about the need to add the Grand Teton and Jackson Hole areas to Yellowstone, but that legislation to extend Yellowstone for this purpose had been defeated in Congress. At Shoshone Point the weather was perfect and we could see for forty miles. The peaks were bright with snow as the president caught his first sight of the magnificent view.

Harding was impressed. He gazed silently at the view, obviously moved, then turned to me and said, "I'll get busy on that extension legislation when I get back."

"You'll have a lot of trouble," I warned. "There's a lot of opposition in Wyoming to the idea of putting the Tetons and the Jackson Hole into the Park, and it could hurt you politically."

"It's worth the trouble," he shot back. "We can do it." With the newspaper reporters and cameras close by, recording it all assiduously, the President announced that he fully supported the plan to add the Tetons to Yellowstone National Park.

The President had jokingly mentioned that he wanted to see "Jesse James" while in the park. I don't know where he had heard, but Jesse James was the name we had given to a bear that hung around the highway south of Lake Hotel. He was notorious for stopping cars for a handout. I told the President that I couldn't promise we'd meet up with Jesse James himself, but that I thought we could show him some other bears. Sure enough, as we approached Lake, Jesse James and another black bear were standing by the road. We stopped the car and the cameramen went into action as the President got out and tossed the bears some snack food.

When we got to Yellowstone Lake, President Harding wanted to know why we hadn't made arrangements for him to do some fishing. I explained that the Secret Service had vetoed it because the park was unable to provide a boat fast enough to keep up with the one the President would use. Starling had said that it would take the Secret Service too long to get to the President if something happened. Dick Jervis, head of the Secret Service detail, was sitting alongside our driver, and the President barked at him that he didn't see why he couldn't go fishing. "I'm on vacation and I want to enjoy myself," he said. But Jervis gently said, "No, Mr. President, I'm sorry, but it cannot be done." It was the first time I realized that where security is concerned, the Secret Service can overrule the President of the United States.

Some of the college girls who worked at Lake Hotel often stopped the busses to sing for the tourists, and I had arranged for them to stop the President's car and sing for him. They presented Mrs. Harding with a bunch of wildflowers, and then focused their full attention on the President. Standing on the running board, they sang song after song, the President obviously enjoying every moment of it. Jervis tried to get the girls to wind up their performance, but the President shooed him off. Finally, I had to tell the girls to bring their songs to a close, which they did with a "Goodbye-Come Again" ballad.

As the car drew away, the President said, "Albright, can we come back this way after lunch?"

I had to tell him that we couldn't, because we would be going in the opposite direction. Mrs. Harding, who had been holding her wildflowers and sitting quietly through the whole performance, said, "Warren, it took you longer to say goodbye to those pretty girls than to run through several hundred tourists yesterday at Old Faithful!"

As we started north along the Loop road, I told the President about the attempts under way to dam Yellowstone Lake, and how it would ruin the park. We stopped at Artist Point overlooking the Grand Canyon of the Yellowstone, where he got a breathtaking view of the Yellowstone River cascading over the lower falls and serpentining eight hundred feet below us. Mr. Harding, with the reporters and newsreel cameras at his side, commented: "There must be no interference with the flow of water through this canyon; such interference would destroy much of its beauty and majesty."

As the President left the park, he made a brief speech at the north entrance arch, and he included another plug for the national parks. "Commercialism will never be tolerated here so long as I have the power to prevent it," he said. At another point in the tour he had commented that the nation had only a few national parks and could afford to maintain them intact for the benefit of posterity.

When the presidential train pulled away, there was a feeling of elation among all of us that the National Park Service had made a valuable new friend who would support our efforts and protect the parks. I immediately set my thoughts in motion to get our friends in Congress pushing again for the Yellowstone extension bill that would add 800,000 acres of the Tetons and Jackson Hole to Yellowstone National Park.

Shortly after the presidential visit I got an invitation that further encouraged me. Some of the movers and shakers in the Jackson Hole area, who were seeking ways to head off commercial development of their beloved country, asked me to meet with them. The group which gathered at Maud Noble's cabin on the banks of the Snake River at Menor's Ferry included Dick Winger, the former owner of a small newspaper, Struthers Burt, who was representing dude ranchers, and two cattlemen and a Jackson Hole businessman. Our spirited hostess was a long-time resident who loved the land. We talked for more than two hours, mostly about a plan Burt had presented to buy up private land and add it to federal land to form a kind of national recreational area that would protect the wild animals, allow roads to remain unpaved, and preserve the status quo.

They did not want it to be a national park, because they wanted the traditional hunting, grazing, and dude ranching activities to continue. I was disappointed that the group still resisted my dream of adding the area to Yellowstone, but I was practical enough to realize that I should support this effort — and I did. Burt and I met separately to talk about how we might locate a wealthy "angel" to purchase private land and hold it until Congress could pass legislation adding the area to the national park system as a recreational area. Between these new developments and President Harding's expression of support, it looked at last like we were going to make some real progress on saving the Teton area.

Then on August 2, 1923, shocking news reached Yellowstone. President Harding was dead. He had taken ill just before leaving Alaska, had been taken by ship and train to San Francisco, where his condition worsened. He died in a San Francisco hotel on the eve of the planned final segment of his vacation trip, a tour of Yosemite National Park. Not only had the nation lost a President, but the national parks had lost a valuable friend.

Without Harding's assistance, our Teton efforts would be more difficult. I helped Burt and his group by writing letters to friends of conservation in the east, seeking their financial support. Mather and I made modest contributions, and Burt raised $2,300 to send Winger and a Jackson businessman to New York in an effort to get funding from the Vanderbilts or Whitneys or Morgans. But they were not able to generate any interest.

Meanwhile, the national park system was continuing to gain new friends and support. The American Association for the Advancement of Science, with its nearly one thousand members in the United States and Canada, adopted a resolution at its 1923 convention. Directed to the U.S. Congress, the Canadian Parliament, and to the people of both countries, it called for the United States to secure such amendments of existing law and the enactment of such new laws "as will give to all units in the international parks system complete conservation alike and will safeguard them against every industrial use either under private or public control at least until careful study shall justify the elimination of any part from park classification."

At Yellowstone I was continually presented with opportunities to make powerful friends for the parks. Seven senators, twenty-five congressmen, and two governors visited Yellowstone at one time or another during the 1923 summer season. I considered it an important part of my job to make their stay as pleasant and informative as possible, and Grace did her part too. Almost without exception, these distinguished visitors departed declaring enthusiastic support for the national parks.

In June a congressional party that had been conducting investigations at the Panama Canal and in Alaska came through Yellowstone on their way back to Washington. I boarded their train before it got into Gardiner so I could greet the party, explaining that busses would meet the train and take them around during their stay in the park. One by one, about four of the congressmen took me aside and said,

"Don't put me on the bus with 'Kodak Charley.' " They were referring to Congressman Charley Abernathy from North Carolina. All
were fond of him, but he was a camera nut. He had brought along
fifty rolls of film and had been making a nuisance of himself, always
asking the crowd to line up for photographs.

I was stumped. I didn't have enough cars to take care of all of
them. Then on the way to headquarters, I got a bright idea: Chief
Ranger Sam Woodring was also from North Carolina, and he had a
new patrol car. So I told Abernathy and his wife that I had made
special arrangements for them to ride through the park with a fellow
North Carolinian, the chief ranger. And I took Woodring aside and
told him to take them everywhere, and give Abernathy a chance to use
up his film. Well, the rest of the party never saw Charley again during
their time in the park, for which they hailed me a genius.

Senator Joe Robinson from Arkansas and Representative William
R. Wood from Indiana, a House appropriations subcommittee chairman, were great fishermen, and had a friendly contest going to see who
could catch the most fish. So I took them in my own car to the best
fishing spot in the park, where Wood won the contest. They both became good allies of the national parks. And as for Abernathy, he was
very grateful for the special private tour we had given him, and became one of the best friends we ever had in Congress.

I had been trying to build some credit with Representative Charles
E. Winter of Wyoming, who had been under pressure from constituents to get the Bechler dam project passed in Congress. We invited
him to dedicate the new 157-mile Howard Eaton Trail, named after
the recently deceased founder of the dude ranching industry in Wyoming's Bighorn Mountains. In his dedication speech, Winter strongly
backed protection of the park against such threats as dams and water
projects. "Here let me say," Winter declared during his address, "that
great as their utilitarian purposes might be, the lakes and waters of this
and other national parks must not be touched or violated for business
or profit. The American people are practically of one mind on that
question. There must be no commercialism of the park waters."

That year we even had a hand, though indirectly and through
happenstance, in getting a friend of the parks elected to Congress. The
previous November, Benjamin L. Fairchild had lost his congressional
seat in Pelham, New York. He had decided to do some traveling,
something he hadn't had much time to do with his congressional re-

sponsibilities. His brother-in-law was Idaho Congressman Addison T. Smith, who was a long-time friend of mine. When Fairchild was visting him in Idaho, Smith suggested he go see Yellowstone, and when he arrived I saw to it that he got VIP treatment. He happened to mention to me that he wanted to go on to California and make a pack trip into the Yosemite back country, then climb Mount Shasta, something he had done once before as a youth. Fairchild told me when he would be in Yosemite and when he wanted to start his Mount Shasta climb, and I got National Park Service personnel in California to make the arrangements. Fairchild soon left Yellowstone and I forgot all about it.

About three weeks later I got a long distance call from Congressman Smith in Washington, asking if I had any idea where his brother-in-law was. Smith was in a lather, and said it was essential that he get in touch with Fairchild. "The man who defeated Ben for Congress last year got killed last night," he said. "We've got to get hold of Ben and get him back to New York right away. If he can register as a candidate in time, he can get back in the race and maybe back into Congress. But there are only a few days left before the registration deadline."

Whether he realized it or not, Smith had called the only person who could have helped him. Fairchild had not told anyone else where he was going or when, and he had told me only because I was making the arrangements for him. I told Smith that I thought I could track him down, and I went right to work on it. I telephoned Chief Ranger Forest S. Townsley at Yosemite, and he sent a ranger into the back country on horseback. When the ranger found him, Fairchild immediately rode out, caught the first train, and got back to New York just in time to file for office. And he was elected. Thereafter, he always introduced me to people as "the man who got me re-elected to Congress."

13

Great Benefactor of the Parks

THE YEAR AFTER PRESIDENT HARDING'S DEATH, YELLOWSTONE HAD IT'S FIRST VISIT FROM JOHN D. ROCKEFELLER, JR., the great philanthropist who was to become one of the best friends the national parks ever had. A representative of the Colorado Fuel and Iron Company, which Rockefeller controlled at the time, contacted Cammerer in Washington and said that Rockefeller wanted to bring his three eldest sons on a trip to the Rockies and visit some national parks incognito. We contacted the people scheduling the trip and helped them lay out a plan that would have the Rockefeller party stop at Mesa Verde, Yellowstone, and Glacier.

Rockefeller had made it plain that he wanted no special treatment on this tour. He would be traveling as "Mr. Davison" (his grandmother's maiden name, and his middle name). He wanted no guides, and there was to be no publicity. As far as possible he wanted the boys to be able to mix with the public without being identified as Rockefellers. So in due time the superintendents of Mesa Verde and Glacier and I received instructions from Cammerer in Washington to make travel arrangements for the "Davison" party. I was to hire two touring cars and drivers, and was told the date and time when they were to arrive by Northern Pacific railway at Gardiner. Under no circumstances were we to tell anyone who the "Davisons" really were. We were to make suggestions about where they might want to go and what they could see and be of whatever service we could, but we were not to interfere with them in any way, and we were absolutely not to talk any business with Rockefeller.

At Mesa Verde they were entertained by the superintendent, Jesse Nusbaum. Jesse was an archeologist and one of the best superintendents we ever had. He had plans for a museum to house the treasure store of Indian artifacts he had collected, and a wealthy widow from San Francisco, Stella Leviston, who had visited Mesa Verde and taken an interest in the museum idea, had made him a gift of ten thousand dollars to get the museum started.

When the Rockefellers arrived for dinner, Nusbaum's house was a fascinating clutter of artifacts and, of course, the boys wanted to know all about them. So as they sat on the porch, Nusbaum regaled them with the background of the various ancient implements and pottery and what they could tell us about the vanished civilization they had belonged to. John, Nelson, and Laurance listened with rapt attention, and then Mr. "Davison" said, "You are familiar with who I am, of course, and I want you to know that I would like to contribute to your museum."

Nusbaum was in a pickle. He hadn't done a thing to disobey the order not to talk business with Mr. Rockefeller, but who would believe him? Yet what was he supposed to say now? While Nusbaum was silently puzzling over what to reply, Rockefeller asked, "Would I be permitted to contribute to your museum?"

"Oh, — er — why, yes, I'm sure you would," Nusbaum said, "and I surely would like to have you do so!" In a short time the museum project received ten thousand dollars from Mr. Rockefeller and the Laura Spelman Rockefeller Memorial.

When the "Davison" party arrived at Yellowstone, I went to meet them. Although I wanted to extend a welcome and get them started on their tour of the park, I wanted to do it with as little show as possible. So instead of having one of the fine big hired cars meet them, I drove our battered five-year-old seven-passagener White motorcar to the station, and pulled up at the end of the platform where the private cars always stopped. But when the train pulled in there was no private car.

I got out my notebook and checked the schedule. This was the day, all right. So I walked up the platform toward the depot. Suddenly I noticed the Northern Pacific detective who rode any train that was carrying somebody important, so I said to myself, if that guy is here, then the Rockefellers must be on this train. When the detective saw me, he said, "Your folks are up in the car next to the engine," and he went up there with me.

"Mr. Davison?" I asked, as I walked up and introduced myself to a man coming down the steps with three teenage boys. Mr. Rockefeller laughed and said, "You know!" He introduced me to his eldest son, John D., III, eighteen, and to Nelson, sixteen, and Laurance, fourteen and told them I was the superintendent in charge of this great national park they were going to visit. He suggested to the boys that they help the black passenger car porters with the baggage and one of the boys said, "Yes, Father," and they went off to help the porters. Rockefeller took out a little notebook and jotted down something, apparently a record of expenses.

I apologized for my disreputable old car, explained why I had brought it, and offered to drive them to the hotel at Mammoth Springs. I told him it was only a five-mile drive to the headquarters at Mammoth Springs where we would get them fixed up and then leave them on their own.

"I'll be glad to ride with you, Mr. Albright," he said, "but I want these boys to go along with the regular tourists. They need to mix with the crowd."

As I drove Rockefeller to headquarters, he asked quite a few questions. As we drove through the arch at the north entrance I told him about the visit of President Harding in 1923, and then sketched some of the history of the park and its main features. I must admit I was tempted to speak to him about my grand passion, the dream of adding the Teton-Jackson Hole area to Yellowstone, and it took all the restraint I could muster to refrain from mentioning it. Rockefeller had already donated land and funds to help establish Lafayette National Park in Maine, and if he could see the possibilities presented by the majestic Tetons and the Jackson Hole area, he undoubtedly could help make my dream come true.

At headquarters I gave him the maps and other materials we had collected for him, and told him that if he needed help at any time, he could get it at any of the ranger stations. I went over all his reservations and accommodations with him to be sure they had his approval, and then got him together with the drivers we had engaged for him. I handed him our suggested itinerary. Right at the top of the list was a visit to Jackson Lake. Of course, seeing the view of the Tetons was considered by many as one of the great scenic adventures of the Rockies, so I wasn't breaking any rules by including it. In going over the itinerary, I told Rockefeller about a small hill at Jackson Lake where if they made a short, easy climb, he and the boys could get a fine view of the area. I did not advise going on down to Jackson Hole, however. (I didn't want him to encounter any of the enemies of the proposed park extension—if I couldn't talk to Rockefeller about adding the Tetons and Jackson Hole to Yellowstone, I surely didn't want the opponents to get to him first.)

That was the last I saw of the "Davison" party until their last day in the park. Just before they were to leave, I called on them to make sure everything had been to their liking and to invite Rockefeller to come back when he could stay longer and do some camping. He replied that he would like very much to do that. Then he questioned me about the bill he had received for transportation, which he thought was rather high. "I don't like to bring up points like this," he said, "but some places have a tendency to overcharge. I expect to pay full rates, but I dislike being overcharged just because of who I am."

I told him how the rate was structured, and explained that in addition to twenty-five dollars per day to cover each car and driver, he also had to be charged a per-passenger tour fee on the basis of full capacity for each of the two seven-passenger cars despite the fact that only four people were in his party.

"Yes, I see," he said. "That makes sense. It's a fair rate and I'm entirely satisfied."

His sons were standing there during the conversation, and I suspect that he had questioned the bill primarily as a means of educating them about fairness and how to avoid being overcharged. He and the boys then departed for Glacier National Park to do some camping.

A few weeks later, Rockefeller wrote to me from New York, thanking me for helping with his trip. He had noticed that the roadsides were very badly cluttered with fallen trees, brush, and logs, and that unsightly telephone poles were on both sides of the road. He said that roadside landscaping had interested him for many years, and noted his particular interest in the roads at Lafayette National Park.

I wrote back to tell him that we had long been unhappy about the conditions of the roadsides, but had never been able to get funding from Congress to clean them up. I explained that at the time the roads were constructed, it had not been considered good economic practice to clear away the brush and fallen trees left by the road builders. I went on to say that Yellowstone had never been allotted much money for its roads. The two sets of telephone poles were there because the government and the hotels each had their own line. The poles had been put up many years before in the least expensive way possible, right at the edge of the road. I added that many other people had commented on the eyesore, and that I hoped someday to be able to have the funds to clear away the clutter.

Almost immediately, Rockefeller wrote back and asked if I had any idea what it would cost to clean up the roadsides and move the telephone poles back into the timber. If I could provide estimates he would be willing to finance the experimental clearing of a mile or so. I made cost estimates for three sections — one with a bad accumulation of dead material, one with a medium, and one with a light accumulation. Rockefeller sent a check for twelve thousand dollars in the autumn of 1924. He directed that the money be used for clearing some of the road. But it was not to be used for moving the telephone lines, because he felt that sort of thing should be done by the government.

We did our preliminary clearing and burning as soon as we received the check, and cleaned up part of the road between Norris Geyser Basin and Mammoth Springs. I then prepared a detailed report of costs and sent Rockefeller pictures of what we had done. He was so pleased that he at once authorized me to go ahead with the large project of clearing the roadsides all around the park. We completed the job in four years, thanks to fifty thousand dollars donated by this "wealthy friend of Yellowstone." Using the road cleanup to demonstrate the value of improving the appearance of the park, I was able to get funds from Congress for moving the telephone lines back into the forest, where they were less conspicuous. Congress later appropriated funds for cleaning up roadsides in other parks, and made it standard operating procedure to include debris cleanup in the funding of all new roads.

In 1926 Rockefeller returned to Yellowstone for a twelve-day visit, accompanied by his wife, Abby, and Laurance, then sixteen, and their two younger sons, Winthrop, fourteen, and David, eleven. This time there were no restrictions and I was free to talk to Rockefeller about anything I pleased, acting as his host and guide.

Laurance was busy most of the time taking pictures with his first camera. His father proudly told me Laurance had bought it for sixteen dollars, which he had earned by raking leaves, bringing in wood, and doing other chores. David, who told me he wanted to be a scientist when he grew up, spent much of his time digging around rocks and collecting beetles. There was great excitement when he found some hard clay with an impression in it that looked like it could be a fossil. No one had ever found a leaf fossil in that part of Yellowstone. Still, it looked real enough for us to send the sample to the Smithsonian Institution in Washington for a test, and for a while his father thought David might become famous for being the first to find a leaf-fossil in Yellowstone. But it turned out to be only a piece of ash in the clay, not a fossil.

I arranged to take the whole family on a tour of the Jackson Hole area. As we started off, Rockefeller commented on how pleased he was at the progress we had made cleaning up the roadsides, and was glad to see that we had been moving some of the telephone poles away from the roads on our own.

We got only as far as Jackson Lake the first day, and spent the last hour on a hillside by the lake watching the sun set behind the Teton Range, while moose fed in the marshes below us. After spending the night at Jackson Lake Lodge, we continued south into the Jackson Hole country. Rockefeller soon began to see things he didn't like.

"Why are those telephone lines on the west side of the road, where they mar the view of the mountains?" he asked. I had to explain that the Forest Service had built them there despite my request that that they be put on the east side, away from the mountains.

We hadn't gone a quarter of a mile farther when he said, "Why is that ramshackle old building allowed to stand over there where it blocks the view?" I explained that it was on private land — that indeed much of the land along the road was privately owned. Mrs. Rockefeller seemed increasingly upset as we passed a woebegone-looking old dance hall, some dilapidated cabins, a burned-out gasoline station, a few big billboards, and here and there a sign advertising cattle range land for sale. The Rockefellers expressed great concern that this spectacular country was rapidly going the way of development and destruction.

"Mr. Albright, what would it cost to clear up all of this?" Rockefeller asked as he headed toward Jenny Lake.

"I have no idea — but we don't have any control over most of it anyway, because it is privately owned." I answered.

"Well, send me an estimate as to what it would take to buy the land and clear the junk out of this area," Rockefeller said, "and send me a map."

I assumed that he was referring to the parcels of land in the rundown areas alongside the road, jotted down a reminder in my notebook, and told him I would get an estimate for him as soon as I could.

We went by Jenny Lake at the foot of the towering, snow-capped peaks of the Tetons, and then visited two dude ranches. As we headed back toward Yellowstone, I told the driver to turn off on a logging road that went to a high point, and there we stopped the car so they could get a panoramic view of the Jackson Hole country.

As we sat on logs and watched another sunset, I began to unfold to Rockefeller my dream for the area, and how I had been trying for years to save the Tetons and the whole valley north of Jackson. I told him about the opportunity we had lost in 1919 when Congress had adjourned without acting on the Mondell bill that would have added the area to Yellowstone. I explained that we were trying to find new ways to save the area, and about the proposal by the dude ranch owners he had just met, who wanted to make the whole valley into a national recreation area, if they could raise funds to buy the private holdings and combine them with the public lands owned by the Forest Service. Then I told him the latest problem we were facing: that the Coordinating Commission on National Parks and Forests, created by the President's Committee on Outdoor Recreation, had studied the area the previous year and had made a very disappointing recommendation that only a small part of the area, about 150,000 acres of the eastern slope of the Tetons, be added to Yellowstone as a separate unit.

Mr. and Mrs. Rockefeller listened quietly as I unfolded the story. When I finished, they remained silent as we watched the sun disappear behind the jagged peaks, casting long, sharp shadows across the valley.

I felt a little let down. Here I had laid out my fondest dream, and there was no word of comment. In fact, during the rest of the time we spent camping together there was no reference to the subject.

On the night before the Rockefellers left Yellowstone, the whole family came to our house for dinner. Grace did the cooking. By now she had so much practice entertaining our many VIP visitors that she took it all in stride, and was not overly impressed at entertaining the Rockefellers. Of course, there was no reason to be shy with them. They were very comfortable people to be with.

When I carved the roast, I cut extra-big slices, thinking that the boys were probably pretty hungry. Grace was motioning to me from the other end of the table, but I couldn't figure out what she was trying to tell me, until she blurted out, "Horace, you've got to quit talking so much and pay attention to your carving, or you won't have anything left for yourself!"

Grace had made some ice cream, and while the dishes were being cleared for dessert, we all could overhear our housekeeper complaining to Grace that she couldn't get the freezer can opened. Rockefeller said, "Well, if it's an old-fashioned ice cream freezer, these boys have plenty of experience. They can get it open for you." So Laurance and Winthrop went to the kitchen and opened it.

Shortly after the Rockefellers left the park I asked Dick Winger in Jackson to assemble some data for me on estimated costs of buying up the private parcels around in the area near Jackson Lake where the unsightly old buildings and abandoned ranches marred the scene. When I went east that winter on my next trip to headquarters, I made an appointment with Rockefeller. I went to his office at 26 Broadway in New York on November 20 with the data and a map Winger had prepared.

When I was ushered into his big office, I gave him the cost estimates and laid the big map on his desk. I felt some trepidation as he looked at the estimates. Would he be shocked at the $397,000 Winger had projected as the cost for fourteen thousand acres, all on the west side of the Snake River?

He studied the papers for a few moments, then with a frown, he looked at the map. "Mr. Albright, is this all there is of it?" he asked.

"This is the property we have been working on," I replied. I recalled for him the conversation we had while going along the road near Jackson Lake.

Teton Range and Snake River, Grand Teton. George A. Grant photograph. National Park Service.

"No, no, that isn't what I had in mind at all," he said. "You took us that afternoon to a hill where we looked out over the mountains and the whole valley. The shadows were falling across the land, and you discussed an ideal project. I remember you used the word dream. *That's* the area for which I wanted you to get cost estimates. The family is only interested in an ideal project. And it would please me very much if you would get me data on that."

I was completely flabbergasted, and protested that I hadn't understood that he wanted figures on all of that. "Why, it might cost you as much as a million and a half or two million dollars to buy all that land," I said.

"Well, of course, you don't know yet what it would actually cost," he replied. "But that is what I'm interested in. I'm only interested in the ideal proposition. I wanted to know about the land on both sides of the river, and to the north. We can't do any more here today, but I would like to have you go across the street to 61 Broadway and see Colonel Woods."

I staggered across the street in something near a state of shock. Here I had gone into the office of John D. Rockefeller, Jr., fearing the reception a four hundred thousand dollar-project would get, and in a matter of minutes had come out with his tacit approval for a two-million-dollar project. I met with Arthur Woods, Rockefeller's chief aide, and his assistant, Kenneth Chorley. They gave me advice about preparing the estimates, and I left New York walking on air.

I immediately contacted Winger, and told him to get to work on the larger project, but to be extremely discreet about what we were doing, and not to mention the Rockefeller interest under any circumstances. Winger sent his estimates to me in Washington in mid-February. He had found that there were about four hundred landowners in the area we were considering, and they held a little over one hundred thousand acres. Winger believed the land to be worth perhaps one million dollars, but did not know what the purchase price would actually be. I sent this information to Mr. Rockefeller, accompanied by a long letter outlining how I thought the process of buying the land might best be accomplished.

I suggested that an organization, perhaps listed as a "recreation and hunting club" or a "land and cattle company" be set up to make the land purchases. It would also serve to shield the Rockefeller interest and the long-range intent, which I identified as removal of the lands from commercial use and turning them over to the National Park Service. I suggested that priority be given to land west of the Snake River. I emphasized that the utmost effort should be given to preventing disclosure of the ultimate intent, since knowledge of it could have an inflationary effect on land prices and would stir up opposition among those who wanted to keep the National Park Service, with its strict preservation policies, from controlling the area. I also cautioned Rockefeller that Congress would have to pass a law setting the final administrative policy for the lands in question. I ended the letter saying I had raised all of these points "not with any idea of trying to urge favorable action but just to give you this big park and wildlife preserve plan as we have visualized it. I think if it could be consummated, it would go down in history as the greatest conservation project of its kind ever undertaken."

I made an appointment to see him the following week. It was a short meeting. He looked at the map and the estimates, and said, "We'll do it." He accepted all of the suggestions I had made in the letter, and emphasized that a way had to be found to keep his name out of it. Then he turned the project over to Woods.

Rockefeller's written instructions to Woods in placing the entire matter in his hands were to purchase about fourteen thousand acres on the west side of the Snake River at an average of twenty-eight dollars per acre, and about one thousand acres on the east side of the river at a cost of ten dollars an acre. The document that went to Woods pledged Rockefeller to purchase lands in Jackson Hole with a view to the land being ultimately turned over to the government for joint or partial operation by the National Park Service and the Forest Service, but eventually to be added to Yellowstone National Park. Rockefeller indicated that I was to be looked to for leadership of the project even though I would have to remain in the background because I was a public official.

As 1926 came to a close I could see that down the road there would be numerous problems involved in acquiring the land while keeping the Rockefeller interest secret and getting the federal bureaucracy moving to withdraw the public land "for classification" to prevent speculative activity in the area. Whatever difficulties lay ahead, however, I was elated that at last there was real momentum toward protecting the Tetons and the northern part of Jackson Hole.

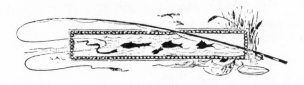

14

The Man Who Tried to Steal Grand Canyon

ADDING THE GRAND TETON AREA TO YELLOWSTONE WAS HIGH ON MY AGENDA, BUT I DIDN'T HAVE THE LUXURY OF CONCENTRATING ALL MY EFFORTS THERE. The National Park Service was involved in other issues that tested Mather and me. Two such problems were the dispute with Senator Ralph Cameron over his mining claims in Grand Canyon, which reached its climax in 1925, and the less serious but potentially damaging situation involving Louis W. Hill, president of the Great Northern railroad, which occurred at the same time.

Hill's company owned Many Glacier Hotel in Glacier National Park, and in early June 1925, he brought a group of newspaper reporters from the east coast to visit the park. If he had let anyone in the Park Service know what he was planning to do, they could have warned him that the park would still be deep in snow, and that it would be June or later before the roads could be cleared and the facilities readied for opening. Although Hill told his staff to open the hotel early, no one mentioned it to park personnel. When he and his reporter friends arrived, they couldn't do some of the things he had planned. Hill was furious, and read the riot act to Superintendent Charles Kraebel. He and his party left ahead of schedule for Seattle, where they spent the rest of the week partying.

As Hill and the press group wound up their Seattle fling, the reporters asked what they could do to express their appreciation. Hill is said to have replied, "Sharpen your pencils and go after Steve Mather and the terrible condition of Glacier Park." A number of the reporters

President Harding, Secretary of the Interior Hubert Work, Stephen Mather, and author at Yellowstone, 1923. Albright collection.

did just that, with the result that articles were appearing in newspapers all over the country attacking Mather and leveling unfounded criticism at the management of the national parks.

Mather was irked by the unfair news stories, particularly when he learned who had inspired them. There had been a running dispute between Hill and the Park Service over a sawmill Great Northern had been allowed to erect in the park alongside Swiftcurrent Lake while building Many Glacier Hotel in 1915. The permit had been given with the understanding that as soon as the hotel was completed, the sawmill would be removed and the site restored to a natural state. But the sawmill remained, and Mather had set a date when the eyesore must be off the premises. Great Northern had asked for an extension, and Mather had granted it.

As it happened, Mather himself was in Glacier giving his daughter, Betty, a nineteenth birthday outing on August 10, 1925, the day the extension expired. There stood the sawmill untouched, and the Great Northern representative there could give no indication as to when they planned to tear it down. Combined with his anger over Hill's publicity attacks, the sight of that sawmill brought Mather abruptly to the end of his patience. He told Kraebel to send in the chief of his trail construction crew with a load of dynamite, and to find some pretext for leaving the area so he would not be blamed for what was going to happen — Mather told Kraebel he was going to blow up the sawmill.

After instructing his driver to take Betty to the station to catch the next train home, he invited hotel guests to stand outside the hotel and see a demonstration. Then he personally lighted the fuse setting off thirteen charges of TNT, a "fireworks display" that reduced the mill to a pile of rubble. When the onlookers asked what occasion he was celebrating, Mather replied, "My daughter's birthday!"

The next day Mather had his driver take him to Great Falls so he could give the story to O. S. Warden, the owner of the Great Falls *Tribune*, who was also the local Associated Press representative. Warden said he didn't want to use in his paper or send out a story like that, and besides, it had happened the previous day so was no longer news. Mather got back in the car and had the chauffeur drive the two hundred miles to Livingston. The AP man there also refused the story on the same grounds, and added, "If I sent this out, Horace Albright would have my head." Mather replied, "What's Horace Albright got to do with it? Does he own these newspapers around here?"

Mather headed for Yellowstone. When he arrived he told me what had happened and tried to talk me into phoning the Livingston AP man and asking him to run the story. I told Mather I would do no such thing, that it would be unwise to give the story to the press and that he should not have blown up the sawmill in the first place. It would cause very bad publicity for the parks if the incident got into the press, I said. The publicity would further exacerbate his relations with Hill. He said he didn't care, that he was going to show that Louis Hill was not running Glacier National Park.

Then Mather switched to the other subject that had been weighing on his mind and giving him even more pain than the Hill episode. He said he had been talking to some prominent people, including Supreme Court Justice Pierce Butler, in regard to what Senator Cameron was doing to Grand Canyon National Park, and that the Justice shared his opinion that Cameron had no business defying the courts that had ruled against his mining claims several years earlier. "I'm going to resign and go down to Arizona and lick Cameron," Mather said, referring to the senator's re-election campaign already under way.

The Cameron affair was a long-festering problem. It had started years before Cameron had become a senator and Grand Canyon had become a national park. Cameron and some friends had taken mining claims within the canyon along its trails and on the south rim, and had tried to control access into the canyon through these claims. He controlled the Bright Angel Trail and charged tourists exorbitant fees. After President Theodore Roosevelt had protected the canyon by declaring it a national monument in 1908, and the Secretary of the Interior Richard Ballinger had ruled in 1909 that Cameron's mining claims were invalid, Cameron had fought the ruling and the U.S. Forest Service. He claimed that President Roosevelt had acted illegally in declaring a national monument, and that the Secretary of the Interior did not have power to dissolve his mining claims. When Grand Canyon National Park was established in 1919, Cameron had turned his antagonisms on the National Park Service and its Director.

The United States Supreme Court had ruled against Cameron in April 1920, declaring that the Secretary of the Interior had the authority to declare Cameron's early mining claims void, and had given him sixty days to get out of the canyon. Cameron had refused to obey the verdict. He also had tried to regain control of parts of the national park through fifty-five new mining claims he had filed illegally within the Grand Canyon in 1919.

In 1920, just when Mather was preparing to have Cameron's properties and personnel removed from the park, the people of Arizona had elected Cameron a United States senator. He had succeeded in keeping himself and his enterprises from being thrown out of the canyon by getting his own people appointed as federal judge, U.S. attorney, and U.S. marshal. Cameron had used the Senate floor as a platform for casting insults at Mather and the National Park Service, claiming we were under the control of monopolistic concessioners.

One of our strongest allies, Representative Louis C. Cramton, was so outraged by Cameron's personal vilification of Mather that he had compiled a dossier on Cameron. In March 1924, Cramton had broken with normal congressional courtesy to make details of Cameron's schemes and shenanigans public.

He had stood in the House of Representatives and poured out the story of "one Ralph H. Cameron." He told the House how the federal government had arranged to buy from Coconino County the toll rights to the Bright Angel Trail in Grand Canyon National Park. He explained that the annual Department of the Interior appropriation measure pending in conference between the Senate and the House was being blocked by this same Cameron over the minor matter of funding to buy up rights to the Bright Angel Trail, and this Cameron had not disclosed that he had personal financial interests in the matter and was himself seeking to secure the lease so he could collect tolls on the trail.

"Enjoyment of the park by the public is actually made hazardous by private interests, trespassers on the public domain, whose claims have been overruled by the Supreme Court of the United States, but who presume upon circumstances and plank themselves in the path of progress, veritable dogs in the manger, snapping and snarling at the national government and endangering every park visitor who goes over the Bright Angel Trail," said Cramton. "These obstacles in the way of progress are, briefly speaking, the Cameron claims."

Cameron, feining righteous indignation, had hastened to make his reply in a Senate speech in which he misrepresented the facts, praised himself, and denounced Cramton, Secretary Work, Mather, and the National Park Service with vague generalizations, since he lacked specific charges.

After Cramton's speech on the House floor, Cameron had held up the yearly appropriation for Grand Canyon National Park. Cramton had been able to work out a compromise and got it passed. By 1925, Cameron had lost most of his political power, yet each week he thought of some new way to attack Mather and the Park Service. The latest was a series of hearings he had promoted to investigate several national parks and national forests.

These investigations, together with the furor over the lumber mill in Glacier, had put Mather in a highly excited state of mind by the time he reached Yellowstone in August 1925. As I listened to him talk in my office at the Park, I wondered if he was on the verge of another spell of illness. As soon as he retired for the night, I wrote an airmail letter to Secretary Work relating Mather's conversation about Cameron. The next morning, however, it was apparent that a good night's sleep had calmed him down and he was himself in every respect. He also seemed to have dropped the Cameron problem.

There was a new and more important mission Mather was about to undertake that I hoped would divert him from the Cameron issue. A blue ribbon commission had been established to study extensions of national parks and work out boundary disputes between the Park Serv-

Author, congressmen Carl Hayden, Louis Cramton, Chas. Carter, and guide on Bright Angel trail in Grand Canyon, 1923. Albright collection.

ice and the Forest Service. Its members had just arrived at Yellowstone to start a tour of several parks. Called the Coordinating Commission on National Parks and Forests, it had been created in February 1925 on the initiative of Secretary Work, as part of the President's Cabinet Committee on Outdoor Recreation. Its chairman was Pennsylvania Congressman Henry W. Temple, and its other four members were Charles Sheldon of the Boone & Crockett Club, Major W. A. Welch, head of the Palisades Interstate Park Commission in New York, Chief Forester William Greeley of the U.S. Forest Service, and Mather.

Whatever the commission recommended would have tremendous influence on the legislation needed to extend Yellowstone, Sequoia, Grand Canyon, Crater Lake, Mount Rainier, and Rocky Mountain national parks. In all these cases the lands adjoining the park borders were owned by the Forest Service. The dispute over the Yellowstone borders was the most crucial of all. It involved two areas, one along the eastern park boundary adjoining Shoshone National Forest, the other the Grand Teton and Jackson Hole lands, which lay in the Teton National Forest. The commission planned an eight-day trip, crossing Lake Yellowstone, then with pack and saddle animals going up the Yellowstone River into the Thorofare country to the south boundary, then up Atlantic Creek to Two Ocean Pass, down Pacific Creek to the Snake River and Teton Lodge. It would then hold public hearings at Moran.

Wyoming Congressman Charles Winter and I were invited along. The third day out Mather and I fell behind the rest of the party and spent the morning talking over park matters as we kept our horses at a slow walk. I told him how pleased I was with the revised statement of national park policy he and Cammerer had prepared and the Secretary had issued in March. Mather said he felt national park policies should be reviewed every few years, and that it was especially important to have the Secretary of the Interior be familiar with them and stand behind them.

The 1925 statement went well beyond the one we had prepared for Secretary Lane to issue in 1918. The new policy stated that cattle grazing was to be gradually eliminated from the parks where presently permitted. It specified the use of trained landscape engineers with a proper appreciation of the esthetic value of parks whenever roads, trails, buildings, and other improvements were constructed. It said that over-development of parks and monuments resulting from construction of roads should be zealously guarded against. It ended with a long definition of the basic difference between national parks and national forests, concluding that "national parks, unlike national forests, are not properties in a commercial sense, but natural preserves for the rest, recreation and education of the people. They remain under Nature's own chosen conditions."

Mather also referred to the study I had completed for him in February, tracing the history of the Forest Service's opposition to the National

Park Service. It showed clearly how the Forest Service had fought the extension of boundaries for Sequoia, Mount Rainier, Crater Lake, Grand Canyon, and Yellowstone, the very areas now being reviewed by this blue ribbon commission. Mather said my report had served as a warning of how vital it was to defend our interests. For that reason he intended to stay with the commission on all of its trips, and would try to impress on the commissioners the need for boundary extensions, especially the Sequoia addition and the extension of Yellowstone to include the Tetons and Jackson Hole lands.

Mather told me how gratified he was at the interest Secretary Work was taking in the national parks. The Secretary himself had come up with the idea of his boundary commission, and had been making some suggestions for improving the educational programs for the national parks. Then Mather startled me by saying that the national parks were now in such good shape that he could afford to quit if necessary so that he could devote his time, his money, and his influence to defeating Cameron in the 1926 election. He said he believed he could do nothing better for the country than to get rid of the obnoxious senator.

I tried to dissuade him, using every argument I could think of, concluding by trying to convince him how politically unwise it would be for an outsider to attempt to influence the Arizona political scene. I could understand Mather's desire to get rid of Cameron, even though I felt strongly that it was not worth Mather's resignation. But no more was said about the matter, and we soon caught up with the rest of the party.

During the pack trip we saw great herds of elk and many deer and other wild animals. The outing gave Mather an opportunity to get to know the head of the Forest Service, and the two men found they had much in common. While packing over Two Ocean Pass, the commission discussed having the Forest Service give up some lands near the headwaters of the Yellowstone River to the park. Forest Service chief Greeley told Mather he would be willing to have the area taken over by the Park Service, if legislation could be passed. "But God have mercy on your soul if you ever build a road in here over Two Ocean Pass," Greeley said. Mather replied that the Park Service was not only against developing the area for roads and hotels, but would welcome something in the law providing that only trails, and no roads or hotels could be built.

The day we returned to Mammoth from our ten-day trip, Mather received a long telegram from Secretary Work. He handed it to me, and I read:

THE SITUATION HERE RELATING TO THE INVESTIGATION BY THE SENATE COMMITTEE OF THE NATIONAL PARK SERVICE IS BECOMING INVOLVED AND DEMANDS SOFT SPEECH OR SILENCE. YOUR MOVEMENTS ARE WATCHED AND WILL PROBABLY BE USED IN AN ATTACK THRU THE PARK SERVICE AGAINST THE DEPARTMENT. THE REACTION TO DYNAMITING THE SAWMILL HAS NOT BEEN GOOD. I THOUGHT WISE TO ADVISE YOU OF WHAT WAS PENDING THAT YOU MIGHT AVOID WHAT MIGHT ORDINARILY BE HARMLESS BUT NOW SERVES AS FUEL TO FLAMES THAT MAY BE KINDLED UNDER THE DEPARTMENT. DO NOT OVERWORK YOURSELF BY PAYING TOO MUCH ATTENTION TO DETAILS. GUARD YOUR TELEGRAMS AND INTERVIEWS AND REGARD YOURSELF AS BEING A TARGET, PARTICULARLY NOW THAT THE COMMITTEE IS MEETING AT SALT LAKE ON THE 26TH. JUST NOW UNFRIENDLY EYES ARE ON THE BUREAU OF RECLAMATION AND THE BUREAU OF PARKS. BOTH DIRECTORS SHOULD PROCEED WITH CAUTION. WHAT IS NOT SAID CANNOT BE MISQUOTED.

I handed it back to Mather, and he said, "Did you have anything to do with this?"

"A little, maybe," I answered, and he didn't say anything further about it. Then he left for Grand Canyon with the other members of the commission.

That very day I got a telephone call from my friend Dan Spencer, general passenger agent for the Union Pacific Railroad in Salt Lake City. He said that Senator Robert N. Stanfield, chairman of the Senate

Senator and "summer ranger" Tasker Oddie (right) and author at Yellowstone headquarters, 1924. Albright collection.

public lands committee, would be arriving the next morning at West Yellowstone to hold an investigative hearing in Gardiner, Montana, concerning my administration of Yellowstone National Park. Stanfield was an Oregon stockman who opposed the National Park Service because of our policies against grazing. The committee was en route from Grand Canyon National Park, where they had been making trouble for Superintendent Ross Eakin. But they had given no public notice of Yellowstone hearings, nor had they given me any notice that they were coming to Yellowstone.

I wasn't afraid of Stanfield or Cameron who by this time had lost most of his political muscle. His ally within the administration, Attorney General Harry Daugherty, had resigned after becoming involved in the Teapot Dome scandal, and his purported friend in the White House, President Calvin Coolidge, had not given Cameron any help. The new Attorney General, Harlan Fiske Stone, had removed the U.S. attorney for northern Arizona who had been doing Cameron's bidding. Cameron had lost control of the local law enforcement people, then the postmaster and other federal and county officials whom he had used to make trouble for Grand Canyon National Park.

Early the next morning I drove down to West Yellowstone and met the committee as they pulled in at the train station. Senator John Kendrick of Wyoming was the only one of the Democratic members of the committee to arrive with the party. All the others had elected to skip the Yellowstone hearings and would rejoin the party at Salt Lake City. Even Kendrick, I found, was not staying, and he went on to make a quick visit in his home state while the others were in Yellowstone. Stanfield informed me the group wanted to go directly to park headquarters at Mammoth for a brief stop and then to Gardiner where they would hold a hearing. They had with them a stenographer and the subcommittee counsel, George K. Bowden. A New York *Times* reporter, L. C. Speers, was also traveling with them.

I knew that senators Stanfield and Cameron had not seen Yellowstone, so I said, "Well, gentlemen, you may not get a chance to see Old Faithful or the rest of these geysers again; why don't you just postpone the hearing until tomorrow and I will take you out. With encouragement from committee member Tasker Oddie of Nevada, they decided to accept my invitation.

Before we left West Yellowstone, the New York *Times* man took me aside. "You're about to be framed," said Speers. "These two birds are very tricky. Can you send me around the park today so I can get an idea of how it is really being run and what the situation is? I'd like to see for myself."

I got my chief engineer to take Speers on a tour of the park while I guided senators Stanfield, Oddie, and Cameron to Old Faithful. After lunch we headed north for the fifty-mile drive to Mammoth, where they were to spend the night. It was four o'clock in the afternoon by the time they arrived at Mammoth, too late to hold hearings that day. Stopping by my office, I found out that while we had been gone, committee counsel Bowden had come to the headquarters, entered my office, and rifled my desk and all of my personal files. He found nothing that could be used against me. I also learned that Bowden had been in Yellowstone earlier in the season under the wing of Dr. J. M. Wolfe, a physician who had worked in the park the previous year. Wolfe had not been hired again this season because of bad conduct.

The next morning they started the hearing at Gardiner. When I arrived I found that the dozen witnesses the committee counsel had lined up to testify on the management of Yellowstone National Park were all people who had reasons of one sort or another for disliking me personally. They included several bootleggers I had thrown out of the park for illegal activities, a disgruntled concessioner, and several former employees.

One of the charges was that I had granted special privileges to members of the firm of J. P. Morgan and Company. The witness claimed that I had helped these New York men to purchase some land and build a lodge just outside the north boundary of the park, permitted them to build a fine road, part of it in the park, then had allowed the road to be marked as non-useable by tourists, and that the owners of the lodge lured bears out of Yellowstone by placing honey and meat along the park border to increase the wild game value of the lodge. Another witness charged that I had ordered park rangers to stampede buffalos "for eight or nine days" for the filming of Zane Grey's *The Thundering Herd*, that many of the animals had been killed in the stampede, and that later the movie people had eaten buffalo steaks and had left the park carrying buffalo hides. The owner of the largest store in Gardiner complained because tourists were not permitted to camp in the part of the park adjacent to Gardiner. Other witnesses testified that I ran the park in a dictatorial way.

Most of the questioning was done by counsel Bowden, who had coached the witnesses beforehand. One speaker, who said he had lived in the Yellowstone country for forty years, complained that he had been barred from the park.

"What reason was given for barring you from the park?" asked Senator Cameron.

At first the witness said he had just been trying to test out the minerals in a placer claim. But Cameron let him go on talking a bit too long, and the witness continued, "Well, you see, in testing the claim I would have had to use dynamite and they said they were afraid if I did, it would scare the dudes."

"What do you mean by dudes?" asked Senator Cameron.

"The city fellows that camp out there around Silver Tip," was the reply.

Stanfield listened silently, but Oddie became increasingly angry as he heard these obviously unfair attacks on me, and he began cross-questioning witnesses, forcing some of them to admit that the reason they had been banned from the park or fired was that they had violated park regulations.

"Were you ever convicted of selling liquor or bootlegging in the park?" Senator Oddie asked one witness.

"No sir," came the reply. "I pleaded guilty."

Stanfield became embarrassed and exercised his position as chairman of the committee, trying to bring the hearing to a close. But Cameron continued to call on the motley array of witnesses that the committee counsel had assembled. I had a messenger standing by with a motorcycle, and after each witness brought his charges, I would send the messenger to the park headquarters five miles away, to bring me files on each case.

From 9:00 a.m. until 5:00 p.m. Bowden's witnesses were put on the stand. Then the chairman let me present my position. The unfairness of the charges had made me extremely angry at first, but as the day wore on I saw I had the best of the situation because one by one the witnesses had impeached themselves. I used some of the law training I had never gotten a chance to put into practice, called a few witnesses to rebut some of the false statements made earlier, then talked for about an hour without interruption from any of the senators.

"I have been on trial all morning with convicted bootleggers, an unreliable doctor, a discharged road foreman, an ex-ranger with a bad record, and other men with personal grievances testifying against me through the convenient method of leading questions from a man who assembled this group of malcontents," I said. "I appreciate the opportunity the committee is giving me to make a statement in my own behalf and in the behalf of the administration of the park.

"The words 'For the benefit and enjoyment of the people' are uppermost in the thoughts of those charged with the administration of the Yellowstone. We construe these words to mean for all of the people of the nation and not just for the people of the town of Gardiner, built here at the line for the sole purpose of deriving private income from park travel. Listening to the testimony this morning, one would think that the great park was set aside by Congress for the 'benefit and enjoyment' of Gardiner. However, there are many good citizens in this town and they are in sympathy with the park administration, although judging from those who testified this morning, one might assume that the citizens were largely composed of ex-saloon keepers, present-day bootleggers, disgruntled ex-employees of the park, and unethical doctors."

I told the committee the major part I had played in organizing the National Park Service in 1917, that I had been superintendent of Yellowstone since 1919, and then I reviewed what we had accomplished. Next I took up some of the complaints they had heard, such as abuse of buffalos during the filming of the movie, the charges of special privilege to the owners of the Silver Tip Ranch, and arbitrary exercise of my powers as superintendent.

As for filming the buffalo stampede, I explained that the animals ranged in the mountains during the summer months and most visitors to the park were unable to see them. Believing that allowing them to be shown in a motion picture would enable millions of people to see a big buffalo herd, I permitted the filming. I certified that no cruelty had been practiced or allowed, and testified that the charge was totally baseless.

"Now, about the Silver Tip ranch located just north of the park in Slough Creek." I told them how the former owner, a bear hunter named Joseph "Frenchy" Duret, had caused the park administration a great deal of trouble, frequently poaching on the park wild life. In 1922, Duret had been killed by a grizzly bear. "Later that summer some public spirited men of New York were touring the park," I continued, "and finding them interested in the preservation of wild life, I induced them to visit the ranch in Slough Creek, which we feared would again become the base of illegal hunting and poaching on the park preserve.

When we approached the Duret homestead, several men with unsavory reputations were just leaving the place, trying to make a tentative deal for the purchase of the property.

"Sensing the gravity of the situation, one of the New York visitors, Thomas Cochran, negotiated the purchase of the property, paying more than it was worth in order to close the matter quickly. The control of the property was then turned over to the Forest Service and the National Park Service, although title was retained by Mr. Cochran and his associates. All improvements of the roads and the trails in the neighborhood of the Silver Tip have been paid for by the owners of the ranch." I added that Cochran and one of the friends with him were from J. P. Morgan and Company. They later purchased some ranches north of the park for winter grazing of elk at a cost of one hundred thousand dollars and gave the land to the park.

Regarding the charge that I arbitrarily exercised my authority as superintendent, I gave my reasons for barring the bootleggers who had questioned my actions, and added that "the man I have threatened with debarring was Dr. Wolfe, my bitterest personal enemy, who has been annoying the administration of the park with reckless driving. One

A pancake breakfast with an old mother bear and her cubs, Max and Climax, Yellowstone, 1922. J. E. Haynes photograph. Albright collection.

night when the ambulance was speeding to the hospital with a boy who had fallen off a cliff and had concussion of the brain, Dr. Wolfe tried to crowd the ambulance off the road. Three other complaints had preceeded this one. Dr. Wolfe hates me because I wouldn't renew his contract covering medical service in the park and because I was instrumental in having him discharged from the U.S. Public Health Service."

Cameron, Stanfield, and Oddie were silent during my entire testimony, and asked no questions. When I finished, counsel Bowden sought to question me, but Stanfield cut him off and abruptly adjourned the hearing.

Instead of proving anything against me or the national parks, the hearing had backfired and the senators were somewhat embarrassed. When Stanfield said he would like to see a buffalo stampede, I readily agreed to show them one.

The next day I took the senators in an old four-horse carriage back into the hills in the northeastern part of the park, where we found that a herd of about four hundred buffalo were grazing in the Lamar Valley. But as luck would have it, just as we came onto a ridge where we could see the buffalo, they suddenly stampeded on their own practically out of sight of the senators. "What's the matter," Senator Stanfield asked me, "can't you control them?"

"Well, sir," I replied, "It's the first time they've had to stampede for senators, and I guess they don't like it."

The senators all seemed to take my quip in good humor, and we finally did manage to get the buffalo to stampede within full view. That evening before he caught the train, I had a long, pleasant chat with Cameron. Away from the hearings, he seemed like a genial, good-natured old-timer, and we talked about the old days in the West. I realized that he had simply been using me as a means of attacking the policies of Work and Mather. As we talked, he never once mentioned the Grand Canyon or any of his troubles with Mather and the Park Service, nor did I mention them. Several times he expressed himself as being very greatly pleased with the management of Yellowstone. He seemed apologetic for the actions of the committee counsel and the choice of witnesses assembled to testify against me, which he blamed on the counsel. I saw him to the train and just before it pulled out, the old scoundrel bent his head down and asked me to examine it carefully. "Albright," he said, "look at me — have I got any horns?" I laughed and told him I couldn't see any.

Bowden, the committee counsel, was silent and gloomy when he got on the train. The day before, on the way to the buffalo stampede, he had confided to the bus driver that he had thought they had the goods on me, but that nobody had told him that I had a legal background and was capable of a quick and clever defense. And Senator Oddie had told me that if possible he was going to have Bowden dismissed because a man of his character was not fit to associate with the committee. Oddie added that any more hearings such as the one at Gardiner would make it hard for the committee to proceed with its investigation.

As they left I had a good feeling that the investigation of me, and the hearing, painful as it seemed at first, would prove beneficial to the parks in the long run. I was gratified a few days later to receive two clippings from the New York *Times*. Reporter Speers, who had interviewed me at length after his tour through the park, wrote two fine articles (August 30 and 31, 1925) that placed the National Park Service and me in a very good light. In his first article, evidently written halfway through the hearing because of his deadline, Steers wrote

> . . . that officials of the park have been unfairly treated by the committee is not denied, and as yet there has not been put into evidence a single word of complaint or protest that will bear the test of a fair investigation. The committee itself — only the Republicans came to Yellowstone — is not harmonious and it doesn't require a microscope to discover that Chairman Stanfield of Oregon and Senator Oddie of Nevada are not in agreement with Senator Cameron of Arizona as to the turn this feature of the investigation of the public domain has taken.
>
> Lots of people, some of them in official positions, do not hesitate to assert that the whole trouble is the result of a feud between Director Stephen T. Mather of the National Parks and Mr. Cameron over the years-long controversy involving the Bright Angel Trail in the Grand Canyon. If everything testified to date regarding Superintendent Albright's administration of the Yellowstone is true, a situation exists that might well justify a Federal Grand Jury investigation; but in justice to Mr. Albright and his assailants, the evidence so far is largely of a flimsy nature.

The next day's article, which appeared on the first page of an inside section, was headlined: ALBRIGHT DEFENDS YELLOWSTONE RULE; CHIDES SENATORS. The article said that the committee members

. . . caught a tartar in the person of H. M. Albright, superintendent of the Yellowstone and Field Assistant of the National Park Service. He was ready to be investigated and gave the committee to understand that if convicted, he wanted it to be on the testimony of men who could themselves stand investigation.

The park superintendent spoke without notes. He was 'mad clear through,' he admits, but kept himself in control. Not once was he interrupted and when he ended, the committee promptly and without another word adjourned.

Steers' long article then gave examples of the charges against me, the records of the people who made the charges, and my rebuttals. Several big eastern newspapers picked up the story, and the Brooklyn *Eagle* carried it on the front page.

Shortly thereafter, I received an envelope from the Secretary of the Interior's office, containing a card with just four words handwritten on it: "You are all right." And it was signed, "H. Work."

Cameron tried to prevent the Yellowstone hearings from being printed along with the other hearings, but after a long delay, they were issued. He had a rough time of it during the following year. The *Saturday Evening Post* and other magazines and many western newspapers editorialized against him. The Los Angeles *Times* ran a series of attacks, criticizing Cameron's attempts to make private gain out of a national park, and also for his attempt to control the site where Hoover Dam would ultimately be built. Harold Baxter, the new U.S. attorney appointed by Attorney General Stone, took Senator Cameron to court while the judge friendly to Cameron was out of the state. He succeeded in having Cameron's last fifty-five placer claims declared invalid, and gave Cameron forty-five days to get all of his property out of Grand Canyon National Park.

In his re-election campaign Cameron tried to cloak himself with the banner of President Coolidge. He also claimed he was protecting Arizona from those outside forces which would deprive the state of its inalienable rights, and attacked the Washington bureaucracy in general and Stephen Mather specifically. The man running against him was Representative Carl Hayden, a staunch supporter of the Park Service. I would be willing to bet that every government man in the West was rooting for Hayden. Secretary Work urged me to go down to Arizona to see how the campaign was going. I didn't go, but I happened to be in Denver the day after the 1926 election, and employees of the Park

Service, the Forest Service, and the Biological Survey got together and had a "hurrah" dinner to celebrate Hayden's overwhelming victory.

Cameron was finished. He ran in 1928 against Senator Ashurst, and again in 1932 against Hayden, but never came close. The man who had "tried to steal the Grand Canyon" had been stopped at last.

In later years back in Washington, Grace and I were invited to dinner several times at the home of then Chief Justice Stone. The men would go into Stone's den for after-dinner brandy, and he would say, "Albright, tell them about Cameron." Then I would recount the whole story, especially the part about how Attorney General Stone had called in the U.S. attorney for northern Arizona to talk about the Cameron problem. He had asked him, "Who is your boss; whom do you report to?"

The U.S. attorney had replied, "Well, you are, of course."

"Are you prepared to take orders from me?"

"Yes, certainly," said the attorney. "All right then," Attorney General Stone had told him, "Go over to that desk and write out your resignation." And he did.

15

Of Princes, Debutantes, Bears, and Just Folks

FROM 1926 THROUGH 1928, WE MADE SIGNIFICANT ADDITIONS TO THE NATIONAL PARK SYSTEM. The highlight was legislation that almost doubled Sequoia National Park to include Mt. Whitney, highest peak in the continental United States. The first three parks in the southeastern United States—Great Smoky Mountains, Shenandoah, and Mammoth Cave — were also created.

In July 1926, Congress passed a bill authorizing a part of the additions to Sequoia that Mather had worked so long to bring about. There was a skirmish over whether to add the name Roosevelt to Sequoia, to honor Teddy Roosevelt, and Congress decided not to do so. A strong recommendation the previous year from the Coordinating Commission on National Parks and Forests, chaired by ex-Congressman Henry W. Temple, a former professor and historian, helped in the legislative fight to extend Sequoia.

While almost tripling the size of Sequoia, however, the legislation gave some parts of the park to the Forest Service, left out the Kings Canyon area we had sought for so many years to include, and contained other objectionable legislative compromises such as authorizing timber cutting and grazing in some areas previously owned by the Forest Service. So we had to continue to work to get the lands and protection needed for Sequoia.

Still, Mather felt a great sense of satisfaction at getting at least a start on the Sequoia expansion, and he mentioned to me again that he really would like to retire and have me take over as Director of the

National Park Service. This talk of retiring had been coming up repeatedly. He felt that the goals he had laid out in 1915 had nearly all been accomplished. We had achieved full recognition for the Park Service as a significant part of the government and had improved the caliber of the ranger force and superintendents. Cammerer had been such a good administrator that Mather had been able to spend much of his time visiting the parks. He continued to focus on improving the facilities of Yosemite and trying to make it a model park — and I was doing likewise with Yellowstone.

Every time Mather would bring up retirement, I would argue against it. His health was reasonably good, he was not quite sixty years old, and still liked to hike, take long horseback trips in the wilderness, and occasionally take part in some not-too-strenuous climbing. Besides, I would tell him, he and I still had a long way to go before all those goals of ours were achieved. We needed more staff and better facilities to serve the ever-increasing patronage of the national parks. We especially needed more professionally-trained rangers, naturalists, wildlife managers, landscape architects, interpreters, park administrators, and maintenance people. For my part, I had a dream I wanted to make real. For years I had wanted to get the many national military parks, battle-fields, and monuments transferred out of the War Department and Department of Agriculture into the National Park Service so we could give proper protection and interpretation to these great historic and cultural treasures.

During a four-day period in May 1926 Great Smoky Mountains, Shenandoah, and Mammoth Cave were authorized. Little land went with the legislation — nearly everything within the boundaries of the three parks was owned privately. We could not even staff the parks for protection purposes until half the land was acquired, so a big task lay ahead for the states and conservation organizations to raise the funds for land purchases.

As early as 1919, Mather had started advocating the creation of national parks in the east (in addition to Lafayette), and in his 1923 annual report to the Secretary he had made another strong plea. In 1925, the Southern Appalachian Park Commission, a high level group appointed by Secretary Work, had surveyed the potential for the south-eastern parks and recommended authorization, although not determining definite boundaries. This commission was also chaired by Congressman Temple.

Our hopes for expansion of Yellowstone, Grand Canyon, Mount Rainier, and Rocky Mountain, and the establishment of Grand Teton also had been given a boost by the report of Temple's coordinating commission. In September 1925, it unanimously voted to extend the eastern boundary of Yellowstone to follow the crest of the Absaroka Mountains, including the land around the headwaters of the Yellowstone River—the Thorofare country. This straightened the park boundary and added summer range for elk and buffalo and the unique volcanic phenomena of the Hoodoo Basin. But the Forest Service balked at the idea of allowing the National Park Service to extend the park southward to include their land.

The commission recommended the creation of a small Grand Teton National Park as a separate unit of Yellowstone, including only the eastern side of the Teton range and Jenny and Leigh Lakes. This was less than half of what we sought, and left out Jackson Lake and the Jackson Hole area within the Teton National Forest. It did not give us a framework for the kind of park that would allow inclusion of the private lands Rockefeller was seeking to purchase and was not a satisfactory solution as far as the National Park Service was concerned. The commission also made recommendations for some modest expansions of other parks — Rocky Mountain, Mount Rainier, Grand Canyon, and Crater Lake.

The years 1927 and 1928 saw continued progress. Early in 1927, Congress extended Grand Canyon National Park north of the Colorado River to include fifty-one square miles of the Kaibab National Forest, as recommended by the Temple Commission. But no action was taken on the recommendations made for Yosemite, Crater Lake, Rocky Mountain, or Glacier national parks.

In 1928 we finally were able to bring Bryce Canyon National Park into the system. Congress had authorized a Utah National Park in 1924 to take in the unique natural amphitheater of colorful spires and minarets that were then being protected as a Forest Service national monument, but the legislation provided that all the land authorized within the boundaries had to become the property of the United States before the park could be established. Mather refused to assume responsibility for the Forest Service lands within the boundaries until the private lands were acquired. In February 1928, after the Union Pacific bought up the private lands and made a trade with the federal government for other public lands, legislation was approved to establish Bryce Canyon National Park.

Again Mather was talking retirement, and I was scraping up more arguments against it. For one thing, I had no desire at all to go back to Washington. In addition to my very full job as assistant director for field activities, there was much yet to accomplish at Yellowstone. I was doing a great deal of behind-the-scenes work to get the land needed for protecting the Jackson Hole area. Our whole family loved the life at Yellowstone. During 1925, I had use of another office in San Francisco for winter field work. When I was working there, we all stayed in Berkeley with Grace's parents. We certainly did not relish the thought of returning to those hot, humid Washington summers.

Where but at Yellowstone could a low-ranking bureaucrat rub elbows with royalty? In the summer of 1926, Swedish Crown Prince Gustav Adolf and Crown Princess Louise came to Yellowstone with a small entourage to start a five-park tour. I took them on extensive trips around Yellowstone over several days. His Highness was an ardent archeologist, loved wildlife, and especially wanted to see mountain sheep. The only sheep were high on Mount Washburn, so we drove as far as we could and then did some hiking. When we finally spotted a band of sheep, Prince Gustav wanted to photograph them.

"Your Highness," I said, "if you want to get close enough for photographs, we'll have to climb around and get upwind of them and then crawl on our stomachs so they won't notice us. It will be pretty tough going," I added, "and we may tear up our clothes a bit."

"That doesn't matter," said the prince. "I would like to go."

So we worked our way around as close as we dared, then dropped to the ground and pulled ourselves along on our bellies until we were about fifty feet from the sheep. Our shirts were torn and filthy, but his Highness got his pictures.

We went fishing at several of the best spots, and he filled his creel to the limit. Just before they left, we had a dinner party at the Lake Hotel, and had the chef prepare the fish Gustav had caught that day in Lake Yellowstone. Grace was hostess and led the procession into the dining-room on the arm of Crown Prince Gustav. But to find me, you had to look halfway down the line behind the Secretary, Mather, and several other high ranking officials.

The day the prince left, we made him an honorary park ranger, which delighted him.

Author and Crown Prince Gustav Adolf of Sweden in Yellowstone, 1926. Albright collection.

The annual governors' conference was held in Cheyenne in 1926. Wyoming Governor Nellie Tayloe Ross was hostess, and she knew that coming to Cheyenne was not much of an adventure for her fellow governors, so she talked to me about our taking care of them for a few days.

The state of Wyoming invited the whole group to Yellowstone, and about twenty-five of them came, along with their families. Funny thing though, there were no sons along, just daughters, and most of them teen-aged.

One of the first events was a dance at the Canyon Hotel, and we had to get some of the young rangers to come so the girls would have partners. One of the rangers was a particularly good looking chap named Karl Hardy. He was so handsome that we called him our Greek god. Well, all the girls at the dance wanted him for their partner. The next day, when we went to the top of Mount Washburn, Florence Trumbell and her sister, daughters of the governor of Connecticut, called me aside. I had been told that Florence was engaged to marry John Coolidge, a son of the President.

"Mr. Albright, we want you to make us a promise," said Florence.

"What kind of a promise?" I asked.

"We won't tell you what it is until you promise to promise!"

"Well, girls, I can't do that, so now just tell me what it is you want me to do, and I'll do it if I can."

"Oh, you can do this all right" said Florence. "At the dance tonight at Mammoth Hotel, we want you to send that handsome Karl Hardy over so we can dance with him."

I protested that I couldn't take a ranger based at Canyon, who had regular duties there, and send him to Mammoth just for a dance. But they said, "You promised! You promised!"

I had been in a lot of tight situations and got out of them all right, but never one quite like this, and I just didn't know what to say. But I told them I would see what I could do. When I got where I could phone, I rang up the Canyon Station and told Ranger Hardy that I wanted him to go to Mammoth that night and dance with the girls.

"Mr. Albright, do I have to?" he said.

"Well, why not?" I asked. "It's a good assignment."

"But, sir, you see, I have been dating Adelaide Nichols, and we're sort of going steady."

Adelaide was the granddaughter of the head of the company that ran the hotel at Mammoth and she lived there. Karl didn't want to be seen there dancing with other girls. "Well," I said, "I realize it will be a little embarrassing for you, Karl, but you'll just have to do it, because I've promised the girls you will." He came all right. I noticed during the evening that he seemed to be enjoying his tough duty.

Gifford Pinchot, by then governor of Pennsylvana, was in the group
visiting the park. I had briefly met this founder of the so-called progressive conservation movement several times before in the east. He had
been the first chief of the U.S. Forest Service, and a frequent opponent
of the Park Service, because we were taking lands from the Forest
Service for parks. For his visit, I had arranged for him to meet in Cody
with several old national forest officers, and I had driven him to the
park along with the governors of Wyoming and Maine.

Pinchot and I had a pleasant conversation over breakfast the last
morning of his visit. Pinchot thought we were doing an excellent job
with the Park Service and had words of praise for Yellowstone. He
did not appear to have any animosity toward the National Park Service.
He wanted to stay a couple of days and have me show him more of the
park but his wife insisted he had to leave that very morning to visit
friends, so we did not get to continue our conversation. I never allowed
the so-called competition between the Park Service and Forest Service
to affect my relations with present or former Forest Service officials, and
I was on good terms with the foresters in charge of the national forests
that surrounded Yellowstone.

The day Pinchot left I received a telegram from Cammerer asking
me to go at once to Glacier National Park where forest fires were raging
out of control. Montana Governor John E. Erickson and I bade a quick
farewell to the others and immediately left for Montana.

Glacier National Park had seen an exceptionally mild winter, followed by a dry and early spring. By May the forests were tinder, and
fires had broken out. Now they had spread and were threatening many
areas of the park. During the train trip Governor Erickson said he was
going to call out the National Guard to fight the fires. I argued that the
Guard were mostly city men who would not know how, and that they

might even make the situation worse. Erickson finally agreed when I explained that I would hire Blackfeet Indians and other people who were better suited to fire-fighting than the National Guard.

When I arrived I found the situation even more serious than I had feared, and I brought my chief ranger and assistant chief ranger up from Yellowstone to help organize the fire fighting. It took three weeks, but we finally got the fires under control. They were the worst in the history of Glacier and served to alert us to the shortcoming of the Park Service fire-fighting capabilities.

Mather immediately set up a new forestry division, headed by Ansel Hall, who also wore two other hats as chief naturalist of the Park Service and head of an education division just being formed. John Coffman, who had spent many years with the Forest Service and was an expert at fire control, was assigned to take charge of fire control training and organizing.

Hall located the new forestry division at his headquarters on the Berkeley campus of the University of California, so along with my wintertime San Francisco office, the Park Service was beginning to have quite a presence in the Bay area. Mather had also moved the landscape engineering division to San Francisco. It had been in Los Angeles, where its chief, Daniel Hull, had established it for his own convenience. Hull refused to move to San Francisco and resigned from the Park Service. Thomas Vint, a trained architect as well as a landscape engineer, who had been Hull's chief assistant, moved into the job.

The engineering division had been located in Portland, Oregon, since 1917, when Mather had hired George Goodwin from the Army Corps of Engineers to form the new division. Earlier in 1926, Mather had ordered Goodwin to draw up new standards for Park Service roads in line with ideas that had been expressed by the Bureau of Public Roads western regional engineer, Dr. Laurence Hewes, who had spoken at our 1925 Mesa Verde superintendents' conference. In reply Goodwin wrote that it would be impossible under the budget then in force to build roads with the new standards that Mather had ordered to be used. It was really quite a sensible letter. But Mather wrote back, "I accept your resignation."

Mather then asked Dr. Hewes to help the Park Service design the new road standards, and in the next few months I worked with him in drafting an understanding of what the Bureau of Public Roads would do in planning and supervision of road construction in the parks. To start the process, Hewes assigned his senior engineer, Frank Kittredge, to complete a survey for the trans-mountain highway across Logan Pass in Glacier National Park. Even though Mather himself preferred to see the parks on foot or horseback, he felt each park should have one good highway—but no more than one—that would allow people to get deep enough, or through, the park so they could have at least a taste of wilderness. Kittredge did such a good job on the Logan Pass survey that I suggested to Mather we have Kittredge work out a program for all the major roads in the parks based on the new standards. I recommended that we hire Kittredge permanently, so Mather offered him the Goodwin chief engineer job and moved the engineering division from Portland to San Francisco.

Roads were a constant source of exasperation to us at Yellowstone. We had to spend so much on visitor facilities to keep pace with the ever-increasing travel to the park that there was never enough left in our budget to give adequate attention to the roads. They were all unpaved and had to be graded and groomed constantly. We pleaded with Congress to inspect the situation. Finally, I got Representative James Good of Iowa (he later became Secretary of War in President Hoover's Cabinet) to bring his appropriations committee to the park. Wanting the congressmen to appreciate how bad the roads were, we even neglected them a bit for a week or so before the committee arrived, and the ruts and dust were terrible.

Then, just the night before they arrived, it began to rain. It rained and it rained. There was no way we could avoid sending the graders out, and by the time they had made the roads passable, they were in as nearly perfect condition as unpaved highways could be — no dust, no ruts, no washboard surface. I constantly told the committee how bad the roads usually were and how desperately we needed funds to get them paved. But they didn't believe a word of it. On the last day of their inspection tour, one of them gave me a big wink and said to his colleagues, "Let's not bring up road improvement, or Albright will start his heart-breaking arguments again!"

It wasn't very many days before another congressional group visited the park, and they found the roads to be just as bad as we had claimed they were. One of the group was a member of the House appropriations committee, Representative Nicholas Sinnott of Oregon, a delightful character who enjoyed declaiming at length on the beauties of the park, often quoting from his favorite authors and poets. Standing on

the Mount Washburn fire lookout station, he surveyed the grand view
and quoted from Isaiah 49: 11, "I will make all my mountains a way,
and my highways shall be exalted." We had a small sign painted and
placed at the lookout station, with that inscription on it, and many
people had their pictures taken alongside the sign. If they were skilled
enough with their cameras, they could get some of the mountain majesty
in the background.

Often senators and congressmen brought their families for visits to
the park. Senator Tasker Oddie of Nevada and his wife came very

William Henry Jackson, photographer of the 1871 Hayden Yellowstone Survey party, upon his return in 1925. National Park Service.

early one season and I invited them to listen as instructions and advice were given to the college boys entering training as seasonal rangers. The following day Mrs. Oddie came to see me and asked whether her husband could work as a ranger part of the summer when the Senate was in recess. As graciously as I could I said I didn't think it would work out. But she said he needed the exercise, and told me he was an experienced horseman and hiker. I didn't really believe she was serious. A day later the senator asked to be given a place on our ranger force, serving without pay. It was pretty irregular, but I decided to give it a try. I loaned him one of my uniforms and assigned him to a mounted patrol. He became a valuable ranger, and that experience turned him into one of our staunchest supporters in the Senate.

Just outside the park on Hebgen Lake, the head of the United States Steel Company, William E. Corey, had a camp. One day he invited me there for lunch. When I arrived, he was in his nightshirt and he kept on wearing it. I found out in later visits that he dressed this way as sort of a joke, and to show his distaste for government officials. I didn't let it bother me, and we became good friends.

A lot of the conversation on my first visit centered on how bad the fishing had become. "There on the Madison River I used to be able to catch the limit in no time," Corey said. "But now, hardly a bite in an hour. You ought to do something about it."

I explained the problem was that the little hatchery we had wasn't adequate to keep pace with the heavy fishing being done by the huge number of visitors we were now getting. "The trouble is, our little hatchery just takes the eggs and hatches them and then plants them as fry." I told him that we needed a hatchery where we could keep the fry and feed them until they grow into fingerlings.

After thinking about it a few moments, he said: "Well, what would it cost — that hatchery you want?"

I told him we'd had an estimate of $27,500.

"Well, get after Congress to give it to you," he said.   I explained we had tried, without success, to get an appropriation from Congress. As we continued our lunch, we discussed other subjects, and no more was said about the hatchery. Then just as I was leaving, Corey said, "Albright, what did you say it would take to build that damn hatchery?"

"Twenty-seven thousand, five hundred," I repeated.

"I'm giving it to you," said Corey. "Go ahead and build the hatchery."

After it was built, I sent him a letter of thanks, and said I would like to put up a little plaque saying that this was a gift from William E. Corey. He wrote back, "To hell with the plaque — raise the fish!"

That was one of the things I enjoyed about my work as superintendent — coming in contact with characters like Corey, who almost on a whim could fulfill a need of the park that cost what to me seemed like a king's ransom. I enjoyed dealing with all the visitors. I genuinely like people, all kinds of people, and I got a great kick out of seeing them enjoying the park.

I would go into the campgrounds on a summer evening and talk with campers about their children and their homes and their towns, what they did for a living, how they got to the park, where they were going next, where they had camped. They would have lots of questions for me, too. As I would talk to a little group at one campfire, more people would drift in from other campfires and sometimes I would stop talking and suddenly realize a big crowd had gathered around me. I would take advantage of it, telling them things that would fan their interest in the park and in conservation. I would tell them about the problems, too, and get their ideas about what ought to be done to correct them.

Going about my business in the daytime, I would come upon people looking in vain to see an elk or a bison. Often there would be one nearby that they simply failed to see. So I would show the visitors how to spot the animals that are so well camouflaged. Sometimes when there was a good band of elk within easy sight of the road, I would see a tour bus pass them right by. So I would stop the next bus, and a whole string of busses, one after another for an hour sometimes, to let the tourists see the elk.

There was one animal the visitors never had any trouble seeing — bears. Even though most of Yellowstone's big population of bears stayed in the wilds, there were a number of black bears that had become what we called "beggar bears," or "hold-up bears." They would hang around the roadsides waiting for visitors to stop their cars and throw out food. These black bears were not vicious, but they were big and powerful, and could be dangerous if provoked, and we constantly warned visitors that the bears were wild animals and should be treated with caution. But visitors would often hold out food with their hand, hoping to get a bear to rise up on its hind legs and reach. Occasionally the bear would bite or scratch the visitor in trying to reach the food. Then, of course, we would get an impassioned complaint about the "vicious" bear.

I would answer such complaints by first telling the visitor that he or she should not have held a hand out to the bear; second, that the wound was only superficial; and third, that the bear's bite was actually a unique souvenir to take home. The third point rarely failed to convince the visitor that the bear bite or scratch was really something worthwhile.

One time my good friend Harold Fabian, a Salt Lake City lawyer who was the law partner of my old college friend Beverly Clendenin, brought his teenage daughter Bunny for a visit. They had been in the park only a short time when Fabian called me from West Thumb demanding that I get rid of a dangerous bear that had just wounded his daughter. I tried my one-two-three routine on Fabian, winding up with what a unique souvenir Bunny now had to take home and show to her high school classmates, and how popular she would be when she showed off the scratch.

"Well, she's not going to be showing off the scratch," answered Fabian. "It's high on her thigh."

So I reasoned that to have gotten that kind of wound, Bunny must have been trying to tease the bear, and Fabian had to admit she probably had been breaking the rules. He made no further complaint.

One day a lady telephoned from Canyon Lodge demanding to speak to the superintendent, and telling my secretary she wanted a black bear "killed at once." I tried to find out what her injury was. All she would say was that no one had ever been hurt or humiliated as much as she had been, and she kept repeating that the bear had to be shot for what it had done. She was almost hysterical, so I sent a ranger over to find out how badly she had been hurt.

When he got there he found out that the woman had been feeding a big black bear all morning, and tourists had been photographing the two of them. After lunch she had been standing on the lodge platform just as several hundred people were boarding the busses. She enticed the same bear to the lodge platform with a handout, and the bear stood up as she fed him from her fingers. Passengers in and out of the busses were taking pictures when somebody called to her, and she turned to answer. The bear, thinking the show was over, dropped to the ground, but in doing so he caught the tip of his claws in her dress, ripping off the dress and her slip, leaving the lady standing there in her underclothes. She admitted to the ranger that she had not been hurt, just humiliated. The ranger didn't give her much sympathy, but instead lectured her on her foolhardiness.

In the late fall of 1926, after I had closed the park, I spent a few weeks at my San Francisco office, then headed east to Washington for the Ninth National Park Conference. Mather had planned this conference to span ten days, by far the longest ever. It started with a reception given at the White House by President Coolidge, and wound up with four days in the New York City area, where we visited Palisades Interstate Park, the Bronx Zoo, and the American Museum of Natural History. Mather and I also took in the Sesquicentennial Exposition in Philadelphia where the Interior Department had an exhibit.

While in Washington we had the kind of in-house discussions that were standard at these annual conferences. We took up problems and administrative matters, with the superintendents and top field people sharing ideas with the Washington officials, experts from other bureaus, and concessioners. In addition, however, Mather wanted his Park Service people to get due recognition as members of one of the best bureaus in government. So in addition to the White House reception he arranged for us to meet with members of Congress at the Capitol, got novelist Mary Roberts Rinehart to give a reception at her home, and staged a big banquet at the Willard Hotel. He invited some of the most illustrious people of Washington, and each park superintendent was host of a table with at least one dignitary as his guest.

At my table were Secretary of Commerce and Mrs. Herbert Hoover. I had met Hoover before, and I had not found it easy to communicate with him. The first time was in 1917, when he was national food administrator and we had had the problem of protecting the national parks from the stockmen. I had not talked with him then because he had immediately turned me over to his assistant, Duncan McDuffie.

The second encounter with Hoover was in 1922, when he had been Secretary of Commerce for about a year. Mather and Hoover were close friends, and Mather asked me to go see Hoover along with Yosemite superintendent Dusty Lewis, to see if we could get a fish hatchery for Yosemite. Mather had gone out of town, so Cammerer called Hoover's assistant, Don Wilhelm, whom both of us knew, and Wilhelm got us an appointment.

When Lewis, Cammerer, and I were ushered into the large office, Hoover was reading some kind of report, and I don't remember him

Author, Jimmie Johnson, Chas. W. Cook (of the 1869 Folsom-Cook exploration of Yellowstone), and Stephen Mather at Cook's home in White Sulpher Springs, Montana, 1925. National Park Service.

saying a word of greeting. He just motioned for us to sit down, and we did. His secretary had prepared a card for him with our names and positions listed, so he looked at Cammerer, whose position as assistant director of the National Park Service was the highest. Cammerer finally realized he was expected to begin, so he tried to explain the need for the hatchery, but he just couldn't get the words out in the chilly atmosphere, and turned helplessly to Lewis. So Lewis began explaining what we wanted in Yosemite, but he also got tongue tied, and blurted out, "Well, Mr. Albright has a hatchery in Yellowstone and we want one like that in Yosemite." So Secretary Hoover shifted his eyes to me. I had the feeling that this man was either in a very bad mood or very busy, and that we had better get out of there. So in one breath I quickly ran through what we had in Yellowstone, what we needed in Yosemite, the estimated cost, and that the item should go into the 1923 budget we were now completing.

Secretary Hoover said, "It ought to be done." That was all he said. No promise, no encouragement, no questions. So we made a fast exit. Wilhelm was waiting for us and said, "What the dickens is the matter with you fellows? You weren't in there three minutes. Did you get what you wanted?" We said we weren't sure, but hoped the Secretary would take up our request with Henry O'Malley, the commissioner of fisheries (we had already consulted O'Malley and knew he favored the hatchery). But we never heard anything more about it and we did not get a hatchery at Yosemite until the state of California built one for the park some years later.

Now, at the banquet table, I couldn't help recalling that previous meeting, and wondering what had been on his mind that day. I still was finding it very difficult to draw him into conversation, but I did get a bit of a response when I brought up fishing, a subject I had heard was close to his heart. I extended him an invitation to come to the park and cast a few flies in Yellowstone Lake. He was noncommital.

Then, finally, something made the impassive Mr. Hoover smile. But it was no human who did it. There had been an overpopulation of deer on the North Rim of Grand Canyon. Some of them were being captured and transferred to other areas, and Mather had personally financed the capture of two of the deer for shipment to the National Zoological Park in Washington, D.C. They had just arrived at the time of the banquet, and one of them was quite tame. Mather got Grand Canyon Chief Ranger Scoyen, who had been handling the transfer, to bring the tame one to the banquet.

Scoyen led the large doe to the entrance of the ballroom, and she walked straight down the center aisle to our table and started nibbling at Hoover's salad. Mr. Hoover laughed delightedly and gave her all of it.

Another guest at the banquet, George Horace Lorimer, editor of the *Saturday Evening Post*, invited Mather and me to lunch the following week at his office in Philadelphia, and to bring several of the superintendents from the conference with us. At lunch, Lorimer asked why we were not doing more about wilderness preservation in national parks, and talked about some problems he had heard about in Estes Park, Colorado, adjoining Rocky Mountain National Park. Mather took exception to Lorimer's comment, explained that Estes Park was not in the national park, and gave him a ten-minute talk on all the things the Park Service was doing to preserve wilderness. Lorimer then asked if I would write an article on wilderness preservation and the national parks and assigned a writer, Frank Taylor, to assist me in polishing the prose. I wrote that the National Park Service had to provide access to national parks, which meant maintaining the few existing roads and building at least one access road into new parks because the parks had been set aside for the enjoyment of the people. But at the same time, we opposed the forces who were seeking to put roads into the wilderness. I cited as proof of the preservation policies of the Park Service the fact that "nine-tenths of Yellowstone is still — and we hope it always will be — an everlasting wilderness."*

*"The Everlasting Wilderness," *Saturday Evening Post*, September 29, 1928.

Devils Tower National Monument. George A. Grant photograph. National Park Service.

16

A Visit from Silent Cal

EARLY IN 1927, MATHER AND I MADE A VISIT TO DEATH VALLEY, THAT STARKLY BEAUTIFUL PIECE OF DESERT, LOWEST SPOT IN THE WESTERN HEMISPHERE, yet practically in the shadow of the continental United States' highest peak, Mount Whitney. We had gone to Death Valley at the urging of the Pacific Coast Borax Company, which had just closed a mine there. They were planning to build a hotel near the site, and wanted our advice on the tourist value of the area. I had seen Death Valley once as a youth, and had often thought of its potential as a national park.

When the Borax people asked whether it might become a national park, Mather was noncommittal, and said that California already had four national parks and would soon have a fifth, Redwood. Later he told me that the reason he had not shown any interest in Death Valley was that with his former involvement in the borax business, he might be accused of conflict of interest if he pushed this former borax mining area as a park. I made a mental note, however, that we should eventually try to bring it into the national park system.

While there, Mather brought up the matter of retirement once again. He wasn't feeling as well as he would like to, and was tired, he said, and he told me I had better start thinking about succeeding him. As usual, I argued that he was nowhere near ready to retire, and said the trip he was making to Guatemala the following week would give him a chance to rest. But when he returned, he was still talking retirement. On our first day together in Washington, though, I felt relieved, because of something he said as we drove across the Chain Bridge on the way to dinner at Cammerer's home. Mather was a member of the National Capital Park and Planning Commission, which was at the time studying a proposal for a hydroelectric dam on the Potomac — a project to which he was intensely opposed. He gazed down at the Potomac as we were crossing, and remarked that saving that river was a job he had to work on. That didn't sound like a man who was planning to retire.

In April, Mather went to Hawaii with Secretary Work for the Pan Pacific Conference on Education, Reclamation, Rehabilitation, and Recreation. Coming home on the ship Mather had a heart attack. It alarmed everyone in the party except Mather. Work cabled me to meet him at the dock in San Francisco so he could talk with me. But Mather, in high spirits, was the first down the gangplank, and insisted I go with him immediately to his room at the Palace Hotel so I could bring him up to date on park affairs.

When I caught up with Secretary Work a few hours later, he said that what he had wanted to tell me was that Mather's physical condition was not at all good. Work, formerly a medical doctor, said that he was afraid Mather might suffer a more serious if not fatal heart attack one of these days. "I want you to take over the administration of the Park Service from outside of Washington, make all decisions and act as if you are Director, subject only to my instructions," Work said.

"I can't do that, Mr. Secretary," I replied. "In the first place it would not get results. More importantly, it would wreck my relationship with Mr. Mather, and that is something too sacred to be tampered with. I'm sorry to go against your wishes on this, but I feel strongly that any limits on Mr. Mather's activities will have to come from Mr. Mather himself." Secretary Work accepted what I said, although he was not happy about it.

In late May, Mather came to Yellowstone for the opening of the park and to check on the progress of the extension of a road the army had started many years earlier from Madison Junction about three miles up the Firehole River. One afternoon he told me he had been trying to decide what to do about Yosemite. Dusty Lewis had suffered a heart attack a few months earlier and would be out of commission a long time. But Mather wanted to keep the Yosemite superintendency open for Lewis if at all possible. What Mather had in mind was for me to go to

Yosemite after closing Yellowstone and then spend the winter there watching over things.

With so many other irons in the fire, I said I guessed one more job wouldn't hurt me, and I wanted to help save the Yosemite job for Lewis. Mather added that he would also like me to accomplish some other things while at Yosemite. I could study the effects the new all-year road from Mariposa to El Portal would have on the park, and also assess whether the development of winter sports was feasible and whether the park facilities could handle the resulting increase of visitors. In the 1926–1927 winter season just ended, Yosemite had drawn seventy-five thousand visitors. Over the Decoration Day weekend, more than ten thousand visitors had entered the park each day, and by noon of May 30 there were twenty-five thousand people within Yosemite Valley alone.

Meantime, there was a full summer season ahead at Yellowstone. In late July we had a visit from Secretary of Commerce Hoover. He had taken me up on my banquet table invitation of the previous year. It was partly a business trip to look at the conditions of the Bureau of Fisheries operation in the park, which came under the jurisdiction of the Department of Commerce. He also wanted to check on our plans for the siting of the new hatchery we were planning to build with the money William Corey had given us for that purpose. Not incidentally, Hoover, an avid angler, wanted to get in some fishing. His office had notified me of the date he would arrive, but not the time or how he was coming. In early afternoon the ranger at the east gateway phoned to say Hoover had just entered the park in a hired car.

Secretary Hoover accepted my invitation for dinner at the Lake Hotel where he was staying. I also invited Captain C. F. Culler of the regional Bureau of Fisheries, temporarily in charge of the present small hatchery, the only federal fish hatchery in a national park. Its main job was to collect eggs, hatch them, and distribute the minnows to other hatcheries where they could be raised or used to stock streams. After dinner we decided to take a walk to the hatchery, about a mile away. We went along the shore of Yellowstone Lake in the warm evening air with the light from a full moon. No one talked as we walked along, enjoying the moonlit view and the sounds of the evening. Hoover picked up a dead branch, broke off the side branches and twigs, and made himself a walking stick.

When we got to the hatchery, Culler explained why he thought the new hatchery should be built right alongside the old one. I presented a

Secretary of Commerce Herbert Hoover with author and Marian and Robert Mather Albright, Yellowstone, 1927. Albright collection.

contrary view, saying that our landscape people didn't want the new hatchery down on the lakeshore, but up the road a little way, out of sight. Hoover asked both of us a few questions, then walked around examining the two sites. Finally he announced his decision by placing his stick in the ground in the middle of the site the Park Service favored. Back at the hotel, with the business part of the two-day trip finished, Hoover said to me, "When do we start on our fishing trip?"

"It depends on when you'd like to have breakfast, Mr. Secretary," I replied.

"About six or six-thirty," he said. I observed that the hotel didn't start serving until seven o'clock and he thought that would get the trip started pretty late. So Culler invited us to eat ham and eggs with the hatchery crew at six-thirty, and Hoover accepted.

As we got into the boat and started off in the early morning, Hoover was still dressed in his double-breasted blue serge suit and a white shirt with the high, stiff collar that was something of a trademark with him. He certainly didn't look much like a fisherman. I told him we would be going through some heavy brush, and handed him an extra pair of leggings I had brought along. But he declined them. He reached down in the boat and brought from under his legs a tin box he had carried aboard, and opened it up. In it were all kinds of lures and paraphernalia for deep sea fishing.

"Mr. Secretary," I said, "I have never seen a lot of stuff like that before, and I don't think it will be any good here, fishing for trout." Then he admitted he had never looked in the box before — it had been given to him as honorary president of the Isaak Walton League of America. I handed him some spinners and flies that he could use, but he kept rummaging around in the box to see if there wasn't something useable there, probably so he could tell the "Ikes" that he had caught fish with their gift tackle. Looking over the equipment reminded him of some deep-sea fishing experiences. Very quietly at first and then with more animation, he took us on a kind of verbal fishing trip to different parts of the world, not bragging about anything, but just telling what bait he had used and what he had caught.

When we got to Clear Creek on the other side of the lake, I insisted that he put on the leggings. He could see the brush and rocks, so he complied. But he still wouldn't take off his double-breasted suit coat and replace it with a jacket we offered him. He was quite a sight in his business suit as he waded into the creek. He caught six or eight trout rather quickly with one of my flies, and was obviously quite pleased. (I wasn't fishing that day, just looking after him.) After catching so many fish, he sat down for a while and talked a little bit more about his fishing experiences. We moved around into another arm of the lake to Peale Island where we could fly fish right off the island shore, and he caught a few more. He wouldn't let anybody take his fish off the hook. He even wanted to clean the fish, but we talked him into letting us handle that messy chore. We fried them over a campfire, and they made a delicious lunch.

On the way back Secretary Hoover was thoroughly relaxed and talked quite a bit. I began to understand that what I had interpreted as coolness was really shyness. By the time I had spent that day with him, I had grown downright fond of the man. The little bit of animosity I had been harboring since that strange session in 1922 had vanished. When we got back to the hotel, he posed for a picture with my two children — Robert was eight and Marian five. It was a picture of a smiling, warm man who genuinely liked children.

Right after Hoover left, Secretary Work arrived on a vacation trip with Governor John S. Fisher of Pennsylvania and George Ogden, vice president of the Pennsylvania Railroad. The three had been schoolmates in the Wyoming Valley of Pennsylvania. Work said he wanted it understood that he was not there officially and didn't want me to put myself out for them. But I said it was my pleasure to show them the greatest national park on earth. As we were finishing lunch at the Lake Hotel, about to drive down to the Jackson Hole country, I was called to the telephone. It was a long distance call from Thomas Marlow, a prominent banker in Helena, who was the Republican national committeeman for Montana.

"Horace, do you have a pencil and paper handy?" Marlowe asked. I said I did, and he said, "I have something to tell you. A message just came over the wires, and it might be a very hot message that the folks in your party up there might be very interested in. It came from Rapid City, South Dakota, and the message is from President Coolidge."

Then he read me the brief statement that stunned the nation:

"I do not choose to run for President in 1928."

I took the message back to Secretary Work and his friends at the table. They were so shocked they could hardly finish their lunch. They talked and puzzled over the true import of the terse message. What in the world had President Coolidge meant by the word "choose"? They were still talking animatedly about it when I finally got them into the open touring car for our trip to Jackson Hole. First they decided the President meant he was still available for a draft, and then they decided they had to draw the opposite conclusion, that it was all over and that he wasn't going to run. But then they would try yet another interpretation, and on and on they went.

As we got near the Thumb Ranger Station about twenty miles down the road, Work said to me, "Albright, do you have an unabridged dictionary — you know, one of those big ones about a foot thick?" I said we had one at headquarters. He asked me to stop at the ranger station, call my secretary, and get her to read me everything the dictionary said about the words "choose" and "choice." It took two full legal-size yellow sheets of paper to write down everything about the two words, and when I brought my notes to the car they chewed on them all the way down to the lodge at Jackson Lake where we were spending the night. Secretary Work had no further interest in his outing, and decided to leave the next evening. When we got to the train, assistant Secretary of the Interior John H. Edwards was just arriving, and gave Secretary Work the news that Secretary Hoover was on his way to Rapid City, where the President was vacationing. Right then Secretary Work changed his plans and decided to go to Rapid City himself. Within a few days, Herbert Hoover declared for the presidency. About a year later Secretary Work would resign to become the national chairman of the Republican party and manage the Hoover campaign.

Three weeks after the announcement, Coolidge made a visit to Yellowstone. Having made his decision not to run, he had thought he

Author and President Coolidge at the Grand Canyon of the Yellowstone, 1927. Albright collection.

might as well add a few days to his vacation and get in some fishing in the park before returning to the summer heat of Washington. Bill Starling of the Secret Service came to Yellowstone with an advance party to check on security procedures, and wanted special protection measures taken. It seemed that the day the President was to arrive, August 22, was the day Sacco and Vanzetti were to be electrocuted, and there was concern that some extremists opposed to the execution might cause trouble. Starling told me not to announce ahead of time where the President would be going, and to be flexible with the planning because they might change the schedule with no notice.

While I wanted to make it possible for the President to get his rest and relaxation fishing, I did not intend to miss the opportunity to push for some of our priorities. Foremost, of course, was to get him to visit the Grand Teton area. At first he agreed to make a trip down there, but at the last minute he backed out in favor of some fishing. I did get him to Shoshone Point, and the view was as clear and spectacular as it had been the day I had taken President Harding there. Mrs. Coolidge was very enthusiastic about the possibility of protecting the Tetons and the Jackson Hole country as a national park, and I think the President liked the idea, too, but he didn't say anything. The next day Grace took Mrs. Coolidge and their college-age son, John, down to the Jackson Hole area for lunch while the President went fishing again. The first lady became a strong booster for the creation of Grand Teton National Park.

The President went fishing in the Firehole River near Old Faithful, but he was using worms and didn't catch anything. I had been warned by the Secret Service not to try to interfere by telling him what bait to use. But the following day I told Bill Starling, "We can't let the President go back without catching any fish, and this time of year you can't catch any fish with worms."

Starling said again, "Don't interfere."

"Well," I replied, "he isn't going to run again, and I don't think he will fire me for interfering. I'm going to tell the ranger who goes out with him to show the President how to use spinners.

The President was receptive to Chief Ranger Woodring's suggestion and started using a spinner. But his line still had several lead sinkers on it for use with worms, and the line was riding so low in the water that the spinner was not performing properly. Woodring explained to the President, and took a couple of the sinkers off the line and put them in his pocket. With the new technique President Coolidge caught fifteen or sixteen large trout, and acted like a man who had accomplished a great feat.

We also took Mrs. Coolidge fishing, and after she caught eight big fish, she suddenly wanted to quit. Grace asked, "It wouldn't be that you don't want to catch more than the President?" She smiled and said, "It could be."

On the next to the last day of the trip, when they were at Grebe Lake, Woodring noticed that the President's spinner was jumping along the top of the water. So he told Coolidge to reel in his line so they could put some more lead on. Sam reached down to the bottom of the boat to get some more sinkers out of the President's tackle box. Mr. Coolidge saw him reach for the new sinkers, and asked, "Mr. Woodring, what did you do with those two pieces of lead you took off the line the other day and put in your pocket?"

He said it with a deadpan expression, Sam told us afterwards, so he couldn't tell whether Coolidge was really being economical or if he was just trying to kid Sam. That day the President hauled in a four-pound rainbow trout, the biggest trout he had ever caught.

A couple of times I was pointing out features of the park, and the President showed me his peculiar style of wry, taciturn wit. We arrived at Roosevelt Lodge and got out to walk to the area where Theodore Roosevelt camped during his 1903 visit to the park. As we walked along, President Coolidge asked, "Roosevelt camp here?"

"No, Mr. President, not right at this point," I answered. "The camp is named in memory of President Roosevelt having been near here when he camped with John Burroughs in 1903. He actually made his camp up the road a little way in a big grove of Douglas fir trees. I'll show it to you in a little while."

"I've got his camp in Washington," he remarked.

On another day as President Coolidge was fishing on Grebe Lake, Sam Woodring saw an enormous bull moose with a huge rack of antlers come out of the woods and stand by the edge of the lake. This was real wilderness, with no roads, and the President had to ride four miles on horseback to get to the lake. Woodring tried to get the President's attention to look away from his line over to where the moose was. "He's coming out on the lake," said Woodring with growing excitement. "He's got his head under the water, eating."

Without even looking up, President Coolidge replied, "Saw three first day I was here."

The President had his meals in his room at the Canyon Hotel and stayed there in the evenings. But Mrs. Coolidge and young John liked to eat in the regular dining room and stay afterward for the evening entertainment produced by the college students working for the concessioner during the summer. The last night of the presidential visit we planned a little party, with music after dinner for dancing. There were plenty of men to dance with Mrs. Coolidge, but we didn't have a partner for John. Then I remembered Adelaide Nichols, the girlfriend of our handsome ranger, Karl Hardy. Adelaide was delighted to fill in as John Coolidge's dinner and dance partner.

Wupatki National Monument, Arizona, 1935. George A. Grant photograph.
National Park Service.

In the course of the evening, I suddenly came across Ranger Hardy in the back of the room.

"Karl, I didn't know you were here," I said.

"Yes sir," he replied, "I pulled duty here tonight."

"What do you think about Adelaide there being in the arms of John Coolidge?" I asked, twitting him.

"Doesn't bother me at all," Karl replied. "After all, you know, I danced with his girl a year ago."

I was under a great deal of pressure from Wyoming officials to have the President leave the park through the Cody entrance on the east, inasmuch as he had arrived through Montana on the north. I told him about the problem, and suggested that if he left through Cody he could see some more of the park. He didn't want to disappoint the Wyoming people, so he agreed. As we drove along a rough stretch of road en route, Coolidge commented, "Pretty bad road. Suppose you're hoping to get a new one?" I protested that I had no such thought in mind, although I did tell him about our road program.

Compared with the presidential visit, most of the other activities in the park that summer were routine. It was a good thing, because all during 1927 and 1928, a great deal of my time had to go into the behind-the-scenes work on acquiring the lands for the proposed Grand Teton National Park. Cammerer and Mather were at the same time working with local and regional organizations trying to acquire the lands for the already-authorized Great Smoky Mountains, Shenandoah, and Mammoth Cave national parks.

State officials of Tennessee and North Carolina estimated that ten million dollars would be required just for the five hundred thousand acres of private land that needed to be purchased for the Great Smoky Mountains National Park. When the authorization bill was passed by Congress, more than one million dollars had been subscribed by the state of Tennessee, the Great Smoky Mountain Conservation Commission, the Great Smoky Mountains, Inc. of North Carolina for Great Smoky, and other local citizen volunteer organizations. Then, with George Dorr paving the way, Cammerer interested John D. Rockefeller, Jr., in the project. After long negotiations, Rockefeller pledged five million dollars through the Laura Spelman Rockefeller Memorial fund, which had been established in memory of his mother. The five million dollars for land acquisition in the Smokies, however, was contingent upon a contribution by the states and other private interests of an equal amount. Both Tennessee and North Carolina stopped all lumber cutting in the area under consideration, and Cammerer decided on boundaries that would, to start with, include 228,500 acres in Tennessee and 225,000 acres in North Carolina.

For Shenandoah and Mammoth Cave, money was harder to come by. The state of Virginia and the Shenandoah National Park Association of Virginia subscribed one million two hundred thousand dollars for Shenandoah Park while Congress was considering the authorization bill. A campaign to involve citizens — "Buy an Acre at $6" — succeeded in raising funds. Also, Cammerer was able to get Mr. Rockefeller to provide some funding for Shenandoah.

Meantime, our Grand Teton activities had to proceed on three levels at once. We had to arrange for the President to "withdraw for classification" all of the federally-owned unreserved land within the proposed park so it would not be subject to mining claims, land speculation, or other development. On another level, we were seeking to acquire the private lands in Jackson Hole that Rockefeller was willing to purchase. On the third level, we had to work with Congress to pass legislation establishing a national park for the Grand Teton area. Secretary Work responded by immediately having a presidential executive order drafted that would withdraw all unreserved federal land north of Jackson, and President Coolidge signed it on July 7, 1928.

The land acquisition process, which was extremely complicated and difficult, was made even harder by the need to keep Rockefeller's name out of things. The corporation his people had set up — the Snake River Land Company of Salt Lake City — had gotten the word spread around the Jackson area that it was a cattle company. I had enlisted Harold Fabian to supervise the land purchasing, but since he was based in Salt Lake City, we needed someone to do the actual purchasing who was respected in the Jackson Hole area, who knew what land might be available, and its fair price. Fabian and his associates settled on the leading banker in Jackson, Robert E. Miller, president of the Jackson State Bank. His bank also held mortgages on many of the properties we sought.

The Snake River Land Company told Miller to pay fair prices, but also had an arrangement that would allow him to make a larger profit if he got all of the needed lands under a certain price. Miller did not know, however, that Rockefeller money was behind the Snake River

Land Company, nor did he know the true purpose of the land purchases he was making. In fact, he personally opposed creation of a Teton National Park and favored the Forest Service proposal to lease parcels of the Teton National Forest to individuals.

I had advised Fabian to put top priority on purchasing the properties on the west side of the Snake River, nearest to the Teton mountains and Jenny and Jackson Lakes—the area whose rundown condition had caught Rockefeller's attention. Miller ignored these instructions and concentrated on getting land on the east side, where his bank held a lot of mortgages. Finally Fabian put so much pressure on Miller that he began buying up property near Jenny Lake and Jackson Lake. But we were not pleased with the way the program was going.

On the legislative front, a bill had been introduced in the Senate to create a Grand Teton National Park as a small, separate unit comprising just the east side of the Teton Range and Jenny and Leigh Lakes, as recommended by the Coordinating Commission on National Parks and Forests. The Park Service reluctantly endorsed this bill as better than nothing, but the Forest Service opposed it because almost all of the land would come from its holdings. Wyoming Senator Kendrick delayed action on the bill because state officials still had designs on the Teton Range for a Wyoming state park. He also resisted the idea of having the Teton National Park be an extension of Yellowstone, even as a separate unit, as recommended by the commission. Another bill, much more to our liking because it would include some of the land the Rockefeller interests were buying, was introduced in 1927 by South Dakota Senator Peter Norbeck, one of our friends, but field hearings were not held until the summer of 1928. Norbeck's bill was opposed strongly by some of the Jackson Hole people.

The Senate committee on public lands scheduled a hearing in Jackson on July 22, 1928. We hoped it would turn local opinion around to our view and win Senator Kendrick's support. We lined up all the people who were friendly toward a Grand Teton National Park, with Struthers Burt rallying the dude ranchers. Burt arranged for the hearings to be held in Jackson in a hall over Porter's drug store on a Sunday afternoon. To my amazement, practically no oppostion to the park was voiced at the hearing. After everyone had been heard, the committee chairman, Senator Gerald Nye of North Dakota called for a show of hands from those at the hearing for and against the proposal for a small separate Teton National Park. The park advocates won seventy-seven

Yellowstone opening ceremonies at Gardiner, 1926. Stephen Mather and author at gate.
J. E. Haynes photograph. Albright collection.

to one. Senator Kendrick now realized that he could safely back the park and said, "We'll go ahead now and have a national park, and I want it to be a spiffy park, not a small, stringy one."

Our joy was short-lived, however. When the opposition, led by Miller and Wyoming State Senator William Deloney, heard about the outcome of our Sunday meeting, they came storming down to the JY Ranch where we were staying. They complained to Senator Kendrick that they had not been told about the hearing, and demanded another one. Kendrick told them he would have an informal meeting with them on Monday. They sent "Paul Reveres" riding through the night, stirring up park opponents, and urging them to come to the JY Ranch.

About twenty opponents showed up at the Monday meeting. Kendrick heard them out, then said, "We have had enough of all this. We are going to have a park."

Realizing they didn't have a chance, Deloney elicited from Kendrick an agreement that the legislation would specify that no new hotels or camps would be allowed within the new national park. They were not interested in preservation, of course, but wanted to placate the present merchants, dude ranchers, and hotel owners, who didn't want any competition. It would however, serve conservation purposes, and I supported the provision on those grounds. After the meeting, Deloney graciously said, "Congratulations, Horace, you're finally going to get a park. And now I suppose you'll go on trying to get the rest of the park you want."

"Of course I will, Bill," I replied. "You know me, I'm not going to be satisfied with this little park."

My winters in 1927 and 1928, after closing Yellowstone, had been spent at Yosemite because Dusty Lewis was not able to return to work in the park. Grace and the children and I stayed in the superintendent's residence. I had to make several trips to other western parks, and in February 1928 I planned the superintendents' conference for Mather. It was a roving affair, with our first meetings and dinner parties held in San Francisco, and a gala luncheon sponsored in Stockton by Elmer Reynolds, owner of the Stockton *Record*, who published a special edition reviewing the progress of the national parks. We wound up the conference at Yosemite with more meetings and discussions on park matters.

One of the problems at Yosemite was a logging threat to a large stand of timber on land owned privately inside the park. We were trying to purchase it, but it had been appraised at about $3.5 million. Cammerer and I had approached John D. Rockefeller to see if he would pay half the cost inasmuch as Congress had already agreed to pay half. But Rockefeller advised us that he had made significant contributions for timber purchases in California (he had recently saved the magnificent Bull Creek Grove of Coast Redwoods in California's Humboldt State Park), and was not inclined to consider the Yosemite timber.

Mather and I also discussed the problem with Nicholas Roosevelt, an editorial writer for the New York *Times* whom we knew. Roosevelt was a kin of Theodore Roosevelt, and himself an avid conservationist. While the Yosemite part of the superintendents' conference was in progress, Nicholas Roosevelt arrived at the park and, accompanied by park rangers, set out on skis and snowshoes to look into the timber problem. He returned to New York and wrote an editorial concerning the large stand of giant sugar pines on the Big Oak Flat Road that was about to be logged.

The *Times* editorial Roosevelt wrote caught Rockefeller's eye, and he wrote Mather for details of the appraisals of the sixteen thousand threatened acres. So in March Cammerer and I went to New York with the material. In a few days he notified Mather that he would equal the federal government's authorized funding and contributed $1.75 million of the $3.5 million total purchase price.

On the first of May, I turned Yosemite over to Assistant Superintendent Ernest Leavitt and returned to Yellowstone for the new season. About a month later Arthur E. Demaray, assistant director of the Park Service for operations, came to the park, and we had talked at length about future activities. Demaray thought the Park Service should be in charge of all recreation programs for the entire federal government. He had been influenced in this by Mather's unhappiness that the Forest Service was getting congressional funding for recreation activities, while we got none, although the idea for the Park Service to be in charge of all recreation was not Mather's policy. I had to leave Yellowstone for Glacier for a few days, and to give Demaray a little experience running a park, I made him acting superintendent while I was gone.

It happened that Don Colton, chairman of the House public lands committee, arrived at Yellowstone the next day with two members of the committee. Demaray looked after them, and tried to sell them his idea of the Park Service being the main recreation arm of the government. When I returned, Demaray told me with great enthusiasm of his conversations with the members of Congress.

"You shouldn't have done that," I said. "Suppose we had all the recreation. The Forest Service would then come in and say, we want to look after all the forests in the national parks, and the Biological Survey would say, we want to look after your game. We have to have a perpendicular operation, and look after our own affairs, and the other agencies can take care of their affairs. There's an awful lot of country,

and the Forest Service is entitled to look after recreation in their national forests."

Demarary was a bit chastened after our conversation, although I don't think I changed his mind.

In late June, Mather asked me to meet him in San Francisco to attend the annual conference of state park officials. Mather had brought together state park leaders in Des Moines in 1921 to strengthen state parks and take the visitation pressure off national parks. At his own expense Mather organized the State Parks Conference and hired Herbert Evison as its director. Because I had been busy at Yellowstone in previous years, this was my first state conference.

Afterward, Mather and I went to see the San Francisco chief engineer of the city's water authority. We confronted him with his agency's failure to comply with provisions of the Hetch Hetchy Act, which had required it to build some access roads to the park. Although the Hetch Hetchy Dam had been completed in 1925 after a ten-year building process, San Francisco was still dragging its feet about constructing the roads, and insisted that when it did get around to building them, it would adhere to the outmoded standards in place in 1913 when the act had been passed. This was unacceptable to Mather, and he was thoroughly irked by the refusal of San Francisco officials to budge on the subject.

Mather was still feeling grumpy about the meeting as we drove to Yosemite. But his mood brightened considerably when we threw a sixty-first birthday party for him on the Fourth of July. We were joined in the celebration by Kenneth Chorley, a member of John D. Rockefeller's staff who had been sent out to take a look at the threatened forest.

As I returned to Yellowstone, Mather headed back to Washington, where he had a whole new set of circumstances to cope with. Herbert Hoover had been nominated at the Republican national convention in June, and Secretary Work resigned so he could run Hoover's campaign against Al Smith. To replace Work, President Coolidge appointed a Chicago attorney, Roy O. West. Mather knew West only slightly, but went to see him at once and tried to get him to visit some national parks. He found West to be more interested in Bureau of Reclamation programs than in national parks, but he told Mather there would be no disturbance of national park plans, policies, or personnel.

West's nomination ran into severe opposition from members of his own party, and the Senate delayed hearings on the nomination. While awaiting confirmation, West assumed the role of Secretary of the

Interior in an acting capacity. In the summer he took a trip to look at reclamation projects, and made a brief stop at Glacier National Park and at Cody, Wyoming. I met him for the first time at Cody. He did not have time to tour Yellowstone, but asked me to show his sister — who had met him at Cody — through the park.

In late September, there was a big celebration to mark the formal dedication of Bryce Canyon National Park. It was held both in the park and in Cedar City, Utah. Many Mormon church officials attended, including Latter-day Saints church president, Heber Grant. The president of the Union Pacific Railway, Carl R. Gray, was also present, because the railway company had just completed lodges at Bryce, Zion, and North Rim of the Grand Canyon.

After the festivities, Mather tried to get me to go with him to Glacier. He seemed worn out, and I didn't think he ought to make another trip, so I said I had to get back to Yellowstone. He changed his mind about Glacier, but decided instead to stay in Cedar City a few days and help celebrate the opening of the new Zion-Mt. Carmel road and tunnel in Zion National Park. He entered the tunnel to watch the construction crews putting the finishing touches on it, walking along in his inimitable way, chatting with the men and admiring their work. Before he realized it, he had walked out the other end, and thus became the first person other than the workers ever to walk the full length of the tunnel.

Mather went from there to Chicago. He was really excited over the prospects of Hoover — a mining engineer, a Californian, and a conservationist — becoming president, and he even did a bit of politicking for him.

On election day, 1928, Grace and I drove down to San Francisco to attend an election night party put on by Francis Farquhar and some other Sierra Club officials. We all listened to the radio as the election returns were reported all across the country. Hoover's victory seemed to us a great boon to the national parks, and when we drove back to Yosemite the next morning, we were in high spirits.

Two days later we received a telegram from Cammerer that plunged us into despair. Mather had suffered a stroke. He was in St. Luke's Hospital in Chicago, and I was to go there and meet Cammerer as quickly as possible.

17

Reluctant Successor

ARRIVING IN CHICAGO IN MID-NOVEMBER 1928, I WENT TO ST. LUKE'S HOSPITAL. Cammerer was waiting, and told me to go in to see Mather, who had been trying to say something but could not make himself understood. The only word they had been able to get was "cascades."

I went to Mather's bedside. He recognized me, but could not speak. I had been hoping against hope that his condition was not too serious, but the doctors had told Cammerer that the paralysis was extensive and they doubted that he could ever have an active life again. I was shaken at the sight of him, but I spoke a few words, trying to be encouraging. Then I asked him what it was he had been saying about "cascades," and his face lit up a bit.

"Cascades in Yosemite?" I asked, referring to some private land near El Portal that I knew he had been worrying about. But that was not it.

"Cascade corner in Yellowstone?" referring to the southwestern part of Yellowstone where the water development people were still trying to build the Bechler dam. But that was not it either. Nor was it the Kepler Cascades on the Firehole River in Yellowstone. Finally I tried the only cascades left.

"Cascade Mountains in Washington?" His eyes crinkled in a smile. That was it! He wanted to know about the new highway across the northeastern corner of Mount Rainier that the state of Washington was planning to name after him. I told him the designation had gone

[222]

through, and that signs were now going up along the highway, designating it "Mather Parkway." A relaxed, satisfied look came over his
face, but he didn't try to do any talking.

Cammerer and I talked a long time that night, a mixture of grief
for our stricken friend and worry over the future. Cam felt I should be
appointed Director. He maintained that I was much better informed
about national park matters than he was, and that his health would
not permit it. He would look forward to working under me. He knew
I had often said I didn't want to be Director, and I told him that
before I had started for Chicago, and not knowing exactly how serious
Mather's condition was, Grace and I had talked things over. I had
told her my decision was that I would not accept the job if it was
offered. I preferred to stay at Yellowstone.

"Horace, you are the man for this job," Cammerer said. "Don't
refuse it."

The next day, Dr. Work showed up in Chicago. Although he had
resigned to run the Hoover campaign, he still carried a good deal of
influence at the Department of the Interior, especially since his successor, Secretary West, still had not been confirmed by the Senate.
Work met me at LaSalle Hotel and we spent a couple of hours discussing what should be done. He knew that Cammerer had talked to
me about becoming Director, and he said: "I agree with Cammerer.
You've got to take the job, and President Hoover will want you. I'm
just in between now and not acting officially, but I know how it should
go. You've got to promise to take the position when it is offered to
you."

When I still resisted, Work put forward a new argument that I
really had not stopped to consider.

"Horace," he said, "don't you realize that if you stay at Yellowstone, and Cam won't take the job, there is no one else who can carry
on in the Mather tradition? They'll bring in someone from outside,
and you could be moved. You think you can just stay in Yellowstone
the rest of your life and enjoy that superintendency, but you can't.
The next Director of the Park Service could move you from Yellowstone down to Platt National Park. How would you like that?"

Platt was a travesty — a tiny mineral springs in southern Oklahoma, well below national park standards, and we had been trying to
get rid of it for years. Work's point hit home. I realized I had been
trying to hold on to something that could very well slip through my

fingers in a moment's time. After a long silence while I thought it through, I said, "All right, I'll go to Washington and talk with Secretary West."

I stopped off in New York to see Mr. Rockefeller, but he was out of town. Ken Chorley, however, told me he knew Rockefeller would want me to take over for Mather (in fact, as soon as Rockefeller returned to New York, he sent me a letter to that effect). Chorley and I talked over some of the Grand Teton land purchasing matters, and I went on to Washington where I had my first real talk with Secretary West, whom I had met only briefly a few months earlier in Cody, Wyoming, when he had asked me to escort his sister through Yellowstone.

He was very cordial, but did not seem to have given much thought to the Park Service succession. He said he was ready to act on Work's and Cammerer's recommendation, and he asked me to become Director pending Mather's resignation. In fact, West wanted me to take over then and there in an acting capacity. I explained that I should go back to Yosemite to be with my family for the holidays, and would come to Washington early in January.

"You can do anything you want," West replied, "but I want to appoint you acting Director right now." I insisted that Cammerer should serve as acting Director until I came back, that he had done so on other occasions, and the Service would be in excellent hands . So West agreed.

The trip back across the continent gave me my first chance to sit still long enough to sort things out, and I felt some qualms at having agreed to take the job. I had done some figuring, and even with the

"Director Mather feeding a bear with bus load of children in the background,"
Yellowstone, 1926. National Park Service.

small increase in salary I would be losing money. I would no longer have a fine house provided me and my family, and would have the expense of building a house in Washington. I would not be able to afford the style of entertaining that Mather had always maintained. Worst of all, I really hated the thought of leaving the West.

Once Grace and I had a chance to talk these things through, I felt better about it. She too was reluctant to break the pleasant pattern our life had been following.

"But, Horace," she said, "you and Mr. Mather have put so many years of effort into the parks. The children and I can certainly make ourselves comfortable in Washington. I just don't know any other way you can finish the things you and Mr. Mather have worked so hard to get started."

Then messages began coming from other superintendents, many of the concessioners, and the national conservation organizations. They all said I was the man who should be the new Director. A letter from Bob Yard helped set to rest my worries about my financial limitations. He wrote:

> Here and there are a few who think the new Director ought to be a rich man, to travel in the wholesale way Mather did, to entertain trail parties, give fine dinners, and associate in general with men of heavy consequence, conferring a super-financial if not super-social aura on the Service. Mather was Mather. The particular creative thing he did with the Park Service no other could have done at the time, nor will any other need to continue. His money was an unnecessary picturesque part in his personality.

Mather had improved enough by mid-December to realize the debilitating nature of his illness, and was ready to consider his successor. He notified West that he wanted me to take over, and formally submitted his resignation early in January. On January 15, Congressman Louis Cramton paid tribute to Mather in a speech on the floor of of the U.S. House of Representatives.

> In Congress, where from time to time we find it necessary to criticize the conduct of public officials, it is well that we should also for a few moments stop in our work to pay tribute to this outstanding figure in the public service who has sacrificed his money, his health, his time, his opportunity for wealth, in order that he might promote that which will mean so much to the people of this country in the future.

Cramton concluded with words that expressed in eloquent simplicity the true contribution of Stephen Mather: "There will never come an end to the good he has done."

On January 3, 1929, I arrived in Washington, and was sworn in as Director on January 12. I had just turned thirty-nine. It was fourteen years since that day in January 1915 when Steve Mather and I started our quest for a National Park Service. It had been a time of growth and development for me, and I had profited from every minute of my time with Mather. The years had prepared me as well as anyone for the job. I knew personally about one hundred members of Congress and was on a first-name basis with about one-third of them. The superintendency of Yellowstone was a position that carried a stature and influence that in some ways paralleled that of the Director. It certainly had more visibility, and during the ten years I had been superintendent, it had embarrassed me, when I would travel with Mather, that I would sometimes get more attention than he. People knew about Yellowstone and the bears and the geysers, and they didn't necessarily know about the National Park Service and its Director.

In the thousands of letters, editorials, and expressions of appreciation to Steve Mather that followed the announcement of his resignation, a little bit of the reflected praise came to me. Many newspapers and magazines, in commenting about Mather's great leadership of the National Park Service, gave him credit for training someone to take his place. Said a New York *Times* editorial, "This means not only that the policies which Mr. Mather developed will be carried on, but that their execution is entrusted to a man who played a large part in framing them." And the Los Angeles *Times* said, "The mantle of Elijah has fallen on capable shoulders."

The list of objectives I set for myself was formidable. I wanted to consolidate the gains we had made and round out the park system, extending boundaries of some parks, establishing certain new parks, and strengthening protection of all parks. I was determined to pursue my dream of bringing into the national park system the national historical monuments, battlefields, memorials, and other historic sites, all presently under the jurisdiction of the War Department. I wanted to improve the administration of the National Park Service, build a larger headquarters staff, improve salaries, and get superintendent positions covered by the Civil Service. We needed to improve the extent and quality of the educational activities in the parks, and I would work to pass whatever legislation was necessary to put the future of the system on a secure, permanent basis so that the power and the personality of the Director would no longer have to be controlling factors in operating the Service.

As an administrative corrective to the Park Service's lack of status I launched a strongly worded appeal to the Personnel Classification Board insisting that the National Park Service be raised from a "major bureau," to the higher classification as one of the "largest and most important" bureaus of government. The other six bureaus of the Department of the Interior had this higher classification. I argued that from the standpoint of appropriations, revenues, service to the public, and constructive work in conservation, the National Park Service was second to no other conservation bureau of the federal government. I said that this discrimination in listing had an adverse affect on officers and employees of the Park Service when they were brought in constant contact with the personnel of other conservation bureaus which had the higher classification. Before the year was out, the Personnel Classification Board had elevated the Park Service to the "largest and most important" bureau status.

I had commissioned construction of a house in the Spring Valley section of Washington. Grace had decided to keep the children at Yosemite for the winter, then go to Yellowstone for the summer until the new house was completed.

To replace me as superintendent of Yellowstone, I assigned Roger Toll, the superintendent of Rocky Mountain National Park. We had been holding the Yosemite superintendency open for Lewis, but he had never fully regained his strength after his heart attack, and Mather had brought him to Washington and assigned him to the position of assistant director. Cammerer was associate director, remaining second in command in Washington. I felt it was no longer practical to hold Yosemite open, so I sent Charles Thomson from Crater Lake to become superintendent of Yosemite.

With less than eight weeks before the inauguration of the new President and the adjournment of the old Congress, I spent most of my first two months working for legislation to complete some of our objectives. Most important, as far as I was concerned, was the bill introduced by Senator Kendrick on January 24 to establish Grand Teton National Park. This was the legislation Kendrick had promised after the hearing at the JY Ranch the previous August. It provided boundaries that pretty well followed those proposed by the Coordinating Commission on National Parks and Forests. It was quite small, only twenty-seven miles long, and from three to seven miles wide. It included just the east side of the Tetons and Jenny and Leigh Lakes, and left out all of the Jackson Hole area we had sought to add.

To ensure the perception of a park exclusively situated in Wyoming, Kendrick's bill did not propose attaching the park to Yellowstone (which lies partly in Montana and Idaho as well as Wyoming). The bill made the Teton park a completely independent unit.

The new park would be exempted from the Federal Power Act of 1920 and thus protected against dams. The bill, however allowed cattle or sheep grazing privileges to those who already had grazing rights. It was far from the park of my dreams — but it was a start, and I worked hard for its passage. The bill went through both houses within three weeks and President Coolidge signed it into law on February 26. I was also trying to get a bill through Congress authorizing a small extension to Yosemite National Park which would be necessary to pave the way for Rockefeller's purchase of the stand of giant sugar pines and other species in the western part of the park, and that bill went through without a hitch.

The 1929 lame duck congressional session also passed a law changing the name of Lafayette National Park to Acadia. The boundaries were also extended to include several gifts of land, some of which was donated by Rockefeller. The largest gift was Schoodic Point, a rugged, scenic area separate from the rest of the park and southeast of Bar Harbor on the mainland. The donors, who were English, did not approve of the park being named after the Frenchman who helped the Americans defeat the British. Superintendent Dorr also disliked the name, and he selected Acadia, derived from an Indian word describing the area. Dorr worked to rally support in Congress for passage of the legislation.

The 1930 appropriation bill included a provision that allowed the National Park Service, for the first time, to use condemnation proceedings to acquire private holdings within park boundaries. The total appropriation was $8,750,000, a far cry from the five hundred thousand dollars Mather and I started out with in 1915. Of course, by now we had twenty-one national parks and thirty-three national monuments, and more than three million visits had been recorded in 1928. Secretary West, who finally was confirmed by the Senate and sworn in by President Coolidge just a few weeks before the end of the administration, was helpful in approving our budget requests.

A little-noticed bill sponsored by Florida Senator Park Trammell passed Congress without debate just three days before the end of the Seventieth Congress. It authorized investigation of the Florida Everglades as a possible national park, but there was no appropriation. So the investigation had to wait for a year, until Congress gave us ten thousand dollars to start the study.

In 1928 the minority leader of the Senate, Joseph Robinson of Arkansas, had introduced a bill to create Ouachita National Park. It was an area in the Ouachita Mountains adjoining the Ozarks, and had a fairly good forest cover and a reservoir, but it by no means met the standards necessary for a national park. It was in Robinson's state, and he had promised his constituents he would get them a new national park. Mather had opposed the bill from the start. Frederick Law Olmsted, Jr., then chairman of the Committee on National Parks and Forests of the American Society of Landscape Architects, spoke out strongly against it. "Society should be prepared," said Olmsted, "to stand firmly against the tendency, which such bills indicate, toward a new and dangerous policy to the creation of National Parks, one concerned with regional needs rather than with proper national purposes."

Senator Robinson had wide influence on Capitol Hill, however, and although we managed to get our friends to delay a vote until the end of the session, Robinson finally got it passed in both the House and the Senate. The chairman of the House public lands committee, Donald Colton, urged a presidential veto, and I got Secretary West to recommend that the president pocket veto the bill, which he did.

Robinson came down to the Department of the Interior a few days later and barged into my office. He would get even with the National Park Service, he said. He never forgave me for my part in having the bill vetoed, although he never actually did anything to harm the parks. But from that time on he refused to help or support us on anything.

We suffered one major defeat in those first sixty days of 1929, and it was a hard one for me to take because it involved transferring military parks and monuments to the National Park Service, one of my principal objectives. In 1928 Mather and I had encouraged Secretary Work to consult with Secretary of War Dwight F. Davis to seek the transfer of the military parks as being in the national interest. We argued that the National Park Service was established to preserve for all time areas of historic, scientific, and scenic importance, which most assuredly should be interpreted to include military battlefields, parks, and monuments. To our pleasant surprise, Davis had agreed that the War Department would turn the areas over to us. He and Work signed the following letter:

> The areas now administered by the National Park Service comprise all the national parks and national monuments of the Nation except those monuments entirely within national forest reserves and those parks and monuments administered by the War Department. It is a logical development of that service to expand along the lines of controlling the national historical parks under a uniform policy and a single administration. It is so organized as to function along these lines, and it would appear desirable to continue to maintain and develop a similar organization upon a much smaller basis under the War Department. We consider that the present divided responsibility for the management of the parks and monument areas coming under the respective jurisdiction of the Interior and War Departments is fundamentally unsound. We believe that one agency should be charged with the administration, management and protection of these areas, and it is this belief which constitutes the basis for our recommendation.

We had succeeded earlier in 1928 in getting bills introduced in Congress to transfer all of the War Department historical parks and monuments to the National Park Service, and the joint letter in April from the secretaries of War and Interior to the Senate public lands and surveys committee had helped win quick committee approval and passage of the bill by the Senate on May 10, 1928. A similar letter went from Secretary Davis and new Secretary of the Interior Roy West to the House committee on public lands in November. Unfortunately, the House committee on military affairs claimed jurisdiction, instead of the public lands committee, which was friendly to the Park Service.

The military affairs committee finally gave us a hearing on January 31, 1929. Neither Secretary Davis nor Secretary West chose to testify, and Davis left the testifying to his assistant secretary of War, Charles B. Robbins, who did a poor job of presenting the issues. Robbins could not come up with any good reasons why the areas should be transferred. He said that Secretary Davis was out of town and had not conferred with him beforehand, and the chief of staff had told him the only reason he knew of for the transfer was that it might consolidate the areas under one head.

In South Calaveras Grove (now named the Horace and Grace Albright Grove, in South Calaveras State Park, California), 1924. Stephen Mather and author third and fourth from left. Albright collection.

The prevailing attitude on the committee was summarized by Representative Frank James of Michigan, the chief spokesman for the opposition, who said, "For sentimental reasons we think these parks ought to stay where they are." One congressman tried to characterize the National Park Service as "keepers of the nation's playgrounds," and implied that if we had control of the military parks there would be hot dog stands everywhere.

I showed how our primary purpose was to preserve areas in their natural conditions, intact for future generations, and not to develop them, and that we were more opposed to hot dog stands and things like that than the War Department was. I pointed out that the War Department had no division charged with the care of these monuments and parks. I added, "If you gentlemen were to ask for information in regard to the military parks, you would find that there is nothing out about them at all; there is no available data." I noted that while the farm on which President Lincoln was born was a military park, no one was there to interpret its history. The National Park Service, however, was able to provide information and interpretive services.

The committee listened to my arguments, but did not even try to understand them. I knew before I left the room that it would not even report the bill out for a floor vote.

A couple of days before the inauguration, I got a call from the White House that the President wanted to see me. I had no idea what it was about, and I had never been to his office, nor had I talked to Coolidge since his visit to Yellowstone in 1927. It was a bright day and the sun was shining into his office. He greeted me cordially, went over, and reached down into the righthand corner of his desk for a cigar, one of those little ones he smoked. He didn't offer me one. I had heard that he never offered any of his cigars to anyone, but he may also have remembered that I didn't smoke. He perched on his desk, put his feet on his chair, and lit his cigar.

"Want to talk to you about fishing," he said. "You know, I was in Wisconsin last summer."

"Yes, I know, Mr. President," I interrupted. "I keep track of you all the time."

"I learned how to fly cast," he said.

"I know that too," I again interrupted. "You've come quite a way from fishing in the Black Hills with a worm."

Then I found out why he had called me to his office.

"Suppose I went back to Yellowstone and I went out to that Grebe Lake where we were, what kind of flies would a rainbow take?" Then he named some of the flies he had been using.

I suggested a royal coachman or a gray hackle, and we were deep in discussion of the best flies for Yellowstone waters when his secretary came in and said that a certain senator was waiting to see him. Coolidge seemed disappointed at having our conversation interrupted, but I quickly excused myself and left, saying I hoped he would come back to Yellowstone soon. But he never did. It was the last time I ever saw him, and I will always cherish the memory of that little interlude, when he was so light-hearted and genial, apparently delighted to be getting the weight of the presidency off his shoulders.

While I was sorry to see Mr. Coolidge leave, I looked with great anticipation to the Hoover administration which came into office on March 4. Hoover had been president of the National Parks Association in 1925, and the talks I'd had with him at Yellowstone in 1927 had shown me that he truly loved the parks. Hoover's selection of Dr. Ray Lyman Wilbur as Secretary of the Interior also held great promise. Like Work, Wilbur was a former medical doctor. He was president of Stanford University, had served on the California State Park Commission, and was an advocate of providing more large wilderness areas for the national parks.

Even after all the good things people had said and written about my appointment as Director of the Park Service, I was not entirely sure I would be asked to stay on. When I had met with Work in Chicago, he assured me that I was Hoover's choice, but after Secretary Wilbur took over he called for letters of resignation from every bureau chief and assistant secretary, and sent them to the White House. I went to see first assistant Secretary of the Interior E. C. Finney, who had been with the department for many years, and had Civil Service status as I had. I asked what he was going to do about his resignation.

Finney told me he was going to include a statement that his resignation was without prejudice to his re-employment or his transfer to some other activity in the government. He would also ask that his Civil Service rating and records be retained. So I wrote the same kind of letter. Finney's resignation was accepted, but then they appointed him solicitor of the department, almost as influential a job as his old one.

There was no word at all in answer to my resignation letter. For almost a month I sweated it out, and I felt even more nervous when I heard a persistent rumor that was making the rounds. It seemed that George Hearst, one of the sons of the newspaper magnate, was being pushed by influential people for the job of Director of the National Park Service.

Some of my congressional friends heard about the delay, and wanted to intervene. Representative Harry Englebright of California, who had been at the University a few years before me, called and said, "It's time they were giving you some sort of word. I'm going to see what's holding it up." I told him I would rather he would stay out of it, and that calling the White House might do more harm than good.

It was only a couple of days later that Secretary Wilbur called me up to his office late in the afternoon and tossed a letter across his desk to me.

"Here's your resignation letter," he said. "The President doesn't want it, and neither do I."

———————— ❧ ✳ ❧ ————————

18

A Formidable Agenda

WITH THE ASSURANCE THAT I WOULD BE REMAINING AS DIRECTOR, I BEGAN THE "EDUCATION" OF YET ANOTHER SECRETARY OF THE INTERIOR. Dr. Wilbur had a good background as a conservationist, liked to hunt and fish, and was a partner in a fishing camp in Oregon. From his experience with California state parks he had some familiarity with national park matters. On his first day in office I sent him a thick looseleaf book containing everything he needed to know about the National Park Service, the background of the major issues we were facing, and a summary of our priorities. While the report could help him learn the issues, it would take time and a good bit of trial and error before he would be able to cope skillfully with some of the problems he faced. He also had much to learn about how to deal with Congress and the Washington bureaucracy.

He liked to open all the mail addressed to him personally. He would have it brought in first thing in the morning and open each letter himself, glancing at the contents, perhaps to see if it was anything important, while talking to his staff of secretaries. One morning about a month after Wilbur had become Secretary, Senator Norbeck came to my office and said, "I want to meet this new Secretary of yours."

"Why don't you go up and see him now," I suggested. "He always keeps an open door, he gets in early, and I'm sure he would like to see you."

Norbeck was a steadfast protector of national parks and had been of great help in getting the Grand Teton legislation passed. I walked with him to the Secretary's office and when we walked in, I said, "Mr. Secretary, I want you to meet one of the very best friends of the national parks, Senator Peter Norbeck of South Dakota."

Secretary Wilbur got up and greeted the senator cordially. I bowed out saying, "Now that I've got you two good fellows together, I'm going to leave." On the way back to my office I stopped for a moment to say hello to one of the people in the Secretary's office, and was waiting for the elevator, when here came Senator Norbeck.

"What's the matter — aren't you going to visit with the Secretary?" I asked.

Norbeck was visibly upset.

"I certainly am not," he retorted. "He isn't interested in me. He's only interested in his mail. As soon as you left he sat down at his desk and started reading his mail, with me just sitting there and waiting. So I got up and left."

"Oh, that's just a habit of his, reading the mail while talking with people," I explained. "He doesn't mean anything by it. Why don't you go back?"

By this time the elevator had arrived, and Norbeck got in. As the doors were closing, he said, "Until he shows a little more courtesy, I'm not going to have anything to do with him." Although Secretary Wilbur finally did get over that rude habit, Norbeck never did go back to see him.

One day not long afterwards, the Secretary called me in and complained about Congressman Cramton, probably the strongest advocate for national parks in the Congress.

"This man from Michigan travels all over our national parks and Indian reservations," Dr. Wilbur said, "goes in just as if he was an administrator, calls in the superintendents and employees and questions them. He acts like he is the Secretary of the Interior."

"Of course he goes out to the parks," I replied. "He has been chairman of our appropriation committee for a good many years and he is extremely interested in the national parks; the Department of the Interior just couldn't ask for a more valuable friend."

Wilbur would have none of it.

"Albright," he said, "in this administration it is the President's policy, as I understand it, that Congress will look after its business, and we will look after ours."

"Mr. Secretary," I said, "you know we haven't got any business that is just our own, and if we insisted on that, we would soon be in bad shape, because Congress holds the purse strings. My advice is to be very careful how you deal with Mr. Cramton. He doesn't tolerate interference. I would like to see you get acquainted with him and be a good friend of his."

The Secretary didn't take my advice. When he testified before the appropriations committee on the budget for the Indian reservations, he gave the committee his line about Congress not meddling with the affairs of the agencies. It was the last time they ever asked Wilbur to testify. My own relationship with the committee remained cordial, though, and the Park Service continued to get the funds we requested.

The Secretary was not above changing when he became convinced that some idea of his would not work. A month after his disastrous appearance before the appropriations committee, he phoned me and said, "I've been thinking of having a little reception for friends of the national parks, and I want to include some members of Congress. Will you give me a list of people to invite?" The reception did help to mend his relationship with a few of our congressional friends.

I had been urging the Secretary to visit some of the parks so he would have a better idea of what his department was dealing with. In late spring he asked me to make a trip with him to some of the far western parks. He had to make an important speech in Boise, Idaho, representing the President at a governors' conference, and he wanted to work in some park visits while in the West. I had to go out to Yosemite to take care of some concession problems, and to Sequoia to discuss with Superintendent John White some matters involving our efforts to get the Kings Canyon area added to the park. So I told him I would go on out ahead, and then meet him at his home in Palo Alto. Secretary Wilbur and I, accompanied by his wife and teenage son and daughter, drove in his old Buick touring car (he insisted on doing all the driving) to Lassen Volcanic and Crater Lake national parks and then to the Pacific Northwest. His family and I stayed behind in Portland while the Secretary took the train to Boise for the governors' conference.

Wilbur was representing the President, and he didn't tell me what he was planning to say in his remarks to the governors. I knew that a number of powerful stockmen and timber and mining company officials would be around so I warned him about the campaign some of the western governors and development advocates had been waging to get the unreserved public lands turned over to the states. It was an early version of the "sagebrush rebellion," and their argument was that the federal government should "give the land back to the states." Yet the public lands had never belonged to the states in the first place.

This whole federal versus state ownership of the public lands was one the Secretary and I had discussed at length, and as he left for the conference, I warned: "Don't give in, not in any way, shape or form, to these promoters." I reminded him that public lands had been over-grazed when federal controls had not been strictly enforced, and that the same thing could happen if the lands were under state control.

But at the conference he did exactly what I had warned him against. I guess he was just following President Hoover's instructions when he told the conference that the unreserved public lands ought to go to the states, except for the mineral rights, which the federal government should retain. It made big news and opened a pandora's box, with every conservation organization in the country coming out in protest. Later, Wilbur tried to put a milder meaning on his statement by explaining that he had only meant to indicate to the governors that the

Stephen Mather with planners, Mount Rainier National Park, 1928. National Park Service.

administration favored turning public lands over to the states under conditions to be worked out later.

The remarks caused political problems for President Hoover, who had to do a lot of maneuvering to get out of the mess. To take the pressure off, the President appointed a blue-ribbon commission to study the situation. It was headed by James R. Garfield, who had been Secretary of the Interior at the end of Theodore Roosevelt's presidency. Mary Roberts Rinehart and *Saturday Evening Post* Editor Lorimer were on the commission, which studied the issue for about two years. Their report recommended that while some minimum surface rights could be given to states, practically every resource should be reserved by the federal government. Hoover himself escaped criticism, but the give-the-land-back-to-the-states advocates continued their fight, and the issue smoldered during the entire four years of his presidency.

When Wilbur returned to Portland to resume our parks tour, he confessed to me privately, "You were right, it was the wrong thing to say." From then on he was somewhat more open to the advice and counsel offered by his agency heads and staff. Our visit to the parks ended with a trip to Mount Rainier National Park.

In the spring, President Hoover had decided he would like to have a country place not too far from Washington, where he could get away, rest, and, if possible, do some fishing. I was summoned to the White House to join a four-man committee to search for an appropriate site. The others were Larry Richey, personal secretary to the President, Bill Starling of the Secret Service, and Henry O'Malley, commissioner of fisheries.

Each of us had a special mission. O'Malley was to find a fine fishing stream that could be racked so the fish couldn't get out of the stream, and where some good fishing holes could be developed. Starling was to judge whether the place could be adequately secured and the President protected with a reasonable number of men. Richey, who knew more about the President's personal likes and dislikes than anyone else on the White House staff, was to rule on whether he thought Mr. Hoover would approve of the site. I was to judge whether the spot was something that could be regarded as scenic and whether it was in an area that ought to be preserved.

We visited a number of places up and down the Potomac River and looked closely at a place in the Catoctin Mountains of Maryland.

It did not meet Hoover's criteria, but it was later developed as a retreat by President Roosevelt, and subsequently used by other presidents (Eisenhower later gave it the name Camp David). Then we investigated a site about one hundred miles southwest of Washington in the Blue Ridge Mountains of Virginia, within the authorized boundaries of the new but not-yet-established Shenandoah National Park. The head of the Virginia Conservation Department, William E. Carson, was a friend of mine and was working with the National Park Service to acquire the private land needed for Shenandoah. Carson urged me to have the presidential retreat committee look at this site on the Rapidan River. It was presently inaccessible by car, but the state would be willing to build an access road to it. It was only five miles over the one hundred-miles-from-Washington limit the President had set.

Carson met us at Criglersville, a little place a few miles from the Rapidan River. He provided each of us with a fine horse. Some local people had made box lunches for us. We rode up and down the Rapidan Valley looking over possibilities, finally settling on a beautiful site that Carson had scouted out ahead of time. O'Malley said the stream was ideal for fishing. Starling said the site could be protected, and Richey was sure it would please the President. I said it was certainly scenic — it was, after all, part of the area slated to be within Shenandoah National Park.

We made our decision and were having our lunch, when all of a sudden it occurred to me that this might be bad rattlesnake country, because I had seen them in nearby valleys. I had learned in looking at park projects to raise questions about snakes. When I mentioned the subject, Carson looked like he could have choked me, but we decided we had better find out. Starling and I consulted with some mountaineers in the area and learned that rattlesnakes were almost nonexistent there because razorback hogs that roamed wild in the area had cleared out most of them.

When we made our report, the President accepted our judgment, approved the site, and arranged to purchase it. The state built a road over a ridge to make the site accessible to automobiles, and Hoover personally financed the twenty-five thousand dollar cost of constructing the camp. When he started using it in the fall of 1929, a small detachment of Marines, instead of the Secret Service, was delegated to protect it.

The search for the presidential hideaway, along with news of what was happening in the parks, went into my frequent letters to Mather. He was making slow but definite progress toward regaining his speech and use of his limbs and, by May, was able to leave the hospital in Chicago and travel to his summer place in Darien, Connecticut. I arranged for him to make the trip on the Baltimore and Ohio line which went through Washington, and the railway agreed to hold the train a few minutes when it arrived. The entire Washington staff of the Park Service was on the train platform to greet Mather, and we shook hands and spoke to him through an open window in his drawing room during the train's fifteen-minute stop. He held up the sturdy walking stick the staff had chipped in to buy him, to show us he liked it. He was not yet able to talk, but he made it clear that he was delighted and encouraged to see us all again.

Mather's condition improved steadily. Cammerer and I kept him informed regularly, and went to see him as often as we could. Representative Cramton wrote long letters to him about what was going on in Congress. We all were betting on that vital spirit of his to pull him through to recovery.

On July 29, with the snow-capped Teton Range as a backdrop, we dedicated Grand Teton National Park with a ceremony at String Lake, between Jenny and Leigh lakes. Wyoming Governor Frank Emerson and many state officials attended, and a large contingent from the National Editorial Association, which had been meeting in Cheyenne, also came to the dedication. I selected my veteran Yellowstone chief ranger, Sam Woodring, as the first superintendent of Grand Teton, and we started administering our newest national park and making it available for public use. At the same time, of course, I was still working behind the scenes with the Rockefeller group to acquire the land needed for eventual extension of the park into the northern part of Jackson Hole.

I found, as Mather had, that with Cammerer capably holding the fort in Washington, I was able to spend a great deal of my time in the parks. During 1929 I inspected the areas proposed for Great Smoky Mountains and Shenandoah national parks and reported favorably to the Secretary on the recommendations that had been made by the Appalachian National Park Commission. I accompanied the new Yellowstone Boundary Commission on an extended pack trip in the park. The commission was under congressional mandate to determine the advisability of adding to the park land in the upper Yellowstone River region in the southeastern part of the park. This was much to be desired, for it would add significant rugged wilderness country and the most favored feeding grounds of moose. The commission also took another look at the Bechler River Basin in the southwestern corner, which eastern Idaho irrigation interests still sought as the site for a dam.

I was at Sequoia in August for more discussions on Kings Canyon when I received a wire reporting that another potentially disastrous forest fire was raging in Glacier, far worse than the fire of 1926. I immediately left for Glacier. The blaze had broken out in slashings outside the park on privately owned land. Our new fire unit had suppressed thirty-nine fires, but this one became a crown fire of the most destructive type and we were unable to control it. It destroyed a large stand of timber on land the park had recently acquired by trade. In a single afternoon fifty thousand acres were destroyed. The flames missed park headquarters by only half a mile, and destroyed homes on a two-mile stretch of Lake McDonald shoreline. The Great Northern railway cooperated by bringing in extra men twice daily to fight the fire, and we sent Superintendent Toll and seven men with equipment from Yellowstone to help out. The fire was then brought under control, too late to save the timber and homes.

In each of the parks I looked into the possibilities for buying the private holdings within the borders. In many parks these private holdings were hindering proper administration and impeding public access to many of the best scenic resources. Congress had recently appropriated $250,000 for us to buy up some of the lands, and authorized the Secretary of the Interior to contract for $2.75 million more, with the condition that these funds be matched by private donations. Private contributions were extremely hard to obtain, however.

In September Secretary Wilbur made another park tour, and I met him at Glacier where he was spending a few days. The Secretary liked to see wildlife, and he especially wanted to see some mountain goats. Several times rangers pointed out to him specks high up on a mountain and claimed they were mountain goats. The Secretary, who had a delightful sense of humor, finally said, "Now I know how to see goats. If a little snowbank gets up and scratches itself, it's a goat."

He then went to Yellowstone where he addressed the Eleventh National Park Conference and stayed all week attending meetings. I

With William O. Owen, first climber of the Grand Teton, at the dedication of Grand Teton National Park, 1929. Albright collection.

had invited railroad officials, concessioners, and representatives of other bureaus. We studied the operations of Yellowstone Park to demonstrate management techniques, and visited Grand Teton Park. One subject that received a great deal of attention was wildlife management. Mount McKinley had problems with poachers who took bears and other big game; Yellowstone had an excess of buffalo and elk; and there were too many deer in Yosemite Valley and on the North Rim of the Grand Canyon. A wealth of new information came from George Wright, a young graduate biologist from the University of California at Berkeley. He was a protege of Chief Naturalist Ansel Hall and had been working as a temporary ranger at Yosemite. Wright, who came from a wealthy family, financed out of his own pocket a two-year survey of the wildlife in all of the national parks . With two people he hired to assist him, Ben Thompson from Stanford and Joe Dixon from Berkeley, the Park Service had the nucleus of a new wildlife division.

After the conference I went with Wilbur to Grand Teton, Bryce, Zion, and the North Rim on the Grand Canyon, and then to the site of the planned "Boulder Dam," where he dedicated the railroad that would bring materials to start construction. The Secretary raised another controversy when he used the occasion to officially change the name of the Boulder project to "Hoover Dam."

When Wilbur returned to Washington, I hastened to Yellowstone, where Grace and the two children had been spending the summer. I helped her finish packing for our move to Washington.

Back at headquarters I continued tackling my formidable list of priorities, particularly the issue of getting the historical sites transferred to the National Park Service. It had become something close to a crusade for me. In addition to my desire to give the sites the superior protection that Park Service management would afford, I must confess that I was motivated by a fascination with history that I had felt from early childhood.

My maternal grandfather, Horace Marden (for whom I was named), arrived in California's Mother Lode in 1851 at the age of nineteen, while the gold rush was still on. My father, George L. Albright, left his native Canada in 1873 for the famous Comstock Lode at Virginia City, Nevada, where he began as a miner and shaft builder. My grandfather and father both served in the Nevada legislature in the 1880s. When the value of silver declined, my parents moved to California's Owens Valley, where I was reared. As a child I loved their stories of western exploration, gold and silver ventures, the Mexican and Civil Wars, and the Indian troubles. I devoured the books of G. A. Henty, the Englishman who wrote stories that had a boy in the midst of almost every outstanding event of history. I also helped out around the Inyo *Register* and picked up quite a bit of western history from its publisher, Will Chalfant, a local historian.

In 1913, when I first arrived in Washington, I spent many a Sunday and holiday visiting nearby historical places. Living at the YMCA, I found that there were several other young fellows who enjoyed going with me on excursions. We visited Mount Vernon. We hiked up the towpath of the old Chesapeake and Ohio canal admiring the lock houses and other historic buildings. We worked our way around the remnants of Civil War forts and searched the woods of the District of Columbia, Maryland, and Virginia for remains of trenches, redoubts, magazines, and other earthworks almost erased by a half-century of rain and melting snows. We managed to get out to the battlefield of the first struggle at Manassas, and to Baltimore for a visit to Fort McHenry.

When Mather came to the Interior Department in 1915, he was pleased that in addition to the famous scenic parks of the West, we also had responsibility for some important historic areas: Mesa Verde National Park with its marvelous cliff dwellings and surface structures; Casa Grande and Chaco Canyon, containing remains of prehistoric dwellings; Sitka National Monument in Alaska, marking the last major opposition to Russian colonization; and the imposing ruin of Tumacacori Mission in Arizona, one of Father Kino's chain of missions extending from deep in Old Mexico to Tucson. When Mather and I learned that Tumacacori Mission was on a privately owned ranch and not on public land as it was thought to be when it was made a national monument, we arranged a land exchange to make it part of the monument.

It was in 1917, while acting Director, that I first brought up publicly the idea of bringing the War Department historic areas into the National Park Service. In the first annual report of the Park Service, writing about removal of army troops from the national parks, I commented under the heading, NATIONAL PARKS IN THE WAR DEPARTMENT TOO:

> This discussion brings me to a similar question that deserves consideration soon. It has arisen numerous times during the past year when this Service has been requested for information regarding the military national parks — where they are located, how they are reached, what trips to them would cost, etc. The question is whether these parks should not also be placed under this Department in order that they may be administered as a part of the national park system. The interesting features of each of these parks are their historic associations although several of them possess important scenic qualities. Many of the monuments and at least three of the national parks were established to preserve the ruins of structures that have historic associations of absorbing interest, or to mark the scene of an important event in history.

Now, as Director, I was determined to find a way to bring those military parks into the Park Service. President Hoover's new Secretary of War was James W. Good. As it happened, I had become well acquainted with Good during his several trips to Yellowstone while I was superintendent and he was a congressman from Cedar Rapids, Iowa, and chairman of the House appropriations committee. Within a few weeks of his appointment, I had talked with him and also with Secretary Wilbur about transferring to the Department of the Interior the historical areas that were under the War Department, and found both to be in favor of it.

Secretary Wilbur told me that President Hoover wanted to obtain broad authority from Congress to reorganize agencies in the executive branch of the government. He said that such authority would make it very easy to have historic sites transferred. I pointed out that such broad authority might not come soon, and that I thought we were now in a favorable position to secure the specific legislation we needed, especially because the chief congressional opponent of the idea, John Morin (who had been chairman of the military affairs committee), had been defeated in the 1928 election. Secretary Wilbur was sympathetic, but advised me that we should wait a while for possible further word from the President. Not long afterward, the President designated a coordinating committee with a staff to assemble and evaluate proposals for reorganization from heads of departments and independent agencies. This program would operate in anticipation of the broad reorganization authority he would seek from Congress.

With other heads of bureaus in the Department of the Interior, I contributed to the Department's reorganization plan. It was based on what the Secretary regarded as the fundamental responsibilities of the Department: conservation and protection of the public domain; development of natural resources of land and water; and federal education affairs (at that time the Bureau of Education was in Interior). The proposal of the National Park Service that historic sites and structures in other departments, especially the War Department, should be transferred to our bureau, was included in the general reorganization plan for the Department which was submitted to the President's coordinating staff in October 1929, near the time of the collapse of the stock market and the beginning of the Great Depression. But Congress refused to grant President Hoover the authority to reorganize the government through executive order, so I would have to find another way.

Toward the end of 1929, Mrs. H. L. Rust of Washington, D.C., came to visit me. She was a great-great-great-grandniece of George Washington, and she was waging a campaign to arrange for reconsrtuction of the house where Washington was born. The foundation was still fairly intact on the land that had been the family farm, ninety miles southeast of Washington in Virginia, where Pope's Creek enters the Potomac. She wanted to commission architects to design a house that would match the original structure. The Wakefield Association, of which she was president, had raised fifty thousand dollars, nowhere near enough, but they hoped to complete the project by 1932, in time for the two hundredth anniversary of Washington's birth.

The War Department owned a few acres of the birthsite and had a small monument there, but did not supervise or maintain it. The original house had burned down in the late 1780s, and the site was now just part of an old farm that had grown wild. When Mrs. Rust had sought help from the War Department, she had been given no encouragement whatever.

She and her colleagues had proceeded with their plans, trying to raise funds elsewhere. Mrs. Rust had called at the White House to seek approval and to request that President Hoover be the dedicatory speaker at the hoped-for 1932 birthday anniversary celebration, but she had been turned away by one of the President's secretaries. As Mrs. Rust told me her story, I immediately warmed to the idea, and took her to meet with Representative Cramton and see if we could get support from the appropriation committee.

Cramton, too, had been interested in American history since childhood. During the Civil War his father had fought at Gettysburg as a Union soldier. Listening to Mrs. Rust, Cramton recognized the Washington birthplace reconstruction as an important project, and also saw it as a wedge that might help open the way for the Park Service to get into the historical preservation business. He introduced legislation to fund the restoration, provided the War Department would agree to turn the site over to the National Park Service. The War Department raised no objection — they did not want to get involved with raising money for the house.

We also got John D. Rockefeller, Jr. interested, and he enlarged the area by purchasing an additional 254 acres of the original farm. Cramton's appropriation measure passed in January 1930, giving us fifty thousand dollars for assistance in constructing the memorial house and thirty thousand dollars more to relocate the granite shaft marking the birthsite and to landscape the grounds. The legislaion also transferred the area to the Park Service, so at last we had our foot in the door and were ready to double our efforts to take over some of the nation's historic sites.

A few weeks after I met Mrs. Rust, another opportunity presented itself. Virginia Conservation Director Carson and I had kept in touch since serving on the committee to find a Hoover hideaway, and in October he invited Grace and me to take part in a visit to historic sites along the James River from Richmond to Norfolk. We were to visit Williamsburg as guests of Colonial Williamsburg, Inc., the Rockefeller restoration project. Also in the group were Representative and Mrs. Cramton, and Ken Chorley and his wife. We started with a reception at the executive mansion in Richmond, where the governor had assembled a group of Virginia historic preservation leaders.

The following day we drove along the James River and visited historic Jamestown and the area where English colonists had landed in 1607. After spending the night at Williamsburg, we drove to Yorktown along the York River, visited the old town, the Revolutionary War battlefield and Civil War fortifications in and around the town, and the Moore House where the articles of surrender were signed in 1781 by the emissaries of George Washington and Lord Charles Cornwallis, the British commander. John D. Rockefeller, Jr. had already acquired the Moore House and had made improvements to preserve it.

Returning to Williamsburg, we gathered in the Wythe House overlooking the old Palace Green to discuss ways and means for the National Park Service to acquire Jamestown and the battlefield of Yorktown, mostly privately owned. Cramton took a piece of paper and sketched out a park at Yorktown and a park at Jamestown, with Williamsburg in the middle. Then, sort of thinking out loud, he said, "Why not connect all three areas with a parkway?" Thus the plan was born that was soon refined and introduced in Congress as a proposal to create Colonial National Monument.

19

Saved by Grace

STEVE MATHER WAS BEGINNING TO REGAIN THE USE OF HIS LEG, ARM, AND FINGERS UNDER A SPECIAL THERAPY PROGRAM, and he had learned to walk again. His interest in parks remained as avid as ever, and as early as six months after his stroke he was writing letters to me suggesting one thing or another. He wired congratulations to Sam Woodring when he became superintendent of the new Grand Teton National Park. In October 1929 Grace and I had gone to see him at his Darien, Connecticut, home and found that he was even doing a little driving around the countryside in his Franklin roadster. Before we left, Mather pulled out his files and reviewed some of the things he had left undone, such as enlarging some of the parks and establishing new ones.

Just when it looked like he might be regaining full use of his faculties, he suffered another stroke and died suddenly on January 22, 1930. The tributes to Mather, the man, and to his achievements in conservation and the national parks were carried in much of the nation's press, and he was memorialized at length in the Congress. "His love of nature became his country's good fortune," editorialized the New York *Times*. The highway through Mount Rainier National Park was officially named the Mather Memorial Highway. An Alaskan peak within Mount McKinley National Park became Mather Peak. Some of his friends arranged for a Mather Memorial Arboretum of redwoods in Strawberry Canyon at the University of California. The National Life Conservation Society launched a nationwide Mather memorial

tree-planting program that resulted in — among other achievements —
a grove of ten thousand trees at Lake George, New York, named
Mather Forest. And a Stephen T. Mather appreciation group was
formed to raise funds for the preparation and placement of bronze
memorial plaques in park and monument areas especially dear to the
late Director. I had misgivings about this, because I knew Mather had
always opposed memorials of that type. But I did not want to stand
in the way of the activity of the Mather appreciation group.

The early part of 1930 brought continued progress in our efforts
to obtain more historical sites. Cramton had followed through on the
concept of an historical park that would encompass Jamestown and
Yorktown, including a parkway connecting them with the Rockefeller
restoration at Williamsburg. We helped him prepare legislation, which
he introduced early in the year, and it was passed by Congress on
July 3, 1930. The law, which provided for creation of Colonial National Monument, also authorized the acquisition of the Yorktown
Battlefield, Jamestown Island, rights-of-way for the parkway, and the
first phase of its construction.

The sesquicentennial of the Yorktown victory would be observed
the following autumn, and we worked with a congressional commission
on its planning. Our land purchases at Yorktown were expedited, and
Congressman Otis Bland of Newport News, who had opposed us in the
military affairs committee hearings the year before, now became our
enthusiastic friend. The Yorktown sesquicentennial celebration took
place on three beautiful days in October 1931, with troops reenacting
the surrender of Cornwallis' army. The French government sent two
ships loaded with champagne and French wines. President Hoover,
who arrived at Yorktown on a battleship, gave the opening speech,
then returned to Washington the following day. Secretary Wilbur also
spoke during the opening ceremonies, and so did I. On the second day
the governors of the thirteen original states participated. One of them,
New York's Franklin D. Roosevelt, actually got more press attention
than President Hoover, and Roosevelt stayed throughout the three-day
event.

When we started to lay out the parkway, we ran into problems
with the naval mine depot on the York River just northwest of Yorktown. The depot controlled a large area from the beach inland, and
had an officers' recreation area along the shore. There were pleasure
boat moorings, blinds for duck hunting, and half a dozen officers'

**Author at left, and Franklin Delano Roosevelt at Yorktown dedication, 1931.
Albright collection.**

homes on a hill overlooking the river. Designing the parkway so as to
avoid the area would have added many miles. Our engineers said
that the shoreline was the most economical and most scenic route. It
would not harm the officers' use of the shore and river, but it would
make it harder and more dangerous to get to the beach. The depot
commander refused to let our engineers even come onto the base. So I
went to see the Secretary of the Navy, Charles Francis Adams. He
was a descendant of the Adams family of colonial days, and he had a
lively interest in history. Adams overruled the depot commander and

gave permission for the parkway. Our engineers then could enter the base, but the commander and several admirals continued to protest the parkway.

Law required that a proclamation had to be made by the President in order for us to acquire the strip of land averaging five hundred feet along the shoreline for the parkway. When the time came to get the proclamation signed, I took the final form up to Secretary Wilbur early in the morning on a day when the cabinet was to meet.

"Mr. Secretary, you know all about our plans for the parkway connecting Yorktown, Jamestown, and Williamsburg," I said. "Now we're ready to get the right of way for our parkway and I have a proclamation here for the President to sign. I'm afraid to use the ordinary channels and send it to the Secretary of the Navy, because the admirals over there will get hold of it and they'll kill it. You would never get it back. Do you think you could take this proclamation to the next cabinet meeting, and before you go into the meeting or afterwards, get Secretary Adams to initial it, and then arrange for the President to sign it? I'm sure Secretary Adams will agree."

I added that the Secretary should tell the President that if he signed this proclamation, it couldn't be undone except by an act of Congress — and that there might be a big rumpus over it.

Secretary Wilbur said he would do it, but didn't say when, so I really didn't expect to see the proclamation again for maybe a month or two. At least I had planted the idea in Secretary Wilbur's mind.

Well, about three o'clock that very afternoon I got a call to come up to the Secretary's office.

"Here's your proclamation," the Secretary said, shoving a piece of paper across the table so hard that it slid off onto the floor. When I picked it up I saw Herbert Hoover's name on it.

"This is wonderful," I said. "But what happened with Secretary Adams? Was he satisfied?"

"Oh, I didn't show it to Adams," Wilbur said. "I told the President about the situation before the meeting and he said, 'I'll sign it and then we'll take it up with Adams later.' After it was signed I told Adams about it."

With the gains we were making on acquiring historic sites, I realized that the time had come for the National Park Service to employ a chief historian. I hired Dr. Verne E. Chatelain, chairman of the history and social sciences department at Nebraska State Teachers College, who headed the Civil Service list of applicants. We also hired a landscape architect and architectural historian, Charles E. Peterson, who had been working in Mesa Verde and some of the other archeological areas of the Southwest. Peterson worked out of Williamsburg, and designed the Colonial Parkway and the first Park Service structures built in Colonial National Monument.

We finished the memorial house at the George Washington birthplace in time for the two hundredth birthday celebration on February 11, 1932 (the birth date under the old calendar), and President Hoover made an appearance at the ceremonies. During the year I went to Morristown, New Jersey, along with Chatelain and Peterson, to talk with Mayor Clyde Potts. Potts and his associates, together with the Washington Society, had a plan for a Morristown National Historical Park. Although Valley Forge has become more famous, the Continental Army's base hospital and main camp site were at Morristown during the winters of 1776–77 and 1779–80, and General Washington was there most of that time. We decided to work for the establishment of a park there, and soon found we could get donations of the Ford Mansion, which had served as Washington's headquarters, and the Jockey Hollow lands.

The need to add historical sites to the system shared priority with the activities to improve the great traditional natural areas. One of our major efforts toward the end of the decade and the start of the 1930s was to enlarge the national park system through getting additional parks and monuments established and acquiring the privately owned land lying within the authorized boundaries of a number of parks. Times were hard, however, and the federal government was in no position to vote funds for new land acquisition. Yet many members of Congress went right on, suggesting new national park areas within their hard-pressed states or districts in the hope of building up tourist business. In 1932 we had fifty-seven separate proposals for national parks awaiting investigation and sixty-eight proposals for national monument projects.

One of the important efforts was to make Shenandoah and Great Smoky Mountains into real parks by acquiring the land within their authorized boundaries. The Park Service tried to help the various state and private groups that were attempting to raise funds for buying land within the Shenandoah and Great Smoky Mountains boundaries.

In February 1930 the governors of North Carolina and Tennessee, on behalf of their states, had presented Secretary Wilbur with the deeds to 158,000 acres of land they had purchased to be a part of the Great Smoky Mountains National Park. That spurred Congress to pass legislation officially establishing the park for administration and protection only — not for full development — although only thirty thousand dollars was appropriated for those purposes. In the spring I made an inspection trip to the Great Smoky Mountain area to look over the administrative and protection problems and to study an area at the summit of the Smokies. I also scheduled some public appearances there to help the local groups raise funds for more land purchases. Inadvertently, I generated more publicity than planned, however.

In the study party were chairman David Chapman of the Tennessee Park Commission, Arno Cammerer, and some scientists. We had arranged for a man from Cades Cove to meet us on the summit with lunch and horses to ride to Cades Cove for the night. We split into two groups and on the way to the summit, one man sprained his ankle and we were delayed. The man with the horses thought we weren't coming and went back. Chapman, Cammerer, and I proceeded to lose our way on the trail, and ended up spending the night in a tree with a cold rain coming down. At dawn we found the trail and reached a mountaineer's cabin where we dried out and had our first food in twenty-four hours. When we walked out, the local newspapers had a good story on the Director of the Park Service getting lost in the wilds of the Great Smoky Mountains, and I got a good bit of kidding when I spoke that evening to the Smoky Mountain Hiking Club.

We added the twenty-third national park to the system in May 1930, when Congress changed Carlsbad Cave National Monument to Carlsbad Caverns National Park. This gave better protection and status to the caverns, which are probably the most spectacular in the nation and possibly in the world. In 1923, after the U.S. Geological Survey had explored the cave and reported on its spectacular size and beauty, President Coolidge had established a small national monument of 719 acres. The cave had been given nationwide publicity in a 1925 *National Geographic* article and in other publications, and Congress had later appropriated funds for a lighting system in the largest cave and for construction of an elevator. Following new authorizing legislation in 1933 by Congress, President Hoover increased the size of the park by 9,239 acres through a proclamation, thus protecting the surface area above yet-unexplored parts of the cave system.

May also saw completion of the acquisition of the private stand of timber in the Crane Flats area in the western part of Yosemite National Park, just in time to save it from the lumberman's axe. It was the stand of sugar pines Nicholas Roosevelt had written about in 1927. With John D. Rockefeller, Jr.'s pledge to match the federal funding, I was able to work out an agreement to purchase the land from the Sugar Pine Lumber Company. In April 1930 President Hoover issued a proclamation adjusting the boundaries of the park to take in the timbered area.

Yosemite benefited further when 956 acres of the Stanislaus National Forest were added to the western boundary of the park. Secretary Wilbur issued an order prohibiting livestock grazing in Yosemite, effective January 1931, to my great satisfaction. However, on another aspect of Yosemite's protection his judgment was not so good.

A cableway or tram had been proposed to give visitors a quick trip from Yosemite Valley to Glacier Point, over three thousand feet above the valley. Glacier Point with its magnificent view could not be reached in the winter. It was a long trip over a not-too-good road in the summer, and space for parking was limited. A new hotel had been built by the concessioner, the Yosemite Park & Curry Company, which was pushing the tram proposal, aided by some prominent businessmen from San Francisco and Los Angeles, who were personal friends of President Hoover and Secretary Wilbur.

A couple of directors from the company took a set of the tramway plans to Washington and got a meeting at the White House where they discussed the idea with President Hoover and showed him the plans. He told them they would have to see Secretary Wilbur and get his approval since Yosemite National Park was under his jurisdiction. Wilbur told them to leave their papers with him and he would take it up with Director Albright. He did take up the matter with me, but I at once told him I would not approve any mechanical means of getting from the valley to Glacier Point. I added that I thought the opposition to the proposed tramway from conservationists would be strong, and also that the public would oppose it. I told the Secretary he would have to approve it on his own, over my objections. This he would not do, although he tried several times to get me to change my mind on the tramway.

Our Jackson Hole land acquisitions, meanwhile, were running into serious new difficulties. Rumors that John D. Rockefeller, Jr. was behind the land-buying had become more intense, so in April 1930, he decided it was time to end the secrecy. We issued a press release giving the story of Rockefeller's involvement and the part the National Park Service had played in the land acquisition activities.

Instead of easing the situation, the disclosure ignited the smoldering fires of suspicion among local people who opposed the idea of the federal government protecting the land and not allowing development. The fact that "eastern" wealth was behind the project further enraged many local ranchers and homesteaders who were struggling to make a living in those hard times. The Forest Service did its part in hardening opposition to expansion of the park by renewing efforts to authorize summer home leases along the shores of Jackson Lake — a plan which the Park Service earlier had managed to stop. A new senator from Wyoming, Robert Carey, who had been elected in 1930 to fill the vacancy caused by the death of Francis Warren, started out as a backer, then turned into an opponent of park expansion when he

Mount Rainier, ca. 1930. Albright collection.

thought it would help him politically. But Rockefeller was stubbornly determined to see the land he had purchased become part of a national park and he continued his support despite the opposition.

We were able to make one improvement in the Jackson Hole area that didn't require buying land. For many years I had been campaigning to remove those unsightly dead trees, about ten thousand acres of them, from the shores of Jackson Lake. Congress appropriated one hundred thousand dollars — half to the National Park Service and half to the Bureau of Reclamation — for cleaning up the lakeshore even though the lake was not within the park boundary.

In February 1930 I took a group to Florida to investigate the possibilities of a park in the Florida everglades, carrying out a survey that had been authorized by Congress in a bill sponsored by Representative Ruth Bryan Owen of Miami, daughter of three-time presidential candidate William Jennings Bryan. Accompanying me on the trip were Representative Owen, Associate Park Service Director Cammerer; Secretary Wilbur's administrative assistant Elbert Burlew; Yellowstone Superintendent Roger Toll; Dr. Hermon C. Bumpus of the American Association of Museums (and a member of the Park Service advisory board for education); Dr. T. Gilbert Pearson, president of the National Association of Audubon Societies; C. H. Reeder, the mayor of Miami; author Marjory Stoneman Douglas; Dr. M. W. Stirling, chief of the Bureau of American Ethnology; Caspar Hodgson, representing the Campfire Club of America; Dr. David Fairchild, famous plant expert and explorer; and Ernest F. Coe, chairman of the Tropical Everglades Park Association, who had been working many years for establishment of a national park there.

We first chartered a plane to fly over the southern tip of Florida, but found we could see very little from the plane. So we hired a dirigible, from which we got a much better view. This particularly excited Pearson and Bumpus, who could even count the birds as we flew over the rookeries. Then we chartered a houseboat — complete with a motorboat and a canoe — to explore the land and rivers. The tropical plant life, the birds, alligators, snakes, and other wildlife fascinated everyone. After the others departed, Cammerer, Burlew, and I drove all around the southern and central part of Florida to get a sense of the state. The report we prepared for Congress became the basis for a hearing of the full House public lands committee on the proposal for an Everglades National Park.

At the hearing, the committee seemed quite impressed by the testimony. Then Representative Owen called on a physician from Johns Hopkins University who had been going to Florida for years and had a famous collection of shells and pictures of plants and birds. He laid it out on a table and put on an impressive presentation. Just as he was gathering up his collection to leave, he said, "Oh, I forgot something," and reached down under the table. He pulled out a live king snake five feet long and tossed it on the table.

There was instant pandemonium. Members of the Congress drew back. The court reporter looked up, saw the snake coming toward him, and toppled over backwards, his stenotype machine crashing down beside him. A woman in the audience fainted and another screamed. Then Representative Ruth Owen, bless her, reached over, picked up the snake and calmly wrapped it around her neck. She had never touched a snake before in her life. The sight of the congresswoman with the big snake harmlessly draped over her shoulders restored calm to the session. The damage had been done, however. Journalists started calling Everglades "The Snake Park." Although the Everglades bill was reported favorably by the committee, it was not passed by the House. Even though I tried to push it every year while I was Director, it wasn't until 1934 that legislation was passed authorizing establishment of Everglades National Park.

That unlucky situation was balanced by what happened on the legislation to create Isle Royale National Park. Mather had long been interested in making a national park out of this Michigan island in the northern waters of Lake Superior. After Mather's death, Cramton had introduced a bill to acquire the entire 131,000-acre island for a national park. It had been logged many years earlier, but had grown over to nearly complete wilderness except for a few scars left by early copper strip miners. A lot of private land would have to be acquired, because only nine thousand acres of the island were in federal ownership, and two thousand acres of it were state-owned. Congress did not want to authorize what looked like an expensive undertaking, and there didn't appear to be much of a constituency for the park, even though Michigan had no National Park Service area. Cramton worked very hard on getting his bill passed, and Michigan's Arthur H. Vandenberg introduced a bill in the Senate. When Vandenberg held hearings, I testified that the island was ". . . a type of scenery utterly distinct from anything now found in our national park system; its primitiveness, its unusual wildlife and interesting flora, its evidence of possible prehistoric occupation, all combine to make Isle Royale and its neighboring islands of national park caliber." In the summer the Senate special committe on wildlife resources visited the island, as did a team from the Park Service, but there was no further action in the House or Senate on the measure.

To the great disappointment of his friends at the Interior Department, Cramton had been defeated in the Michigan Republican primary. It seemed his outspoken support of prohibition was unpopular with his constituents. With his defeat, our hopes of getting Isle Royal authorized as a national park in that session faded away.

On the morning of March 2, 1931, just one day before Congress was due to adjourn, and the end of Cramton's days as a member of Congress, he telephoned me. He was fretting because he had never managed to create a memorial of any kind to Stephen Mather, something we had talked about for a long time. The Park Service had prepared several versions of a bill for Cramton to create a Mather memorial, but he had not gotten around to introducing any of them.

"There isn't really enough time left to get it enacted, but I would like at least to introduce a bill," Cramton told me. "Why don't you pick out the version you feel is best and send it over to me, and I'll see what I can do."

The one we selected was a very general bill calling for the establishment of a memorial in or near Washington, but not designating a site. I had several copies made and put them in my pocket intending to go to the Capitol late in the afternoon on my way home. After dinner, when I went to hang up my coat and felt something in the pocket, there were the copies of the Mather memorial bill. I had forgotten to take them to Cramton!

It had been a long, exhausting day and I dreaded going back downtown. Grace asked if there was anything she could do to help, so I asked if she would mind taking the housekeeper with her and going to the Hill to give the bill to Mr. Cramton. It was then about eight o'clock, but Congress was working late to wrap things up the next day, and I knew that Cramton would have time to introduce it, which was all he wanted to do, so Congress could have a bill to work on in the next session.

As she and the housekeeper were leaving, Grace asked, "Is that all you want me to do?"

"Well," I replied, "Senator Norbeck has been just as good a friend of Mr. Mather and the Park Service as Mr. Cramton has. Maybe he would like to introduce it in the Senate, so why don't you get him off the floor too and give him a copy."

At the House of Representatives, Grace called Cramton off the floor as she knew how to do, gave him the bill, then went over to the Senate and got Norbeck off the floor. He told Grace he would be glad to introduce the bill. She thanked him and was starting to leave when Norbeck called her back and said, "You know that Congress is going to adjourn tomorrow; Horace doesn't expect this bill to be passed, does he?"

"I think he does," Grace replied. "Otherwise he wouldn't be sending me up here at this time of night."

When Grace came home and told me about the conversation, I was upset. "For gosh sakes," I said, "don't you remember any of the procedures? Norbeck couldn't do anything but introduce the bill. It has to have a number. It has to go down to the Department of the Interior for a report, then go to a committee for a hearing, and that would take weeks!" Poor Grace looked so crestfallen. I assured her no harm had been done, and that I would explain to Norbeck and Cramton that she had misunderstood.

The next morning about half past nine, Grace phoned me at my office and said, "Senator Norbeck just called. He said to tell you that conditions had been just right, and about one o'clock in the morning he had brought up the Mather Memorial bill he had introduced a few hours earlier — and it passed!"

"The bill didn't have any number, hadn't been to committee, and he said he passed it?" I asked incredulously.

"Yes," Grace said. "And Senator Norbeck told me to tell you that it is up to you now to get Mr. Cramton to get it through the House."

I immediately got in touch with Cramton, who said Norbeck had already called him. The passage of the Mather Memorial bill so quickly in the Senate had surprised him even more than it had me.

"I told Norbeck I would do my best to get it through in the next few hours before we adjourn," said Cramton, and added that as long as he was trying for this bill, he would make one more attempt to get the Isle Royale National Park bill passed too. He said he would try for a suspension of the rules, something very rarely granted when Congress is preparing to adjourn, and he warned me that he didn't hold any real hope for passage of either bill.

When Cramton went to Speaker of the House Nicholas Longworth and explained the situation, Longworth commented, "I knew Mather and thought very highly of him. I would like to see the bill pass. You have been a good congressman for many years and I know this is your last day, and I would like to do something for you; I'll recognize you if you'll stand up and ask for suspension of the rules."

Cramton, always the canny politician, asked if the speaker had any objection to his bringing up two bills; if the Mather Memorial passed, he wanted to bring up the Isle Royale Bill.

"Bring them both up, Lou," the speaker answered. "Why not?"

Of course, a suspension of the rules required unanimous consent — a single objection from anyone could prevent passage.

Just before noon, Cramton rose, was recognized by the speaker, and asked for suspension of the rules to pass the two bills. Representative Robert A. Green of Florida, a Democrat, commented that Cramton's request was unfair because a few days earlier, when Green had tried to pass a bill to establish an Everglades National Park, a lot of Republicans had prevented the bill from passing. Now here was Cramton, a Republican, trying to sneak the Isle Royale bill through. Cramton replied that he would be more than glad to vote for the Everglades bill. Green seemed to be mollified, and did not object to the suspension of rules. Both bills passed without debate!

Overjoyed, Cramton rushed the Isle Royale bill over to the Senate, and Vandenberg had just enough time to bring up his own bill, which had failed to pass the previous month. He substituted the House-passed Cramton bill for his and got it passed by the Senate without debate a few minutes before adjournment.

Unaware of all this, I went up to the Hill early in the afternoon to see if I could get in for the closing session of the House, which in those days was quite an affair. Nick Longworth would take out his violin and play some pieces, and Ruth Bryan Owen would sing, and then they would adjourn. I spoke to the doorkeeper, who was a friend of mine and often called members off of the floor when I needed to speak to them. I asked if he would open the door when they got around to adjourning so I could hear. He told me to go right on in and stand in the back.

I was just about to go in when along came Maurice Latta, the White House legislative clerk, who was there because President Hoover had gone up to the Hill and was at his Senate office signing last-minute legislation, trying to clear all of the bills he could that day.

"Albright, the President has just signed a bill that would interest you," Latta said.

"Is that so?" I replied. "What bill was it?"

"Well, it was about a memorial to Mr. Mather," Latta said. And that was the first I knew that the bill actually had been passed by both houses. I think it must have been some kind of legislative record — getting a bill introduced, passed and signed by the President all in about twelve hours time! And all because of Grace's wide-eyed diligence.

Later in the day, after the Senate had passed the Isle Royale bill, President Hoover signed it too. That is how we got Isle Royale National Park. The enabling legislation, however, was similar to that of the Great Smoky Mountains and Shenandoah national parks, in that it provided no federal funds and required that most of the authorized lands be acquired before the new park could be officially established, a process that was to take until 1940 to complete.

Ironically, thirty-seven years passed before Mather was memorialized under the provisions of the 1931 legislation. In 1968 the big gorge on the Potomac River below Great Falls, Maryland, was officially named Mather Gorge.

20

On a Firm Footing

THERE IS NO DENYING THAT I RARELY PASSED UP AN OPPORTUNITY
TO LEAVE WASHINGTON BEHIND AND GET INTO THE PARKS THEM-
SELVES, for that was where I longed to be. There was ample reason
to spend time in the field. We were badly understaffed in Washington
and in the field, and communication was difficult. So countless matters
could best be handled on the scene. In addition, there was a steady
stream of congressmen making inspection trips or visits to the parks,
and they tended to feel they should be escorted by the Director. A
great deal could be accomplished during these one-on-one discussions
with politically powerful persons. In 1931 the House appropriations
committee's subcommittee on Interior Department appropriations, led
by its acting chairman, Frank Murphy of Ohio, made two extensive
trips to eighteen national parks and three national monuments. Several members of the House public lands committee went along on some
of the park inspections, and some members of the special Senate committee on the conservation of wildlife resources joined them for tours
of Mount McKinley, Yellowstone, and Grand Teton national parks.

I could not afford the time to accompany Representative Murphy's
group on the whole trip, but I sent Senior Assistant Director Demaray
in my place on the first trip. They went to Mammoth Cave (not yet
operational), Hot Springs, Carlsbad Caverns, Mesa Verde, and Grand
Canyon national parks, as well as Aztec Ruins, Petrified Forest, and
Casa Grande national monuments. They paid particular attention to
our budget requests for fiscal 1933. I joined the committee on their

summer trip to Rocky Mountain, Zion, Bryce Canyon, Grand Canyon (North Rim), Sequoia, General Grant, Yosemite, Lassen Volcanic, Crater Lake, and Mount Rainier national parks.

On the way to Mount McKinley, we stopped at Ketchikan, Juneau, and Seward, where we transferred to the Alaska Railroad. The congressional party wanted to see Anchorage and the Matanuska Valley, so I left them in Anchorage. I rode to Mount McKinley in the special car of the administrator of the Alaska Railroad, a large old Buick automobile fitted with railroad wheels. I took a pack trip to the Wonder Lake region, an area we wanted to add north of the park. A former ranger of mine at Yellowstone, Harry Liek, who was Mount McKinley superintendent, met me at the McKinley Park station, and I spent the night at the concession tent camp. The next day, Sunday, Superintendent Liek, two rangers, and I started out with some horses and pack animals on the trail to Wonder Lake. We had gone about ten miles when I began experiencing pains in my abdomen, and I realized that I probably had some fever. We decided to turn back to the Savage River camp, where Liek endeavored to summon a doctor in Fairbanks, about 150 miles away, to fly out to the park. The three doctors in Fairbanks were out of town, so Liek left word for A. R. Carter, the Railroad Administration doctor, to telephone when he returned. Early in the evening, Dr. Carter called and, on being told of my symptoms, said it was "probably appendicitis," and left at once in a small plane with a nurse and instruments, prepared to operate. The plane landed on a river sandbar near the Savage River camp about 10:00 P.M., as it was still light in the long summer Alaska days.

The doctor examined me and said he thought I had appendicitis. He felt it was safe to sleep during the night at the camp and go to the Fairbanks hospital in the morning. I insisted on seeing the Wonder Lake country from the air, this being my first trip to Alaska. But Doctor Carter said flying made him sick and he wanted to go right to Fairbanks. I suggested that if we got up to the height to get to Fairbanks and there was no air turbulence, we should fly to Wonder Lake, then Fairbanks. Carter reluctantly agreed. So we flew over the Wonder Lake country until bush pilot Sammie Robbins said he only had enough gas to get to Fairbanks.

We made it to Fairbanks and I was in the hospital by early afternoon, and the next day the young doctor took out my appendix (it was only the second appendectomy he had ever performed). Meanwhile, the congressional party visited Mount McKinley National Park, then Fairbanks, and every member of the party came to see me in the hospital. Chairman Murphy joked, saying he had heard of a good many schemes to rid one's self of congressmen, but I had certainly picked a successful one.

The committee returned to the States by steamer to Seattle and then continued on to Yellowstone and Grand Teton, where I wanted most to be with them. Instead I had to return to Mount McKinley for ten days of recuperation. While in the park I saw an abundance of wildlife, and also got to see Wonder Lake and Mount McKinley from its forelands before heading back to California where Grace was spending the summer.

The appropriations committee members must have been satisfied with their trip, for they gave us all the funds we requested. In fact, the Park Service's success with the budget committees gave me a problem later that year. I picked up the early edition of the Washington *Evening Star* one day and read an article that quoted Secretary Wilbur as saying that the national parks were getting too much money while the other bureaus in the department were being starved. I went to the Secretary's office and asked Wilbur if he had actually said that.

"Well, I don't think I put it exactly that way," he replied. "But I am angry at what the appropriations committee has done. We can't run the department on our current appropriations; men will have to be discharged."

I said that while he might feel that way, it was not right for him to complain publicly about a bureau getting too much funding. Wilbur admitted he had been indiscreet, and gave me permission to see if I could get the story killed in later editions of the paper and in the next morning's Washington *Post*. With a couple of phone calls I was able to do so.

Then I went to the appropriation committees the following week and testified in favor of legislation granting Secretary Wilbur the authority to redistribute to other bureaus in the Interior Department approximately 10 percent — or about $450,000 — of the funds that had been provided for National Park Service roads and trails.

I had made improvement of roads and trails one of my priorities when I had become Director, and was able to convince Congress of the necessity. In addition to the roads within the national parks, I also asked for funds to improve approach roads outside the parks, between park entrances and nearby highway points. In the fiscal 1932 appropriation that was passed in January 1931, we received $1.5 million for approach roads, plus another $6 million for road and trail improvements within the parks, and got an additional $3 million the following year. It was the first time Congress had ever allowed funding for approach roads.

During 1931 we pushed ahead on a number of major road projects, including the Wawona Road and tunnel in Yosemite, the Going-to-the-Sun highway in Glacier, the Trail Ridge Road in Rocky Mountain, the Generals Highway between Sequoia and General Grant parks, the Colonial Parkway between Jamestown and Yorktown, and the Red Lodge-Cooke City approach to the northeastern corner of Yellowstone. I had opposed this last road while superintendent of Yellowstone, but in 1931 it was forced on us by the Montana congressional delegation.

President Hoover was responsible for another of our new road projects. In May 1931 all of the bureau chiefs in the Interior Department and their wives were invited to spend the weekend at the President's place on the Rapidan. It was not to be entirely social. The President wanted to discuss with us ways of trimming the budget in these days of the Depression.

We arrived on a Friday afternoon, and it was the first time I had seen the Hoover camp since it had been finished. On Saturday morning the President called us into his cabin and had us sit in a big semicircle of chairs around his desk.

He began by saying, "I guess I have more seniority in the Interior Department than any of you, because I was in the Geological Survey many years ago."

Well, Geological Survey Director William C. Mendenhall begged to differ, saying that he believed he preceded Mr. Hoover at the Survey. So the President said, "Let's compare dates." It turned out that Mendenhall had a few weeks' edge in seniority. The President accepted the challenge in good humor and said, "Well, I guess I'm a second-rater here after all."

We spent almost all day on our budget discussions. Hoover had an excellent grasp on the work of the department and asked very perceptive questions. We ended up finding ways to cut several million dollars from both the current year's budget and the fiscal 1933 budget. After dinner, Mr. Hoover told us that Sunday would be kept free for

HORACE M. ALBRIGHT
DIRECTOR OF NATIONAL PARKS
SIGNS SIERRA CLUB REGISTER ON MT. WHITNEY
HIGHEST MOUNTAIN IN THE UNITED STATES
LONE PINE, CALIF   FRASHERS PHTO - POMONA

On Mt. Whitney, September 1930. Albright collection.

fishing, hiking, horseshoe pitching, horeback riding, or whatever we would like to do. He said that anyone who wanted to ride with him and Mrs. Hoover should be out at the hitching rack at eight o'clock sharp.

Grace wasn't a rider and made other plans for the morning, but I was at the hitching rack waiting when the President and Mrs. Hoover arrived. No other guests showed up. After President and Mrs. Hoover waited a few minutes, his personal secretary, Ted Joslin, and one Secret Service man joined us. We rode all morning on many trails and over some of the territory the state of Virginia was buying for the new Shenandoah National park.

After a while, the President led us up a trail to the summit of the Blue Ridge directly west of his retreat. On reaching a crossing trail, he turned south on a trail that gave us views in all directions — east into the Rapidan Valley with meadows and forests, west to the Shenandoah Valley, and ahead to occasional hills and mountain crags. The President called for me to bring my horse up alongside his. We looked at the view for a moment. Then, pointing out the flat, even contours of the ridge, he said, "You know, Albright, this mountain top is just made by God Almighty for a highway. There's nothing like it in the country, really, where you can see such vistas." He paused for a few moments, gazing at the beautiful scene. Then he added, "I think we should get a survey made for a highway here, and I think it can be built at a reasonable cost."

I explained that while it was an excellent idea, we didn't actually have a national park established here yet — even though it was within the authorized boundary of the Shenandoah National Park, we didn't own the land. Also, the nearest state highway with which such a road could connect was thirty miles away. But I promised to discuss the proposal with the director of the Bureau of Public Roads and report to him on the results of the survey.

"The state of Virginia is very cooperative," Mr. Hoover said. "Why don't you talk to Will Carson and see what you can work out?"

"But if we build a road up here, Mr. President, that's the end of your privacy," I replied. "When tourists come here they'll be going right down into your front yard."

"Well, of course they will," Mr. Hoover said. "But after all, I have no right to tie up a place like this. I may not be down there anyway when they come. Even if I was, I would take that chance. I would like to see a road up here."

A few minutes later, Mr. Hoover again called me to his side and said I must know of the plight of the drought-stricken farmers of the Shenandoah Valley, and that we ought to be able to employ them and their horses, plows, shovels, fresnos, and other equipment. He said that he had had Congress appropriate funds for Shenandoah Valley farmers, which we could use to get the project under way. But he asked me not to make any public statements about it until we were quite sure it could be built. President Hoover never was given credit for his sensitivity to the problems of the unemployed, yet he was responsible for a number of projects that provided jobs for people who were out of work.

I got in touch with Will Carson, and the state bought a strip of land along the mountain top and connected it with land the state already owned so that a road could be built. I also contacted the Bureau of Roads, and their engineers ran a survey line. Hoover kept the project in mind and helped us get the funds to build it.

Construction began in the summer of 1931 at the crest of the Blue Ridge, on what was to become the Skyline Drive, one of the nation's great scenic roads. Very little heavy equipment was brought in, since the road was built, as the President had directed, mostly by local farmers and unemployed workers, not by imported road crews and heavy equipment. The President enthusiastically followed the road's progress.

William J. Showalter, a *National Geographic* editor who had a great love for the Blue Ridge, wrote a fine article in which he described the potential of the highway, calling it "The Skyline Drive." The name stuck.

Senator Kenneth McKellar of Tennessee read about the Skyline Drive during the fall of 1932 and decided that the Great Smoky Mountains National Park had to have the same kind of road along the top of the mountains. He called me up and told me I must plan such a route, that the Smokies were entitled to any development that Shenandoah had been promised or was receiving. I told him the circumstances under which the Shenandoah project was undertaken but emphasized that a summit road like the one being built in the Blue Ridge could not be built in the Smokies. There, its construction would cause enormous destruction of the mountain scenery and would be more costly. Besides, the Great Smoky summit lands were not yet acquired in their entirety, there was no demand for such a road, there were no funds in sight with which to build it, and it would be contrary to Park Service policies to build such a highway in mountains of the character of the Smokies. I told him he must not expect us to plan any such project. The Senator grew more furious as I talked. I asked to discuss the matter with him. He rejected this and concluded by saying I would *have* to build the road. Then he slammed down the receiver.

He telephoned me several times more and asked when I was going to have the Great Smoky Mountains summit road surveyed. I had to tell him I was not going to do anything about it and told him again that such a road was not feasible and would be too destructive to the beautiful Tennessee and North Carolina region we were trying to save. Each time McKellar called he was in an angrier state of mind, and he punished me with his language. Several times he warned that he would have me dismissed from my position as Director if I did not promise to get the road built.

Meanwhile, we completed several other important road projects. The year 1932 saw the finishing of the 4,200-foot-long Wawona Tunnel at Yosemite. We also finished surfacing the road to the top of Cadillac Mountain in Acadia National Park, and opened the Trail Ridge Road in Rocky Mountain National Park. The long-standing controversy with San Francisco officials over Hetch Hetchy was finally settled in 1932 when I was able to work out an agreement with them. The City of San Francisco had gone on for years insisting that if it built any roads in fulfillment of the requirement of the 1913 legislation granting the approval of the Hetch Hetchy dam, they would be built according to 1913 standards. I didn't want roads built in the Hetch Hetchy area anyway. So in 1932 I finally got the city to give the Park Service a sum of money equivalent to what it would have cost to build the Hetch Hetchy roads, and we used the money in Yosemite rebuilding the Tioga Road eastward from Crane Flat.

A good deal of my thought as Director went into tightening the administration of the Park Service, enhancing the professionalism in the ranger service and among superintendents, and improving the standards for protection of the parks and park resources. I also put renewed efforts into educational and wildlife management activities.

Inclined railway up Mt. Le Conte, Great Smoky Mountains National Park. Author and Arno B. Cammerer third and fourth from left. Albright collection.

I reorganized the headquarters office, reclassifying the staff officers to bring their positions more in line with similar positions in other bureaus of the Department of the Interior.

I established four major branches, each under the supervision of a staff officer. Under the operations branch I placed all the financial affiairs of the service, including accounting and personnel. The use, law, and regulation branch was charged with all matters relating to legislation, contracts, permits, leases, and rules and regulations. The lands branch handled all land acquisition matters, mapping, and administration of the national monuments. I also started an education branch to coordinate and supervise all the educational and research work of the service, including nature guiding, lectures, and museum work, plus supervision of publications.

To head the new education branch, I brought in from the field Dr. Harold Bryant, who had started the nature guide work in Yosemite ten years earlier. Establishment of an education division had been one of the recommendations of the blue-ribbon Educational Advisory Board appointed by the Secretary of the Interior in 1929, and chaired by Dr. John C. Merriam, president of the Carnegie Institution. Bryant had served on the committee. I promoted Yosemite Park Naturalist Carl Russell to a new position of field naturalist, with the specific assignment of directing our museum planning. A pillar of the educational program was Ansel F. Hall, who had developed the Yosemite museum and was now in Berkeley heading the field educational and forestry headquarters of the Park Service. I had obtained funding for the new education division in the fiscal 1931 budget, which allowed Bryant to move to Washington in September 1930, when he completed his natural history research work in the field.

The enlarged education program (which we later called "interpretation") was based on four policies: simple, understandable interpretation of the major features of each park to the public by means of field trips, lectures, exhibits, and literature; emphasis on leading the visitor to study the real thing itself rather than depending on second-hand information; utilization of highly-trained personnel with field experience, able to interpret to the public the laws of nature as exemplified in all the parks, and able to develop concepts of the laws of life, useful to all; and a research program that would furnish a continuous supply of dependable facts suitable for use in connection with the educational program.

To meet the public demand for conducted nature tours and lectures, and to further our scientific research, we expanded the interpretive programs in the parks. Year-round naturalists were hired for Mesa Verde, Zion-Bryce Canyon, Crater Lake, Rocky Mountain, Lassen Volcanic, and Hawaii national parks, and for several national monuments. The naturalist activity had been given a boost at the First Park Naturalist Conference, held in November 1929 on the campus of the University of California, and planned and directed by Ansel Hall. All six of the year-round park naturalists — from Yellowstone, Yosemite, Grand Canyon, Glacier, Sequoia, and Mount Rainier — were there, as well as members of the wildlife research team, the Park Service fire control expert and chief forester, the Park Service photographer, and a number of professors, researchers, museum technicians, and others with involvement in park interpretation.

The new museums at Norris Geyser Basin and Madison Junction in Yellowstone were opened during the summer of 1930, and an exhibit of hydrothermal activity was added to the Old Faithful Museum which had been opened in 1929. We also opened a museum on the south rim of the Grand Canyon where, aided by telescopes and exhibits, visitors could learn the geological story of how the Grand Canyon was formed. Merriam did much of the planning for the Grand Canyon museum, and a large part of the funding for the Grand Canyon and Yellowstone museum projects came from the Laura Spelman Rockefeller Memorial.

In the first year of a two-year wildlife study financed and led by George M. Wright, a team traveled eleven thousand miles to make studies at Yosemite, Yellowstone, Sequoia, and Zion national parks. Among their achievements were observations of the trumpeter swan in Yellowstone which furnished hitherto unknown life-history data on a species that would become extinct unless causes for their diminishing numbers could be found and corrected. An important study of the life history, habitat, and diseases of elk was conducted in the Jackson Hole country by Dr. Olaus Murie and the U.S. Biological Survey.

The emphasis on wildlife reesarch was especially necesary if the Park Service was to carry out one of its main objectives, preservation of the parks in their natural state and as near as possible to the condition they were in when white men first saw them. The status of animal life was changing with such alarming speed that in many of the parks it would soon be too late ever to determine what the original conditions might have been. In some parks, many of the birds and mammals had already vanished. It was apparent that with the increasing encroachment of civilization, the national parks might be the only hope for a number of threatened species. With that in mind, I established a new wild life division under George Wright in 1933.

I was able to get President Hoover to issue an order in 1931 bringing park superintendents and custodians of national monuments into the Civil Service. Most of these officers were given grades and salaries more nearly commensurate with the dignity and responsibility of their positions. At the same time, we started systematic planning for the future by requiring that each park develop a master plan and a six-year development program, to be worked out by the park superintendent in cooperation with the landscape architects and the engineering staffs, and to include cost estimates and justifications. We also increased the number of landscape architects, and by 1932 had twenty in the National Park Service.

Despite Congress' generosity in providing funds needed for roads, construction, and operation of the parks, the Park Service, along with all the other Interior Department bureaus, had to take personnel cuts across the board in 1932 as the national economic situation worsened. By this time, however, I had an excellent management team in place and the Park Service no longer had to depend on one person. I could spend most of the summer — as I did in 1931 — inspecting the parks, without hindering the effective operation of the service. When I worked in the field, I required that the park superintendent relay to Washington immediately any decisions I had made in the park. Over the years, Associate Director Arno Cammerer had grown into one of the best administrators in Washington, and in his quiet, unassuming way saw to it that things got done. He was also the person most responsible for getting private funding and bringing the southeastern parks into the system.

Senior Assistant Director Demaray, who had begun as a draftsman with the Geological Survey and had been with the Park Service since its inception, was in charge of the branch of operations and did much of the budget and congressional liaison work. In 1931 Secretary Wilbur appointed Conrad L. Wirth (a landscape architect and planner who had come to Washington in 1928) as a planner with the National Capital Park and Planning Commission, on which I served. Wirth (who was to become the Service's sixth Director in 1951) was appointed an assistant director in charge of planning, and soon took charge of the lands branch. Isabelle Story, who had come over from the Geological Survey at the start (she had been my secretary in 1916) had become editor-in-chief and head of the division of public relations, which supervised all the Park Service publications. Rounding out the top staff were George Moskey, assistant director, lands and use branch, and R. H. Holmes, chief clerk.

In January 1931 Congress passed legislation "to provide for the uniform administration of the national parks." We had instigated the bill and helped write it. We called it the "parks purification bill," and got two strong supporters of national parks, Senator Gerald Nye of North Dakota, chairman of the Senate lands and survey committee, and Representative Don B. Colton of Utah, chairman of the House public lands committee, to sponsor it. The bill provided for important adjustments to individual park organic acts which, when originally created, had included authority for the Secretary of the Interior to grant certain privileges that were inconsistent with the purposes for which the parks were established. For instance, mining had been permitted in Grand Canyon and Mesa Verde, and summer homes allowed in Glacier and Lassen Volcanic national parks. The provisions were the "price" that we had been forced to pay politically at the time in order to get the parks set aside. The Nye-Colton Act corrected some of these problems — prohibiting mineral prospecting in Mesa Verde and Grand Canyon, denying rights for any new permits for summer homes in Glacier and Lassen, and repealing authorizations for railroads in several parks.

We would have preferred a law bringing all of the national parks under exactly the same maximum degree of protection given the ideal park, Yellowstone. Although our hope was to have a national park system of primitive lands free from all present and future commercial utilization, we realized that this was not possible at the time. I stated our policy in the 1931 annual report:

> In the few remaining park projects involving the public domain, there can be no doubt about the advisability of adding their lands to the system. If park status is not accorded them soon it will be too late to do so. In each case the scenic features are outstanding and the project is in every way worthy, but there may be, and probably will be, a local requirement inconsistent with the ideal park that must be met. We take the position that it is better to bring these areas into the system on this basis than leave them with

all their natural glory to subsequent general utilitarian exploitation. Such a policy is exactly the one that Congress followed in establishing the present national park system. Any other system would probably have netted us just one park, the Yellowstone. Moreover, any other policy, strictly applied to existing parks, would require fatal delimitation of boundaries in order to exclude small areas affected by commercial development.

With the Depression rendering many people unable to afford long trips to national parks, a number of policy changes had to be made to keep the operators of concessions within the parks from going bankrupt. Restrictions were adopted to prevent companies or persons from engaging in the business of motor transportation except those operators licensed by the Secretary of the Interior. Park concessioners were given greater freedom to make changes in existing services, such as putting in cafeteria service or European-plan rates in hotels and lodges. With the decline in railroad travel, facilities such as Mammoth and Lake Hotels and Lake Lodge in Yellowstone, and the Cut-Bank and St. Mary's chalets in Glacier, were closed down for the 1933 season. Despite loss of gross revenues, however, concessioners made extra efforts to main-

Alaska Range, Glacier Creek area, Mount McKinley National Park. John Kauffmann photograph. National Park Service.

tain the high standard of service that had come to be expected in the national parks.

During these years, and despite the extreme economic difficulties being experienced all over the country, we made some definite progress in expanding national monuments in the West and Southwest. In 1929 President Hoover had set aside by proclamation Arches National Monument in east-central Utah. The monument featured gigantic arches, natural bridges, windows, spires, balanced rocks, and other unique sandstone formations shaped by erosion. In 1930 the President issued an executive order giving temporary protection to two million acres in Death Valley, pending classification of the land and determination of the advisability of declaring it a national monument.

We wanted to protect within the national park system some beautiful natural lands in Arizona that also had archeological and historical significance. These were Canyon de Chelly and Canyon del Muerto, the sacred red-rock areas owned by the Navajo tribe. The area included ruins of some five-hundred ancient cliff dwellings dating between 350 and 1300 A.D. Canyon del Muerto (Death Canyon) was so named because in 1805–6, when the Navajo warriors were away, Spanish troops massacred one hundred Navajo women, children, and old men. The Navajo Council wanted to have a national park declared so the Indians could guide people, supply horses, and sell crafts. Working with the council and the Bureau of Indian Affairs, we were able to develop legislation that would establish a national monument and also allow the Navajos to continue owning the land and live there. (Although the legislation was passed in 1931, we discovered to our dismay that an error in surveying had been made and the monument was technically established ten miles away from its historic location. The mistake was corrected in new legislation that was enacted in March 1933.)

We persuaded President Hoover to issue a proclamation adding 1,609,000 acres to Katmai National Monument in 1931, making it the third-largest area within the national park system. The addition was made to protect the brown bear, moose, and other wildlife of the area, as well as to protect the rich scientific and historical values of the Valley of Ten Thousand Smokes, formed by the 1912 eruption of Novarupta Volcano. With several years of negotiations completed, Bandelier National Monument in New Mexico was transferred from the Forest Service to the National Park Service. The site with its cliff dwellings and archeological treasures had been explored in the 1880s by archeologist Adolph Bandelier. In 1906, when Congressman Lacey had introduced his bill that became the Antiquities Act, he had intended it to be used to declare Bandelier a national monument. In issuing the 1932 proclamation ordering the transfer, President Hoover also provided for enlarging Bandelier, using public lands to increase the area from 22,000 to 26,000 acres.

In 1932 Congress extended Mount McKinley National Park, adding 246,000 acres and including the Wonder Lake region. The added acreage, mostly lowlands, provided excellent winter pasture for the wildlife. This helped protect animals from hunters, as they had formerly migrated to low altitudes outside the park in search of food and could be legally killed. Inclusion of the Wonder Lake land also provided one of the best scenic areas for viewing Mount McKinley.

We were delighted to subtract one area in 1931 — Sully's Hill National Park in North Dakota. We had been trying to get rid of Sully's Hill for years without avail, but Congress finally voted in 1931 to abolish it as a national park and turn it over to the Biological Survey as a game preserve. It did not conform in any respect to established national park standards, and should never have been in the system. We were not able to do away with Platt National Park in Oklahoma, the other sub-standard national park, which years later was incorporated into the Chickasaw National Recreation Area.

While new land acquisition was not involved, we dedicated the Waterton-Glacier International Peace Park in 1932. Rotary clubs in Montana and Alberta had backed the establishment of this "peace park," and legislation was approved by the Canadian Parliament and the U.S. Congress. Waterton and Glacier national parks would maintain their own administration and national individuality, but the international park was decreed as a symbol of permanent peace and friendship between the two countries.

In the last ninety days of his administration, President Hoover added to his excellent conservation record by approving our recommendations and signing executive orders declaring four new national monuments that added more than two million acres to the national park system. The largest new area was Death Valley. This was the culmination of several years of planning. The unique natural area in eastern California, near the Nevada border, was made famous by early pioneers and prospectors. It includes the lowest point in the United States.

I had sent Yellowstone Superintendent Roger Toll to make a thorough study of the Death Valley area after the land had been temporarily protected through a presidential withdrawal in 1930. Early in 1933 I was working on the presidential proclamation for Death Valley National Monument when Congressman Samuel Arentz of Nevada called to say he wanted to see me. Arentz was a close friend, and a great story teller. He brought with him a man he introduced as Albert M. Johnson. Arentz didn't tell me anything about Johnson at first, and just started spinning a few stories. After listening to several of his long yarns, I said, "Gentlemen, it is getting late in the afternoon. What did you want to see me about?"

Then Arentz came to the point. Johnson, it turned out, was the wealthy backer and partner of Death Valley Scotty and had put up the money to build a castle in the upper end of the valley. They had just discovered a surveying mistake, with the result that instead of being built on the land they had filed on, the castle was located on land President Hoover had withdrawn in 1930. Johnson, with Representative Arentz helping to plead his case, asked me to excise from the government withdrawal the small parcel on which the castle was built.

It was my turn to have a little fun, so I asked them to describe the castle, and Johnson did so with great enthusiasm. "Well," I said, "I'm sure not going to do what you've asked. The way you describe it, that castle would be wonderful for a park headquarters, and that big room you talked about would be just right as my office when I am out there."

You should have seen Johnson's face.

Then I laughed and said, "All jokes aside, if you just get a map and send it to me with your request, we will take the castle land out of the area we are setting aside in the national monument. Do it quickly because the President is going to be signing the proclamation very soon."

Two weeks passed with no word from them, so I called up Arentz. He told me that he had discovered that if the castle site was removed from the withdrawal, veterans could file on the land, including the castle, as they had first call under a veterans' aid law. Arentz suggested that we just let things stand as they were, until after the proclamation was signed, then he would try to get a bill through Congress allowing Johnson and Scotty to purchase the land within the monument as an inholding. The President signed a proclamation establishing a 1,609,800-acre Death Valley National Monument. Arentz later got a bill passed allowing Johnson to buy the land where the castle stood. Scotty and his castle, of course, became part of the legend and the charm of Death Valley National Monument.

The other new areas established by President Hoover during his last ninety days in office were Grand Canyon National Monument, which comprised 273,145 acres west of and adjacent to the national park; White Sands National Monument, New Mexico, featuring dunes of pure gypsum and an area of scenic, scientific and geological value; and Black Canyon of the Gunnison National Monument in Colorado, which included the most spectacular ten-mile section of the Black Canyon of the Gunnison River, with sheer, high walls and unique geological formations. President Hoover also proclaimed Saguaro National Monument in Arizona, an eighty-three-thousand-acre park with unique Saguaro cacti sometimes reaching heights of fifty feet. Saguaro was proclaimed on March 1, 1933 under jurisdiction of the Forest Service, but was transferred to the Park Service a few months later.

On balance, Herbert Hoover had a good conservation record, especially protecting lands in parks. The four years of his presidency saw twelve new areas established within the system.

My work took me eighteen thousand miles in 1932. While traveling with Assistant Secretary of the Interior John H. Edwards, we passed through Chicago at the time of the Republican National Convention that nominated Herbert Hoover for a second term, and I attended some of the sessions. As I visited various parks and talked with people, I found sentiment going overwhelmingly toward Franklin D. Roosevelt. When I told Secretary Wilbur what I had been hearing, he refused to believe it.

After the landslide election of Roosevelt in November, I again suffered a bit of trepidation about my future. The position of Director of the National Park Service was not protected by Civil Service — yet it had never been treated as a partisan political appointment, and I had come through one change of administration unscathed. While I had been closely associated with the Hoover administration, I enjoyed strong bipartisan support among members of Congress and hoped that the position of Park Service Director would remain free of politics. Grace and I did give renewed consideration to other possibilities, however, especially to leaving the Park Service. For several years I had been under consideration to head a large mining company.

In 1930 two individuals, Richard C. Baker, the chairman of Borax Consolidated Limited of London, and Christian Zabriskie, a vice president and chief operating officer of Pacific Coast Borax Company in the United States, had approached me about taking over the United States Potash Company which was developing large potash deposits in New Mexico. Zabriskie had known my family, had known Mather well, and was a longtime friend of mine. While I was superintendent of Yellowstone, Zabriskie had brought Baker to the park a couple of times and I had showed them around.

When I had met with Baker and Zabriskie in 1930 in New York, Pacific Coast Borax Company had just bought half of the common stock of United States Potash and was responsible for the New Mexico development of the potash holdings. They needed someone to head U.S. Potash, which would be an independent company. They had thought of me because I was from a mining family, had a legal background and had specialized in mining law, and I had long experience in Washington and with the Interior Department, and most of their potash deposits were in lands leased from the federal government or state of New Mexico. They offered me more than double what I was making as Director of the National Park Service, but I had not seriously considered taking the job because there were so many things I still wanted to accomplish for the Park Service. They had kept the job open, however, and from time to time they repeated the offer.

Late in November 1932, Zabriskie invited me to lunch in New York City. He wanted to know if I would consider taking the job now that there would be a change in administrations. This time I said I would give serious consideration to the offer. I had accomplished most of my objectives with the National Park Service except bringing the military parks and historic sites into the system and seeing the service achieve a nation-wide constituency. By continuing to work in the government for almost two decades, I had sacrificed the opportunity to save any money, and I had my two children's education and my family's future to think of. However, I told Zabriskie this was a very critical time for the Park Service and I couldn't promise anything until I saw what happened in the new administration. Zabriskie said the position would be kept open for me a while longer.

I did take the precaution of confiding about the offer to one person in the Department, Assistant Secretary Edwards, whom I had

**Wawona tunnel inspection with congressional committee, Yosemite, 1931.
National Park Service.**

known and trusted for many years. I asked Edwards to check for me
to see if the mineral leases held by United States Potash were honest
and valid. I knew that the company had obtained more than fifteen
thousand acres of public domain through the Department of the Interior. Although I, of course, had nothing to do with those leases, I
would not have continued to give consideration to the United States
Potash offer if there was any taint of illegality in their operations.
Edwards reported back to me that the leases were clean.

During the waning days of the Hoover administration, we still had
important work to finish. In addition to preparing the way for the
declaration of four new national monuments during the last ninety
days, we brushed up our reorganization recommendations, as President Hoover had finally decided to send his long-awaited reorganization plan to Congress. When it was presented in December 1932 it
included provision for bringing the War Department's military parks,
historic sites, and cemeteries into the National Park Service. We tried
to persuade our congressional friends to approve Hoover's reorganization plan, but Congress had other ideas. In the last few days of his

administration — too late for Hoover to do anything about it — Congress enacted a law giving the President blanket authority to reorganize the executive branch of the government, but not including any specific plans.

Hoover supported the legislation to establish the Morristown National Historic Park in New Jersey, which he signed into law as one of his final acts as President. He offered to give his Rapidan camp to the government for the enjoyment of future presidents, and suggested that the camp and the land around it be added to Shenandoah National Park. He also made a special inspection of progress on the Skyline Drive, and wrote to Secretary Wilbur that "it is a good road — and a very beautiful one."

After Roosevelt's election various people offered to help ensure that I would keep my position, and as prudently as possible, I accepted their help. Also, a number of newspapers carried editorials supporting me to remain as head of the Park Service, and to keep the service from the spoils of partisan politics. Although I wasn't really worried, I still had Senator McKellar on my back, threatening to get me fired if I did not get a Skyline Drive built in Great Smoky Mountains National Park.

I had tried several times to arrange a face-to-face confrontation with McKellar to explain in more detail why we couldn't build his road, but he never seemed to be in his office and would not come off the Senate floor to see me. I went to his committee rooms when I knew he was in them, but he would not come out. He would find out at which door I was standing and would sneak out another door. One morning in February 1933, I had tried all the doors without success and was standing in front of the main door to the Senate, when along came Ray Baker of Nevada, an old friend of mine. He was married to a very rich heiress, was a power in Democratic politics, and a friend of FDR, and had been named chairman of the inaugural committee.

I told Ray my story about the McKellar situation and that I had sent in my card to the senator but he had not come out.

"I'll get him out for you," Baker said, and sent in his card.

Senator McKellar came charging out, ignored me, but stuck out his hand to Baker, who grabbed it in an iron grip and held it. Baker said, "Kenneth, my friend Albright tells me you are not treating him right, won't see him, won't listen to him!"

The senator tried to withdraw his hand, but Ray Baker held it tighter. Baker continued, "Kenneth, I'm holding you until Horace

Albright again tells you why he cannot do what you are demanding. Go ahead and tell him, Horace."

I did this as quickly as I could, but the enraged McKellar fairly shouted, "I'll get you before my committee, and you put all that stuff in the record, and we'll see whether I get what I want."

I said, "Senator, that is exactly what I want to do. I want the whole story in the record with you there to hear because you are not going to get that road!" With that, Ray Baker let go of McKellar's hand, and he returned to the Senate floor.

Baker then said, "He certainly is mad, and he probably will try to get you fired when the new administration begins. I'll do what I can to help you. I'll put you on the inaugural committee. And I'll tell the new President not to listen to McKellar on this subject; that he's wrong and unreasonable and you're right."

I never heard from McKellar again on that or any other subject.

Shortly before the inauguration, I got a call from my old friend Huston Thompson.

"Horace, do you know a man in Chicago named Ikes or Ikis? I've never heard of him, but he is likely to be your new Secretary of the Interior. I think he belongs to the Bull Moose people who voted for Roosevelt." I told him I had never heard of him but that Mather might have known him, and I asked him to let me consult Mather's personal files, which were still in my office. I hurriedly checked, and sure enough, there were two letters to "Harold L. Ickes" about some civic or social problem in Chicago, and Mather and Ickes had been on a first name basis. Neither Thompson nor I could figure out just how to pronounce the name! A day or two later his name appeared in a newspaper as having been under consideration for a place in the administration, even the Cabinet.

A day or two later I received a phone call from first assistant Secretary of the Interior Joseph Dixon, asking me to come up to his fifth floor office because he had someone in the office who wanted to meet me. Dixon had been governor of Montana during four years of my superintendency of Yellowstone, and we saw each other often and helped each other from time to time. When I arrived, I found that the "someone" was Secretary-designate Ickes. Dixon was the only official in the Department that Ickes knew and trusted — they had been friends since they worked together in the Teddy Roosevelt campaign of 1912 — and Ickes had come to him for some information about the Department he would soon inherit.

Ickes greeted me with: "There's no reason in the world you should remember me, but in the early twenties I made a horseback trip out through Yellowstone National Park with Howard Eaton as my guide," Ickes said. "And one night you came down and made a speech to us around our campfire — I think it was at Gibbon Meadows. I remember that talk very well. I was impressed with you and I was impressed with your administration of the park. Of course I had a deep affection for your former chief, Mr. Mather. I've kept track of you, and I'd like to have a long talk with you as soon as I can. I hope you are prepared to stay on with me."

Secretary Dixon emphasized for me the proper pronunciation of Mr. Ickes' (ik'ez) name, and I repeated it several times to be sure I had it. I told them of my conversation with Huston Thompson and of looking up correspondence with Steve Mather. Dixon joked that perhaps he and I were the only residents of the District of Columbia who could pronounce the name Ickes.

Although I tried to leave, Ickes wanted to talk about Howard Eaton, so I stayed for almost an hour. I reminded them that Eaton was regarded as the "founder" of the dude ranch. He and his brothers, Alden and Bill, had a ranch or ranches in the Badlands of North Dakota, and had taken in guests, one of whom in the early 1880s was a young hunter named Theodore Roosevelt. I told how Howard and I had visited Colonel Roosevelt in his office at the beginning of World War I. He had enlisted us as volunteers in the corps of Rough Riders, which he was trying to organize (although he thought President Wilson would not accept the corps — and he didn't!). Colonel Roosevelt had already listed my name on his roster but told Howard that at sixty-five he was too old, wouldn't look good in a uniform or do a good job of fighting. However, he assured him that if his "outfit" was made a part of the armed forces, he would take Howard along. As we left Colonel Roosevelt's office, he said, "Howard, you'll be with me, be sure of that!"

Ickes asked where the phrase "dude ranch" came from. I told him that Eaton always said "Our guests got into cowboy clothes as soon as possible after arriving at the ranch, and then the only way you could tell the dudes from real cowboys was to look close, and if they washed behind their ears they were guests." Ickes and Dixon had a good laugh over that. A short time later I received a fine picture of Howard Eaton on horseback from Jack Haynes of Yellowstone and gave it to Secretary Ickes. He had it hanging on a wall of his office for years.

When I left Dixon's office I breathed a bit easier about keeping my job.

Ray Baker did manage for me to be appointed on the inaugural committee, although the position was not very significant. I was grateful to Baker for his attempts to help me. My principal task on the committee was to supervise construction of spectator stands for the parade along Pennsylvania Avenue, and to see that decorative flags were posted all along the route. I met some fine people on the committee that I had never known, but my appointment came too late to be printed on the programs. Nevertheless, I was awarded a number of tickets for the inaugural address at the Capitol, and Grace and I had good seats in the grandstand near the White House. And I was able to have my son, Robert Mather Albright, then fourteen, made an usher in a VIP grandstand. Membership on the committee also brought an invitation to a reception in the White House right after the parade. We arrived just as Mrs. Roosevelt was arranging lines to the refreshment table, and she asked Grace to help her "round up" the stragglers and get them in one of the lines.

I had a slight acquaintance with President-elect Roosevelt and felt that he knew and approved of what had been happening with the Park Service. I had first met Roosevelt in 1915 when he was assistant Secretary of the Navy and had come to the Interior Department to see Secretary Lane. In 1930 I had done him a favor. After the Governor's Conference in Salt Lake City had ended he had asked me to come to his hotel suite. He said he had to cancel his plans to go with some of the other governors on a trip we had planned for Bryce and Zion and the North Rim of the Grand Canyon. He and Mrs. Roosevelt asked if I would chaperone his young boy, Franklin, Jr., on the trip. "If Franklin does anything wrong or does not obey your insrtuctions, he has tickets in his pocket, and you should send him right home," Governor Roosevelt said. But young Franklin gave us no trouble at all. In 1931 I had a further talk with F.D.R. when he attended the Yorktown sesquicentennial.

So as the new administration took over, I felt I was on a pretty good basis with the President and the new Secretary of the Interior.

21

A Ride with FDR

THE DAY AFTER HAROLD ICKES WAS SWORN IN AS SECRETARY OF THE INTERIOR, HE CALLED ME TO HIS OFFICE. I gave him the briefing book I had prepared for him and reviewed the various Park Service issues that I thought he should know about. I put special emphasis on the need to bring the military parks and historical sites under the Park Service, and explained our efforts to date, including the unsuccessful Hoover reorganization plan.

I explained how much more efficient and economical it would be for the National Park Service to administer the park areas then under four different federal agencies. I told him that the War Department had responsibility for more than a dozen large military parks and monuments, to which it gave scant supervision. Little in the way of educational programs was provided to interpret the sites to the public (an activity the National Park Service did so well). Parks, historic buildings, and monuments in the nation's capital were administered by the Office of Public Buildings and Public Parks, an independent agency. The U.S. Forest Service had a number of natural area national monuments, mostly in the West, with resources similar to those in the Park Service national monuments.

Ickes said he agreed that all of these park areas should be under one jurisdiction and that the National Park Service was the logical place. President Roosevelt would soon be using the blanket authority to make organizational changes in the executive branch, he said, and added that we might be able to arrange the transfers by executive order of the President. If not, we could try again for legislation. But Ickes confided that what he really wanted was a much larger reorganization that would shift the entire Forest Service and other elements of government into a large Department of Conservation which would then replace the Department of the Interior.

This general idea had been presented to Congress many times over the years, but was so controversial that it never succeeded. I assured Ickes that I was in favor of such a move, and also told him my secondary motive for the military sites transfer: it had been rumored in the past that the Forest Service and one or two other agencies had proposals for adding the national parks to their jurisdictions, and although there was no present danger, this was always a possibility as long as the National Park Service remained a comparatively small bureau with areas mostly in the West. But acquisition of the military parks situated in many eastern states would bring a much larger constituency and much broader base, and thus the Park Service would be perceived as a truly national entity. I went on to explain that my primary motive for wanting the military sites transferred was, of course, my conviction that the Park Service could do a far better job of caring for the military parks and interpreting them to the public. I wrapped up my "sermon" by pointing out to the Secretary that protecting historical sites was part of the National Park Service mission as outlined in the organic act of 1916.

Ickes listened with lively interest, then began confiding to me some of his plans. "I have a feeling there is something awfully wrong with this department," he said. "Ever since the days of Ballinger and Fall, I've had the feeling it wasn't run the way it should be. I want to make sure it is being run honestly, and I will be making a lot of changes. But I have great confidence in the National Park Service. I think it is all right. And I want you to help me in straightening things out in the department."

"Mr. Secretary, there's nothing really wrong with this department," I replied. "It's a very good department. There are many very conscientious, loyal, faithful people here, just as good as you'll find in any department. Whatever it was that happened in Secretary Ballinger's time, I never felt that he did anything very seriously wrong, though he's been criticized a great deal. As for Secretary Fall, he may have used very bad judgment, but it did not affect the rest of the department. You'll find that out."

As we wound up our conversation, I told the Secretary he could count on me to help him, although I didn't know for how long — and added that he might not want me around for too long anyway. I did not mention to him that I was seriously considering leaving the government. There would be time for telling him later, when I made a final decision, and I was not ready for that yet. I wanted to stay long enough to ensure that the Park Service would fare all right in the Roosevelt administration while remaining free from political manipulation.

The Secretary soon showed his "progressive conservationist" sympathies. As his personal assistant he hired Harry Slattery, who had been associated with Gifford Pinchot at the U.S. Forest Service since the time of the Pinchot-Ballinger controversy, and had helped to uncover the Teapot Dome scandal. Ickes also acted quickly on his suspicions about the Interior Department personnel by setting up his own detective force. He organized a division of investigation in the department, hired Louis R. Glavis to head it, and gave him an office next to his. Glavis had been involved in bringing the original charges that touched off the Ballinger-Pinchot fight in 1911. He didn't have a very good reputation, and many resented him and his bureau. Glavis became a super-detective and built up quite a force. People in Interior began to worry that they were being followed and spied on, and there were unsubstantiated rumors of telephone wiretapping.

To build up a staff for his new bureau, Glavis got Ickes' backing to commandeer people from all the bureaus. He took three National Park Service people who worked on concessions, and put them to work going through the accounts of concessioners to look for fraud or wrongdoing. When I protested to the Secretary about losing three men from my small headquarters staff, Ickes refused to send Glavis in to settle the argument, but told me to go to Glavis. I fought it out with Glavis and ended up getting two of the people back. I had to let him have one man, however, so I loaned him Noble Wilt.

It was a miserable period for the department, but I suppose Ickes wanted to make certain everything was regular and honest, as befitted his reputation as "Honest Harold." In one early speech, he stated, "I have one consuming ambition, so to administer the affairs of the Department of the Interior that it will be restored to the public confidence and at the end of my administration be on a parity in the minds of the people of the United States with any other department of the government."

Ickes didn't have much of a social life and appeared to be rather lonely, inasmuch as Mrs. Ickes, who was a Republican member of the Illinois legislature, didn't come to Washington to live. I suggested to Secretary Ickes that if he would like to do it, we could take some rides on weekends. He was interested in historical sites as well as natural areas, but didn't know too much about Revolutionary and Civil War history. He had a big Packard limousine and a driver, and our first trip was around the Washington and Baltimore areas on a Sunday near the end of March. I showed him the Washington, D.C. parks and many of the old forts around the city, and some Baltimore historic sites including Fort McHenry, whose defense in the War of 1812 inspired Francis Scott Key to write *The Star Spangled Banner*.

Possibly because I was one of the few officials in the department whom he knew and felt he could trust, Ickes frequently called me to his office to discuss legislative problems and his long-range plans. Out of these talks came a good many assignments that took me away from my Park Service duties. The most important and rewarding, and the one that took up a great deal of my time, was my part in development of the Civilian Conservation Corps.

The CCC was one of the earliest of the emergency initiatives Roosevelt launched in his first one hundred days. The Civilian Conservation Corps Act was introduced on March 21, just over two weeks into the session of Congress called early by FDR, and the act was passed and signed into law ten days later. It was an idea Roosevelt had diagramed on a piece of paper. In his acceptance speech at the Democratic National Convention, he had talked of plans for conserva-

tion of human and natural resources on a national scale. Ten days after his inauguration FDR had called to the White House Ickes, Secretary of War George H. Dern, Secretary of Agriculture Henry A. Wallace, and Secretary of Labor Frances Perkins. He told them to consider themselves an informal committee of the cabinet to coordinate plans for the CCC, with Ickes acting as the coordinator of the group.

Ickes selected me to serve as his representative on the four-member CCC advisory council, working with the CCC director, Robert Fechner. The others on the council were Colonel Duncan Major of the War Department, Forest Service Chief Forester Robert Stuart of Agriculture, and Frank Persons of Labor. At first we met almost every day in Louis McHenry Howe's office in the White House. Each of us had basic tasks. Persons was to work out a way of selecting the boys who would go into the camps — there were to be two hundred thousand boys in camps of two hundred each. Major was to furnish uniforms, set up and supply the camps, and buy needed equipment. Stuart and I were to specify the work to be done, designate where the camps were located, and supervise the camps.

I had a head start because a colleague in the Interior Department, Judge Finney, had been one of the drafters of the $500 million bond issue relief bill, and he had told me it contained authority for all kinds of public works, including road and trail building, cleaning up of forest areas, removal of dead and down timber, installation of protection facilities, and planting of young trees. Park Service funding for many of these things, except roads, had been so limited since the start of the depression that we had a big backlog of things that needed to be done. We also had started working on preparing a master plan of future needs and programs for each national park. I asked Demaray to wire our chief forester, John D. Coffman in Berkeley, to quickly put together a budget for forest improvement and road cleanup, and to include reservoirs such as Jackson Lake at Grand Teton and Sherburne Lake at Glacier.

Originally the idea was to have the camps on federal land, but there wasn't enough of it, especially in the East, so state parks were included in the program. Inasmuch as they were "parks," the state program was put under the National Park Service, and I assigned Assistant Director Wirth to head the program. I brought Coffman, Chief Engineer Frank Kittredge, and Chief Landscape Architect Tom Vint to Washington to help plan the Park Service work to be done.

I sent a memorandum to all of our field people stating the principle of the CCC idea:

> While this program involves hard work placed on the shoulders of every one of us, a large responsibility and a great deal of hard work, it also permits us to play a very important part in one of the greatest schemes ever devised for the relief of our fellow citizens in this present crisis and the rehabilitation of many young men of the nation who have as yet had no opportunity for decent occupation and have been the subjects of unfortunate attitude toward their native land and conditions in general. We therefore have a wonderful opportunity to play a leading part in the development of a wholesome and patriotic mental attitude in this younger generation.

Our advisory council was meeting in Howe's White House office one morning when a secretary opened the door a few inches and said in a stage whisper, "Colonel Howe, Mr. Farley wants to see you." Howe, of course, had to let Jim Farley come in right away. As the Postmaster General strode up to Howe's desk, the rest of us retreated to the back of the room. When Farley got up to leave at the end of their brief conversation, Howe motioned for us to come forward. He introduced us and told Farley about our CCC project. Farley greeted us cordially and walked on out. In about five seconds the door opened and the Postmaster General (who not incidentally was in charge of political patronage for the administration) stepped in and directly addressed the four of us on the council: "I want to see you boys one of these times pretty soon."

That really scared the daylights out of us, because we had not yet hired our technicians, camp foremen, and others to prepare the camps and train the people. As soon as we left Howe's office we got together and decided to hire technicians and specialists immediately, before Farley could get his hands on the jobs and give them out as political plums. I think the Park Service hired more than one hundred landscape architects, engineers, historians, foresters, and supervisors in the next few days. Farley never got around to tackling us for those jobs, and we got the first camps set up without interference.

On April 7, the first man was selected and enrolled in the CCC, and at Luray, Virginia, on April 17, the first two hundred-man camp was established. Three months later, three hundred thousand young men, plus twenty-five thousand veterans, had been placed in 1,468 CCC camps.

In early April I received a message from Colonel Starling, chief of the White House Secret Service detail, that was the beginning of one of the most momentous experiences of my Park Service career. Starling sent instructions that I was to be at the south entrance of the White House at 9:00 A.M. on Sunday, April 9. I was to go with President and Mrs. Roosevelt and others to look at the Hoover camp on the Rapidan. Hoover was in the process of deeding the camp to the government for inclusion within Shenandoah National Park, and I had earlier urged Secretary Ickes to suggest to the President that he consider using the place for rest and recreation.

I drove to the White House in my own car, a guard parked it, and Starling assigned me to one of the cars. At the head of the motorcade, just behind the motorcycle Secret Service escort, was Mrs. Roosevelt's new blue Buick roadster, an open car, in which she and the President would ride. Then came the usual seven-passenger open car carrying Secret Service men, and another open touring car in which the President's chief secretary, Colonel Howe, and members of the family household would ride. The fourth car was another open touring car, and Starling put me in its back seat between two ladies whom he introduced. I was excited about the whole business, however, and didn't catch their names. I talked with them a little bit, but in a few minutes I saw Ickes arrive in his Packard limousine, and I excused myself to go and speak to my chief. As I stepped out of the car, Bill Starling came up and said, "What are you doing? I put you where I want you and I want you to stay there."

I said I needed to speak to Secretary Ickes, and Starling said, "All right, go ahead and speak to him, but get back in that car."

Ickes was delighted to see me and asked me to ride down with him. "We could do a lot of talking today," he said, "and nobody else is going down in my car."

I told him I'd see if it was possible, but that Bill Starling had been pretty insistent about my staying in the other car. I went back and got in the car with those ladies, but I couldn't stand the idea of missing this chance for a long talk with Ickes. So I explained to the ladies and excused myself. Starling saw me leave and bawled me out, "Go on and get in there with Ickes if you want to, but this is the last time I'm ever going to try to help you. I give you a fine opportunity and you won't take advantage of it.

What I had not realized was that the two women were Marguerite

("Missy") Le Hand and Grace Tully, the President's private secretaries. Starling, who had known me through the years since the Harding and Coolidge visits to Yellowstone, was trying to give me a good "break" by having me ride with the two women closest to the President! The two ladies became distinguished for the capabilities and charm that made them so valuable to the President. If I had had the faintest inkling of their potential power and influence, nothing could have moved me from that automobile, and later I kicked myself for missing the chance to get acquainted with them. I did have a good talk with Ickes, however, and we accomplished quite a bit of business on the way down.

At the Hoover camp, President Roosevelt got out of his wife's roadster, ready to walk to Mr. Hoover's house in the camp complex. It was an unpretentious place with a wide porch where Mr. Hoover had loved to sit and entertain guests as they enjoyed the view of the Rapidan Valley. I jumped out of the Ickes car and ran to help guide the President and party to the Hoover home. Mr. Roosevelt soon found the ground too uneven and rough for his weak legs, and three of us carried him to the house.

The spring day was clear, mild, and sunny, with dogwood, redbud, and other flowering trees in full blossom. We all gathered on the porch for a picnic lunch. Will Carson joined us there and told the President about the efforts under way to get the land needed for the Shenandoah National Park project. There was also some serious discussion of national issues, but the President was mostly in a mood for good-natured banter and fun, and there was much informal conversation.

From time to time I was brought into the discussions to answer questions about the park or make comments. I told the President about my visit here with President Hoover, and the horseback ride to the crest of the mountains when Hoover had suggested creation of the road along the summit of the Blue Ridge. I told him that one section was now finished but not yet paved.

After luncheon the President said it was time to return to Washington, but that he wanted to go through the park and see the new road on the way. To Starling he said, "Put me in one of those touring cars, and let Eleanor pick up somebody else to take back. I want Albright in the jump seat." So the President got in the front seat, where there was more room, and they took the braces off of his legs.

He put a cigarette in his long cigarette holder, sat back, and relaxed. I sat behind him on the jump seat, just a few inches from his ear. A Secret Service man was on the other jump seat. Three guests were in the back seat — one of them Henry Morgenthau, who then had a position in the Department of Agriculture but was soon to become Secretary of the Treasury.

As we began the drive, I thought to myself, this may be my chance to talk to the President about the reorganization and getting the military parks from the War Department. I hadn't asked Ickes if I could do it, but I knew he was for it, so I decided I would try, if I saw an opportunity.

From the Hoover camp we were driven up a narrow, winding old wagon road to the partially finished highway in Shenandoah National Park. The President would motion to me every once in a while to bend over nearer him when he had a question or comment, and then I could talk into his ear over the noise of the car.

At first he asked questions about the establishment of the National Park Service and its policies relative to new national parks in the East,

George Washington Birthplace dedication, Wakefield, Virginia, February 11, 1933. Secretary of the Interior Ray Lyman Wilbur delivering address. Author directly behind him in doorway. Marian Albright is little girl next to Wilbur in eighteenth-century costume. Albright collection.

and about the new road over which we were slowly traveling. He seemed surprised when I told him that President Hoover had insisted that the road be built largely by impoverished farmers from the Shenandoah Valley, as a make-work program. I said the area had suffered a severe drought, and the men were paid with relief funds secured by Hoover with the help of powerful Virginians in Congress. Roosevelt was impressed by the alignment of the highway, the beauty of the route, and the hand-built rock embankments and parapets which allowed cars to be driven safely right up to the edge of the precipitous dropoffs, thus allowing panoramic views into the Shenandoah Valley on the west and the forests and valleys on the east.

At the first two or three of the strong but attractive guard walls, Morgenthau's voice came rather loudly from the back seat with remarks about President Hoover's extravagance in permitting the building of such elaborate stone structures. He evidently had not stopped to think that they were built by competent stone and brickworkers who were out of work until employed on this project. As we approached yet another stone parapet, and Morgenthau again began his harangue,

President Roosevelt, Gifford and Mrs. Pinchot, 1934. National Park Service.

the President turned and said sharply, "Oh, shut up, Henry. If it were not for these protective walls you would get out and walk — you are the scariest one in the crowd." That was the last we heard from Morgenthau. Roosevelt praised the rock work and commented on the road alignment on the curves. "Albright," he said at one point, "the superelevation on that curve ahead must permit a speed of forty-five miles an hour." It was my turn to be impressed with the President's knowledge, for that was exactly the scale of the superelevation.

As we left the park area at Panorama (the pass in the Blue Ridge traversed by the Lee Highway) and turned toward Washington, I called attention to a heavily eroded farm, apparently abandoned, north of the road. The President got a little excited about this glaring evidence of erosion. He stopped the motorcade and pointed out the farm to staff people who gathered around our car.

We moved on down the road at moderate speed, and as we approached the Rappahannock River I began thinking — if I'm going to talk to the President about getting the military parks, I had better get to it. Now was the time.

"Mr. President," I said, bending over and talking into his left ear, "you are a longtime student of history. Did you know that this is where the second battle of Manassas, or Bull Run, began, way up here where we are crossing the Rappahannock?"

"No," he said, "that's impossible. We're miles from there."

"That's right," I replied, "but this is where the battle actually started. General Pope and the Union Army were pursued from here down to Manassas. It was a running battle fought all down the railroad." The President said he did not recall any such distance being involved. Well, that got us onto the Civil War. Then I took a deep breath and started on the military parks.

I told the President that since 1917 Mr. Mather and I had been trying to get the military parks and battlefields transferred to the Park Service. I told him how wasteful and inefficient it was to have several different organizations handling parks, and why the Interior Department and the National Park Service should have control over them all. We had the great parks in the West, and now we were getting the Great Smoky Mountains and Shenandoah, I said. We had just acquired Yorktown, Jamestown, and Morristown, and were moving into preservation and interpretation of historic areas. On the other hand, I said, there were also some national monuments under the Forest

Service that were equal in size and natural value to many national parks. All of these other areas needed the better protection the National Park Service could give them. I added that President Hoover had been willing to make the transfer, but that Congress did not approve his reorganization plan.

Having hardly taken a breath between sentences, I quickly wound up by saying, "The National Park Service ought to have charge of administering all of those parks. It's right."

"That sounds sensible," the President said. "I've never heard about it before. I'm awfully glad you got into that."

I breathed a great sigh of relief. The President was interested. I quickly said that we had all the plans ready for a reorganization that would accomplish the transfer.

The President did not ask any questions, he simply said it should be done, and he told me to take up the plan with his office and find out where to submit our papers at the proper time.

Then he asked, "What about Saratoga battlefield in New York? Have you ever been there?"

I said I had, and told him what I knew about that historic site, and that a bill had been introduced in 1930 to create the Saratoga National Monument, but that it did not emerge from committee. I also told him that a War Department report to Congress, transmitted by President Hoover in December 1931, had contained a recommendation that the Saratoga battlefield be studied for possible military park status.

"It ought to be a national military park or a historical park," I said.

"I know," the President shot back. "When I was governor I pestered them to death to make a state park out of the Saratoga battlefield, but they didn't do it." Then he told me — ordered me, really — to "get busy" and have Saratoga battlefield made a national park or monument. Just a moment or two later, he turned his head, and with that famous grin, said, "Suppose you do something tomorrow about this. We'll help you at the White House. And if you get one battlefield, why shouldn't you get the others?"

I was so elated I hardly heard the rest of what the President said. He continued to talk about historical figures and places associated with them — Robert E. Lee and Ulysses S. Grant and Appomattox. He mentioned John D. Rockefeller, Jr., and the restoration of Williamsburg. We also talked about the CCC and how the young men could perform valuable work for the national parks while having a job. He seemed to be enjoying the ride immensely.

As I got out of the car at the White House, I thanked him for the privilege he had accorded me and for his promise to see that the historic sites we coveted would be transferred to the National Park Service. I hurried home to share my excitement with Grace. It had been one of the most stimulating and valuable afternoons in my life, and I will never forget Franklin Delano Roosevelt's intense interest in American history and his memory of men and events.

The next morning I told Ickes about the conversation with the President. Then I got my staff started on the gathering of facts about the Saratoga battlefield, and preparing legislation for it to become a national historical park. We also prepared for the President's reorganization team the necessary data on the War Department military parks and historic areas we wanted. I was advised that I should see Lewis W. Douglas, who had resigned as Arizona's congressman to become director of the Bureau of the Budget, and who was directing the reorganization. I arranged an interview with him in early May. It was brief, yet long enough for me to see that he was entirely in favor of our cause. He told me when and where to submit our proposals.

The last of my major objectives for the Park Service was nearly accomplished. Transfer of the military sites would make the National Park Service a truly national bureau, with holdings in every part of the country. What is more, my talk with the President and my association with Ickes gave me confidence that the national parks and the Park Service would remain on a good footing. I felt the time was drawing near when I could comfortably leave the government, perhaps by the end of the summer.

22

In My Heart I Never Left

LATE IN MAY I WAS SUMMONED TO THE WHITE HOUSE TO DISCUSS
WITH LEWIS DOUGLAS THE REORGANIZATION PROGRAM as it related to
the Interior Department. He handed me the draft presidential proclamation. As I read it I was stunned by its scope. It not only gave us
the War Department historic sites of all kinds — battlefields, parks,
monuments, and still-active cemeteries (including Arlington National
Cemetery), but the District of Columbia parks and public buildings
too. It gave the Secretary of the Interior and the National Park
Service considerable authority over the National Capital Park and
Planning Commission, and the national Commission of Fine Arts,
both of which had always been independent, and it even changed the
name of the National Park Service to the Office of National Parks,
Buildings, and Reservations.

Although it was gratifying to have so much confidence placed
in the National Park Service, I was very much upset at the name
change and worried by the extent of the proposed transfers. "You're
giving us too much," I protested to Douglas. "We don't want the
public buildings; we're in the park business. And we shouldn't have
the active cemeteries such as Arlington." I begged him to let us keep
the name National Park Service.

Douglas impatiently observed, "Albright, take my advice and don't
try to meddle with this thing. If we start changing, there's no telling
where we will end."

I had known Douglas since his days as a congressman, and had a pretty good relationship with him, so I felt I dared press my case a bit more. I added that Frederic A. Delano, President Roosevelt's uncle, who was the chairman of the National Capital Park and Planning Commission, certainly ought not be subordinated to the Secretary of the Interior. None of my arguments seemed to impress Douglas. When I said I ought to talk to Delano and Ickes about the reorganization, he agreed. He wanted an answer within twenty-four hours, however, and as I departed he again advised me to let the program go through without formal protests that might delay it.

Ickes had not been consulted on the contents of the proposed executive order. The White House was keeping it all very secret. His reaction to the contents was, "That's great!" When I complained about the cemeteries, public buildings, the two commissions, and especially the loss of our name, the Secretary said, "I think we should just take it, and then we will see what we can do later about the things you don't want."

When I saw Delano, I told him, "This just can't be. You have to go to the President about the National Capital Park and Planning Commission and save it. Otherwise, you'll be reporting to me someday, and that wouldn't be appropriate."

"That's all right," Delano said. "The way things are around here these days, I'd say take the whole business, Horace, and we can cut it down afterwards. I will speak to the President about it later, if necessary, and I'm sure we can get the commission situation straightened out."

So I let Douglas know that we thought he should proceed with his program. On June 10, President Roosevelt signed Executive Order 6166. Unless Congress acted to block it, the order would become effective sixty days later, on August 10, 1933.

The executive order affected a number of agencies and functions, but the part dealing with the National Park Service was Section 2, which said:

All functions of administration of public buildings, reservations, national parks, national monuments, and national cemeteries are consolidated in an Office of National Parks, Buildings, and Reservations in the Department of the Interior, at the head of which shall be a Director of National Parks, Buildings, and Reservations; except that where deemed desirable there may be excluded from this provision any public building or reservation which is chiefly employed as a facility in the work of a particular agency. This transfer and consolidation of functions shall include, among others, those of the National Park Service of the Department of the Interior and the National Cemeteries and Parks of the War Department which are located within the continental limits of the United States. National cemeteries located in foreign countries shall be transferred to the Department of State, and those located in insular possessions under the jurisdiction of the War Department shall be administered by the Bureau of Insular Affairs of the War Department.

The functions of the following agencies are transferred to the Office of National Parks, Buildings, and Reservations of the Department of the Interior, and the agencies are abolished:

> Arlington Memorial Bridge Commission
> Public Buildings Commission
> Public Buildings and Public Parks of the National Capital
> National Memorial Commission
> Rock Creek and Potomac Parkway Commission.

If the executive order went through, it would transfer from War Department to Park Service jurisdiction eleven national military parks, including Gettysburg in Pennsylvania, Petersburg in Virginia, Shiloh in Tennessee, Vicksburg in Mississippi, and Chickamauga and Chattanooga in Georgia and Tennessee; two national parks (as classified by the War Department, Abraham Lincoln (birthplace) in Kentucky and Fort McHenry in Maryland; nine battlefield sites, including Antietam in Maryland, Appomattox in Virginia, and Kennesaw Mountain in Georgia; eleven national monuments, including Cabrillo in California, Fort Pulaski in Georgia, Mound City Group in Ohio, and the Statue of Liberty in New York; four miscellaneous memorials, including Kill Devil Hill Monument National Memorial in North Carolina, site of the Wright Brothers first flight; and all national cemeteries in the United States, including Arlington in Virginia.

From the Forest Service, we would get fifteen national monuments, including the vast wilderness of Mount Olympus in Washington (later to become Olympic National Park), Oregon Caves in Oregon, Lava Beds in California, and Chiricahua in Arizona.

In all, the Park Service would gain forty-eight areas. But the order made no mention of our taking over the National Capital Park and Planning Commission or the national Commission of Fine Arts, so I assumed that Delano had spoken to the President about them. We would be responsible for about seven hundred buildings in the District of Columbia and the Rock Creek and Potomac Parkway Commission.

It was overwhelming. It would put the Park Service in charge of the administration of historic and archeological sites and structures all over the United States, expanding our influence to most states of the Union, and would make such a strong bureau with such a distinctive and independent field of service that further attempts to merge or consolidate it with another agency would be squelched.

I wondered why the parks and monuments of the District of Columbia were assigned to us rather than to the District of Columbia government, or even continued under the Office of Public Buildings and Public Parks as authorized in a reorganization during President Harding's administration. This question was never debated or even asked in 1933 or earlier, so far as I ever knew, but I believe two reasons could have accounted for it. First, the parks and monuments of the District of Columbia belonged to the people of the United States in the same way that all the areas under the National Park Service did. The District had a locally oriented administration that was not respon-

East side of old bridge and monument at Moores Creek National Military Park, North Carolina. National Park Service.

sible to a cabinet officer or the President, even though it was a federal territory. Second, the National Park Service had the administrative, engineering, landscape architecture, and interpretation experts needed for managing and protecting the District areas in harmony with the nationwide system of scenic and historic parks and monuments. Whatever the reasoning was, I was delighted, because our management of the District parks and monuments in the front yard of Congress and the President would serve to broaden the interest of members of Congress in the whole national park system.

The President's executive order aroused opposition in a number of places, as could be expected. While the Secretary of War had assured me in March that he would agree to a transfer of the military parks and sites, others in his department had some objections. The most vigorous came from Colonel Howard L. Landers, who had been investigating battlefields for commemorative purposes for the War Department. Landers even wrote a memorandum to President Roosevelt. Another letter to the President in opposition to the transfer was sent by Acting Secretary of War Harry Woodring, who requested that all military cemeteries, including those on or adjacent to the military parks and battlefields, be excluded in the executive order. He wrote the President that the Department of the Interior could not possibly be as interested in the proper maintenance of these cemeteries as the War Department.

I myself was campaigning behind the scenes to change some things in the executive order before it became final, especially the general provision that would give Arlington National Cemetery to the Park Service. In late June I visited Quartermaster General John L. DeWitt, who had charge of the War Department burials, asking him to get the order modified. He was scared to death of Roosevelt, and refused to do anything. "It's all right with me," said the general, "and I don't want to get mixed up in it."

"Let me tell you one thing," I replied. "If you don't help me get rid of Arlington and get it back into your hands, we in the Park Service are not going to worry about burying generals by themselves. We're going to bury them the same as if they were privates, and let God Almighty decide if there is any reason for carrying rank after death." Then I took out of my wallet a clipping I had been carrying around and read it to him. It was a newspaper story about a Civil War soldier who had been buried in Gettysburg Cemetery. Someone had studied his record and learned that he had been a deserter, so they disinterred him and moved him to Potters Field.

"Now, the Park Service wouldn't have done a thing like that," I said. "The man might not have been a deserter. His mother might have been sick, or his wife, or something. There might have been some very good reason for his being away for a day or two. Why go through digging him up and putting him in Potters Field, disgracing his family at this stage of the game? We would have left him in Gettysburg. That's the way the Park Service would run Arlington."

General DeWitt's military sensitivities were quite ruffled by my story. A few days later he called me and said, "If you will bring over a draft order for giving Arlington back to us, I will go along with it and try to put it through."

Mr. Delano helped out by going to see the President, suggesting a few changes in the executive order. On July 28, the President issued Executive Order 6228, which clarified section 2 of Executive Order 6166, "postponing until further order" the transfer of Arlington and other cemeteries not specified in the order, and confirmed the independence of the National Capital Park and Planning Commission and the Fine Arts Commission from National Park Service oversight, except for some administrative and housekeeping functions, which would remain in the Department of the Interior. We were not relieved of the responsibility for the care of public buildings in Washington, which was retained by the Park Service through 1939. I was also unsuccessful in my efforts to have our name restored.

Strangely enough, we didn't hear anything from the Forest Service until shortly before the end of the two-month waiting period. Assistant Chief Forester L. F. Kneipp finally wrote a mild letter to the Budget Bureau complaining that the executive order as written might cause some national forests, in which national monuments existed, to be transferred to the National Park Service.

Early in May, in the midst of trying to get the President's executive order straightened out, Secretary Ickes and I made another weekend sightseeing trip. We started out on Saturday with a visit to Gunston Hall, George Mason's home, then went to Richmond, where we stayed overnight. On Sunday we visited Jamestown, Yorktown, and Williamsburg, looking over the work John D. Rockefeller, Jr.'s people were doing on the restoration of Williamsburg.

On the way to Williamsburg, I decided I could not put off any longer breaking the news to Ickes that I would be resigning.

"Mr. Secretary, I think this is as good a time as any to tell you that I want to leave," I said. I told him about the offer to head United States Potash, that I had been putting them off for several years, and that I had my family's financial future and my two children's education to consider.

"I wish you wouldn't do it, I wish you would reconsider," the Secretary said, adding that he had been counting on me to help him. I explained that I felt I had been in government long enough — it was now twenty years. It was too late for me to practice law, and if I didn't move out of government now it might be too late for any kind of career. He realized that on my salary, which despite several raises was still only $9,000, I could not continue to live in Washington, fulfill the social obligations of the directorship, and set aside any money for the family's future.

On the way back to Washington, we stopped at George Washington's birthplace, and spent so long a time there that Ickes was late for dinner with Senator Hiram Johnson. Nearing the capital, Ickes decided to stop at a store so he could telephone Johnson. I got out to buy a *Washington Evening Star* because it was running a series of articles on cabinet officers, and I had promised my little girl, Marian, that I would pick up the paper so she could clip the article for her scrapbook. When I glanced at the front page, I saw a big picture of Ickes, as he was the featured cabinet officer that day. Turning to the article, my eye fell on a little item noting that Secretary Ickes had changed the name of Hoover Dam to Boulder Dam. The writer apparently didn't approve of the action.

As I got back into the car I showed the Secretary that he was the cabinet officer featured this week. He looked at his picture and liked it. Then I said, "I noticed an item in here, Mr. Secretary, something I hadn't heard about," and I started to read it to him.

"Let me see that," he interrupted, snatched the paper, and quickly skimmed through the article. "Well, now, that's a nasty story. I never changed the name of Hoover Dam. I never called it Hoover Dam; I call it Boulder Dam. I never will call it Hoover Dam. But I didn't change the name of it."

"It was named Hoover Dam in the approriations bill," I reminded him, "and that is what it has been called."

No more was said about it. Then the first thing next morning, the Secretary sent for me.

"What rights have I got in changing place names?" he asked.

"Have you got in mind changing Hoover Dam to Boulder Dam?" I asked.

"Yes," he said. "Haven't I got a right to change the name of that dam?"

"Let me explain this naming business," I replied. "It's something that hasn't come up before, but under the law, you cannot name or change the name of a natural feature of any area under your jurisdiction. You've got to submit the name to the Board of Geographic Names, a group made up of representatives from agencies having public property under their jurisdiction. In the case of man-made structures that are not natural features, the Secretary has a right to name them after living people, and that is what Secretary Wilbur did. But to change it to Boulder Dam, you would have to go through the Board.

"Well, I'm going to change it," he said.

"You probably can, Mr. Secretary, if you want to do it," I said. "I don't think anybody could stop you, but I certainly advise against it. The name has been used now for four years, and if you insist on changing the name, you can be sure the Republicans will return some day and change it back again. Besides, if you do change it there will be an awful lot of mean things said about you."

"I'm changing it," he snapped. And he did.

I heard several years later from a pretty good source about an incident that occurred one night shortly after President Roosevelt dedicated Boulder Dam in 1935. The President was attending a banquet, and was chatting with the master of ceremonies, who was a Republican. The man asked the President, "Why didn't you call it Hoover Dam?"

According to my source, FDR replied, "You know, when I left Washington to go to Nevada for the dedication, I had in mind to do just that. It would have been good politics, wouldn't it?"

The master of ceremonies said, "Yes, it would have been awfully good politics, and it would also have been righting a very great wrong. Why didn't you do it?"

"Because that man over there wouldn't let me," the President said, pointing to Ickes at the other end of the dinner table.

Several times in the weeks after I had notified Ickes I was leaving, the Secretary tried to get me to change my mind. However, I went ahead and set August 9, 1933 for my departure. That would be the day before Roosevelt's executive order was to take effect, and a new Director could thus start out clean with the enlarged National Park Service.

I told Ickes that Arno Cammerer was well equipped to take my place, but the Secretary flatly refused to consider him. Ickes said that he didn't want someone who was "lock step in the Civil Service," and I couldn't change his mind. I did get the Secretary to agree to appoint an informal advisory group to help him select my successor. The group was composed of John C. Merriam, Hermon Bumpus, J. Horace McFarland, Frank R. Oastler, and me.

Ickes continued to seek my advice on departmental matters and still wanted me to accompany him on weekend trips. Just before Memorial Day 'he phoned and said he was bored and wanted to go someplace for the holiday weekend. I said I wanted him to see Acadia National Park. No, he said, that was too far. "Not if you can get hold of a plane," I said.

"Where could I possibly get a plane?" he replied.

I told him Attorney General Homer Cummings had a small, two-engine plane, which could be used by others in the cabinet.

Ickes was able to borrow the plane and we took off on Saturday morning for Acadia, with stops planned. At Poughkeepsie, we got a car and drove back to Palisades Interstate Park to attend a ceremony dedicating one of the bronze plaques in honor of Stephen Mather. The site overlooked the Hudson River just below Bear Mountain. Eleanor Roosevelt was there, and so was Mrs. Mather and their daughter, Betty. Mrs. Roosevelt and Ickes made brief remarks.

Ickes wanted to fly over the homes of both Franklin D. Roosevelt and Theodore Roosevelt on the trip, so we flew over FDR's home, Hyde Park, on the way to Boston, where we spent the night. On Sunday, Acadia Superintendent George Dorr met us when we landed at Bangor, Maine. We spent two days touring the park, and were overnight guests at Dorr's Bar Harbor home.

On the way back we flew over Baxter State Park in Maine, where the Appalachian Trail starts, and then headed south for Long Island to give Ickes a view of Sagamore Hill and the Teddy Roosevelt home. I had the pilot fly over Concord, Massachusetts, so we could follow the route of Paul Revere's ride, and it took us only ten minutes. The pilot didn't know where any of these places were, so I had to guide him. The fog started rolling in, but I was able to spot Sagamore Hill and pointed it out.

The weather suddenly turned so bad that the pilot had to find a place to land, so he picked out a small naval station airport on Staten Island he knew about. Ickes and I played a few games of table tennis at the recreation hall while waiting for the weather to clear. When it became obvious that flying conditions were not going to improve, we took a train home from nearby Jersey City.

On the Fourth of July weekend Ickes was to make the dedication speech opening the Morristown National Historical Park, one of the accomplishments of the last days of the Hoover administration. It was a great day for me because this was a park for which I had been responsible. I got a Pullman compartment for the Secretary and myself to share, and thought we would have a good chance to talk on the three-hour train trip. The train had hardly left the yards at Washington before the Secretary was sound asleep. Ickes slept the entire way to Philadelphia, and I didn't get any chance to talk with him. He gave a good speech, and enjoyed hearing about the Continental Army's two winters at Morristown.

I looked forward to some good talk on the return trip. As soon as we got into the diner, he looked at me and said, "What do you think about my firing Burlew tomorrow?"

"Fire Burlew?" I asked, incredulous. That was the worst thing he could have done at that time. Elbert Burlew was the Secretary's administrative assistant, and Ickes couldn't have run the place without him. Burlew was a holdover from the Hoover administration, and Ickes thought he must be a Republican, although he had been in government for many years and was definitely not a political appointee.

I argued with the Secretary all the way back to Washington, insisting that he should keep Burlew. We parted with Ickes still insisting he was going to fire him. Either my argument did some good, or something else caused Ickes to have a change of mind. Not only did Burlew stay, but Ickes promoted him later to the post of assistant secretary of the Interior.

A great deal has been written about the meanness of Secretary Ickes. There is no denying that he could be very hard to get along with. He could be impetuous and unreasonable. Also, he constantly

Secretary of the Interior Harold Ickes (center) and author, 1933. Albright collection.

kept his associates off-balance. None of us could ever be sure that we wouldn't walk in one day and get fired. However, he could also be very kind and thoughtful. On inauguration day, my little Marian had caught a bad cold and it turned into rheumatic fever. She was a pretty sick little girl. Ickes found out about it and every morning for a week or two until she was better, the minute Ickes got to his office each morning he would phone me and ask how my little daughter was. He sent her flowers, and also sent stamps to my son, Bob, who was an avid collector, as was Ickes.

As the time of my departure approached, a successor still had not been selected. The informal search committee called a meeting in my office on July 9, a month before my departure date. Just as the meeting was to start, however, I was called to the White House for an emergency meeting of the CCC advisory council, and I was there all morning. So I didn't get a chance to sit in on the meeting to pick my successor. I had told committee chairman John Merriam, however, that I wanted Arno Cammerer. When I returned to my office about noon, they told me they had agreed on Newton Drury. I had a high regard for Drury. He was a classmate of mine at the University of California, and was head of the Save-the-Redwoods League, and probably the most prominent conservationist in California. So the only thing I could do was to make it unanimous, and cast my vote for Drury. I told the committee I would present Drury's name to Secretary Ickes, even though I still preferred Cam.

Cammerer was actually rather relieved. I had had a hard time convincing him to let me present his name in the first place. His health was never very good, and he did not really want the position.

I took the committee's report to Secretary Ickes, and he was quite pleased. He knew of Drury, although he had never met him.

"Before you offer the job to Mr. Drury you had better get in touch with your friend, Senator Johnson, and get his endorsement," I advised Ickes. I said Johnson would be in favor of it since his son was a classmate of Drury's and mine. I added, however, that I had my doubts that Drury would accept the directorship.

As I had predicted, Senator Johnson was enthusiastic. And as I also predicted, Drury turned down the job.

Ickes then said, "Get your boys together again, and see who else you can come up with."

"Mr. Secretary," I said, "would it be possible for us to meet in that little office next to yours? Then you could come in yourself and give your own views." He agreed, so we met in his side office. This time I stacked the deck a little bit. I got Frederick Law Olmsted, Jr. and Frederic Delano to join us, although they were not members of the original committee. The meeting went on all morning, and many names were put up. Most of them were not acceptable, and the committee just couldn't agree on anyone. I went in to tell Ickes about the impasse and advised that we would have to pick Cammerer. Ickes relented, and the committee officially selected Cam.

I made my departure from the National Park Service as quietly as possible, asking that there be no goodbye ceremony. I tried to put my thoughts about the future of the Service into a farewell message which was sent to the field just before I left.

In this letter, perhaps one of my last official statements to you, let me urge you to be aggressive and vigorous in the fullfillment of your administrative duties. The National Park Service, from its beginning, has been an outstanding organization because its leaders, both in Washington and out in the field, worked increasingly and with high public spirit to carry out the noble policies and maintain the lofty ideals of the service as expressed in law and executive pronouncement. Do not let the service become "just another Government bureau;" keep it youthful, vigorous, clean and strong. We are not here to simply protect what we have been given so far; we are here to try to be the future guardians of those areas as well as to sweep our protective arms around the vast lands which may well need us as man and his industrial world expand and encroach on the last bastions of wilderness. Today we are concerned about our natural areas being enjoyed for the people. But we must never forget that all the elements of nature, the rivers, forests, animals and all things coexistent with them must survive as well.

I hope that particular attention will be accorded always to that mandate in the National Park Service Act of 1916 and in many organic acts of the individual parks which enjoin us to keep our great parks in their natural condition. Oppose with all your strength and power all proposals to penetrate your wilderness regions with motorways and other symbols of modern mechanization. Keep large sections of primitive country free from the influence of destructive civilization. Keep these bits of primitive America for those who seek peace and rest in the silent places; keep them for the hardy climbers of the crags and peaks; keep them for the horseman and the pack train; keep them for the scientist and student of nature; keep them for all who would use their minds and hearts to know what God had created. Remember, once opened, they can never be wholly restored to primeval charm and grandeur.

I also urge you to be ever on the alert to detect and defeat attempts to exploit commercially the resources of the national parks. Often projects will be formulated and come to you "sugar-coated" with an alluring argument that the park will be benefitted by its adoption. We National Park men and women know that nature's work as expressed in the world-famous regions in our charge cannot be improved upon by man.

Beware, too, of innovation in making the parks accessible. For a half century, elevators, cableways, electric railways and similar contrivances have been proposed from time to time and have been uniformly rejected. The airplane while now an accepted means of transportation should not be permitted to land in our primitive areas.

Park usefulness and popularity should not be measured in terms of mere numbers of visitors. Some precious park areas can easily be destroyed by the concentration of too many visitors. We should be interested in the quality of park patronage, not by the quantity. The parks, while theoretically for everyone to use and enjoy, should be so managed that only those numbers of visitors that can enjoy them while at the same time not overuse and harm them would be admitted at a given time. We must keep elements of our crowded civilization to a minimum in our parks. Certain comforts, such as safe roads, sanitary facilities, water, food and modest lodging, should be available. Also extra care must be taken for the children, the elderly and the incapacitated to enjoy the beauty of the parks.

We have been compared to the military forces because of our dedication and esprit de corps. In a sense this is true. We do act as guardians of our country's land. Our National Park Service uniform which we wear with pride does command the respect of our fellow citizens. We have the spirit of fighters, not as a destructive force, but as a power for good. With this spirit each of us is an integral part of the preservation of the magnificent heritage we have been given, so that centuries from now people of our world, or perhaps of other worlds, may see and understand what is unique to our earth, never changing, eternal.

When I left, a number of newspapers were very kind to me, but the comment that meant the most to me came in a personal letter from John D. Rockefeller, Jr., written from his home at Seal Harbor, Maine. He wrote:

> Surely no man knows better than you the abiding satisfaction that comes from worthwhile service well rendered. The spirit of unselfish devotion to high ideals of service which has characterized your public life ever since I first knew you is an inspiration to all who have had the privilege of being associated with you.
>
> As I look back over this period which is now ended for you, the things that have been accomplished so largely through your efforts, seem almost unbelievable. While relatively few people will know that it is you who have been chiefly responsible for the development of the national parks, there are hundreds and thousands, yes millions of people whose lives have been made happier, richer, better because you — their unknown friend — have opened to them nature's treasure store of beauty. This you have done at the sacrifice of your own advancement, ease, comfort, even health and

other personal considerations. It gives me the greatest satisfaction thus to review your public service and to speak this word of gratitude, admiration and friendship. And now that you have turned to a new field of endeavor, I hope you may have the opportunity of realizing your desires and dreams for yourself and your family to a degree that has not heretofore been possible.

I left government service on August 9, 1933, and on August 10 I became vice-president and general manager, and the chief operating officer of United States Potash Company. But in my heart I never really left the National Park Service, and for the half-century since then I have tried to help out whenever and however I could with its problems and opportunities.

Epilogue: A Continuing Alliance

STRANGE AS IT SEEMED TO BE WORKING IN INDUSTRY INSTEAD OF THE
FEDERAL GOVERNMENT FOR THE FIRST TIME IN MY ADULT LIFE, the
break was clean. I had severed all official connections with the National Park Service. But the devotion of a lifetime could not be so
easily set aside, and my lively interest in the parks, the Service, and the
Department of the Interior continued. This was actually part of the
agreement I had with United States Potash Company. When discussing their offer to me to join the company, I was assured that they
hoped I would continue my activities in the field of conservation of
natural and historic resources as time permitted and as a private citizen. They also said they would be most willing for me to serve on
unpaid committees or commissions if requested to do so by either a
government agency or by industry.

The company had mineral leases on public domain in New
Mexico, where it had discovered potassium deposits and where it was
completing a mine for their extraction. The leases were granted by
the Bureau of Land Management to which royalties on mined ores
were to be paid, and the Bureau of Mines and the U.S. Geological
Survey had responsibility to oversee mine plans, protect miners, and
review published statistics and reports on operations. In my new work
I was involved in conservation of a resource for use, as contrasted with
the duty of the National Park Service to protect scenic and historic
resources for the benefit and enjoyment of present and future generations. For many years I had been seeking to protect the resources

intact, only allowing for access of visitors and providing facilities for them. Now I was engaged in exploitation of a mineral resource important in agriculture and industry, and under the supervision of experts in three bureaus of the Department of the Interior.

My successor in the Park Service, Director Arno Cammerer (always "Cam" to me), wrote frequently, telling me what was going on. It was a great day, for instance, when I learned that the rightful name of the Service had been restored officially. Cammerer had been able to get a good friend of the parks, Senator Carl Hayden of Arizona, to tack an amendment onto the 1934 Interior Department appropriations bill to abolish the much-hated name "Office of National Parks, Buildings and Reservations" and restore the name National Park Service.

Occasionally Cammerer asked my advice. I was delighted to give it, and must confess that I could not resist volunteering opinions now and then, even when not asked. My old congressional connections still proved helpful to the Park Service, and I was glad to do some citizen lobbying from time to time, or work behind the scenes on such matters as establishing Everglades National Park and Kings Canyon National Park. My many personal friends in Washington included a number of congressional and executive branch officials such as senators Harry Byrd of Virginia, Pete Norbeck of South Dakota, Carl Hayden of Arizona, Bronson Cutting of New Mexico and Hiram Johnson of California, representatives Harry Englebright and Clarence Lea of California and Edward T. Taylor of Colorado, Director W. C. Mendenhall of the Geological Survey, Frederick A. Delano, chairman of the National Capital Park and Planning Commission and assistant Secretary of the Interior Oscar Chapman. Secretary Ickes himself was not a close personal friend, but I did have frequent contacts with him.

In 1935, Congress passed the Historic Sites Act, which declared it a national policy to preserve historical sites and antiquities of national importance. To handle the new program, a branch of historic sites and buildings was established, headed by a Park Service assistant director. Ickes decided to appoint a retired University of Chicago professor to take charge of the program, passing over Verne E. Chatelain, who was chief historian and an acting assistant director. Under Civil Service procedures, however, a job opening had to be filled from among the top three people on a list of applicants. Chatelain was at the top of the Civil Service list. The man Ickes proposed to hire had no Civil Service standing and had not even applied. When Cammerer objected, Ickes ignored him. Ickes often failed to seek Cammerer's advice when he really needed it, and I felt the Secretary never appreciated Cam's abilities. On the other hand, Cammerer seemed to be afraid of Ickes and, when meeting with the Secretary, failed to state his views strongly, or accepted their rejection and withdrew from the discussion. I had learned early in my acquaintance with Ickes to argue with him when necessary and not to accept defeat readily.

When I heard about the historian appointment, I was determined to see justice done. Knowing that it would do no good whatever to try to get Ickes to change a decision already made, I wrote instead to the Civil Service Commission and told them they would have to notify Secretary Ickes that his action was illegal.

I was sure that Ickes would resent my letter to the Civil Service Commission and that I would invite his ire, but was also quite certain that we had been together so often, and had so much confidence in each other, that it would not jeopardize our friendship.

After the Civil Service Commission notified Ickes, he had an aide telephone me in New York to say he wanted to see me. I made the trip to Washington, and the minute I walked into his office, Ickes pounded the table, shook his finger, and demanded that I withdraw the letter.

"I knew you wouldn't like the letter when I wrote it," I replied, "but I am not going to take anything back. Besides, I'm right and you're wrong."

"I have a right to put men in high positions in whom I have confidence," Secretary Ickes shouted.

"You certainly do," I said, "but for this position you are required to select from the Civil Service list."

We went round and round, and he was verbally abusive. When I asked who this man was that he wanted to appoint, he replied that it was none of my business.

"I think it is my business," I said, "as a citizen and as a former Director of the Park Service."

Finally, when I saw we weren't going to resolve it, I got up to leave. Reaching across his desk to shake hands, I said, "Let me just say this final word to you, Mr. Secretary. You know that the National Park Service is close to my heart. I helped establish it. I was here when it was born, and I am very much interested in seeing that it is protected. Now your man may be very good, but he should have taken the Civil Service examination — everything should have been done within regulations."

Ickes replied quietly, "Certainly you don't think I would do anything to hurt the Park Service, do you? I am only doing this in the best interests of the Service. It is nothing to me personally." He got up and put an arm around my shoulders as I walked out.

Since the Civil Service Commission would not let Ickes appoint the man he wanted, he left the position vacant. Chatelain meanwhile resigned to take a position with the Carnegie Institution, and a Park Service historian, Ronald F. Lee, took his place, but not with the title of assistant director. Lee, however, later became chief historian.

Another example of the Secretary's relationship with people who stood up to him concerned the making of a motion picture in a national park. While I was Park Service Director, we permitted a few motion pictures to be made, but always with the provision that natural and historic features could not be used except as background scenes. As part of this policy, we had permitted filming of the wildlife picture "Bambi" in Sequoia National Park.

After I had left the Service, Ickes found out about that filming, in some way never known to me. He had been told that the park superintendent and several of his employes had helped the motion picture company, and that when the picture was finished they all had received modest presents or cash in compensation for the time they devoted to the picture. Colonel John R. White, superintendent of the Park, had received a horse and saddle from the movie company. All of the employees had worked on their own time, never on government hours.

When Ickes found out about this, and even though it had taken place before he was Secretary, he had superintendent White come to Washington to tell just what happened. The Secretary took the position that the park personnel should not have had anything to do with the picture. He told White that the value of the presents or cash payments should be computed and deducted from their wages. Superintendent White vigorously defended himself and his employees, insisting that in no way were the Park Service people deserving of criticism or penalty for service rendered to the picture company on their own time. White did not mention the horse and saddle given to him, but which he had in turn given to the Park Service. When Ickes insisted that they pay back to the government the value of the gifts, White agreed to have the value deducted from the wages of all the involved personnel, including himself. Ickes said that because White had told him the whole story, he would not make him pay the penalty.

Already enraged by the Secretary's decision, White replied to Ickes, "You cannot make an exception in my case. Since you insist on penalizing my people, you will have to inflict the same treatment on me that you have ordered for them."

White stalked out of the office and fumed all the way back to California. In Visalia he looked up a newspaper reporter and told him the story. The reporter's article raked Ickes over the coals for the mean thing he had done. White sent the clipping to Ickes, fully expecting to be fired. Instead Ickes brought Colonel White to Washington, where he served for a while as an acting assistant director of the Park Service, later going to Santa Fe as regional director for a while before returning to Sequoia.

A few years after our run-in over the historian position, Ickes phoned me to ask if I could do a "job" for him. He warned that he couldn't pay anything other than expenses, but I assured him that I couldn't and wouldn't accept pay for any services to the government anyway, as long as I was working for industry. Ickes wanted me to help him sell an "idea" he had for acquiring the Kings Canyon land adjoining Sequoia National Park, so that the area could finally be made a large national park.

Since 1915, when Mather became assistant to the Secretary of the Interior, and later during his administration of the National Park Service, as well as during my administration, we had sought national park status for the watersheds of the canyons and high country to the summit of the Sierra Nevada and the south and middle forks of the Kings River. In 1926, Sequoia National Park had been extended to the summit of the Sierra Nevada, excluding the Mineral King canyon, but we were never able to secure favorable action on the canyons and back country of the Kings River. Opposition had come from livestock growers, sportsmen, and hydroelectric power interests, including the city of Los Angeles. The Sierra Club had always supported the plans for acquiring the land, as did many people in and near Fresno.

By 1935, a growing demand had peaked for a large dam on the Kings River below the proposed new national park. Secretary Ickes had decided to do something about both the proposed Pine Flat dam as well as the Kings Canyon National Park. The new park would adjoin Sequoia, and would include the existing General Grant National Park, a small area with giant sequoia trees which had been established in 1890, along with both Sequoia and Yosemite. Ickes could do this wearing his hat as Public Works administrator.

"I'm planning a banquet in Fresno and will invite opponents as well as the advocates of the Kings Canyon National Park," Ickes told me. "I need your help in assuring that the friends of the park will come, and I want you to be there to help me."

Ickes went to Fresno ahead of time and talked to opponents of the park. I had done some telephoning and letter writing, and Ickes discovered that Park Service regional director Frank Kittredge, the Yosemite and Sequoia park superintendents, Sierra Club officers and other local leaders had many park proponents committed to attending the dinner. Then at the banquet, without actually promising the dam, he indicated that if the local people would back the park, and the conservationists would go along with the dam, he would work for both projects. The two factions cooperated, and with strong backing from President Roosevelt the Kings Canyon National Park bill was enacted by Congress a few months later, and was signed into law on March 4, 1940.

When Ickes fought his long and losing battle to have Congress create a Department of Conservation, I gave behind-the-scenes support. To get such a department, Congress would have to include the national forests, which had been transferred from Interior to the Department of Agriculture in 1905 by President Theodore Roosevelt. Gifford Pinchot, who had been behind the 1905 action and was the first chief forester of the Forest Service, was by this time governor of Pennsylvania and had great influence in Congress. Several previous secretaries of the Interior had also thought about making a Department of Conservation out of Interior, and getting the Forest Service away from the Department of Agriculture.

At Secretary Ickes' request, I was part of a group of conservationists that met in Chicago in 1937 to see what might be done to counteract misrepresentations then being circulated by the Forest Service, which tenaciously resisted the proposal for a Department of Conservation. The group agreed to send a letter to President Roosevelt, signed by five of us who would represent the group. As a result, Walter L. Fisher, Jr., son of the Secretary of the Interior at the end of the Taft administration, Irving Brant, an historian, Tom Wallace,

Carlsbad Caverns National Park. Frank Jenifer (Pacific Coast Borax), Harry Palmer and Tom Cramer (U.S. Potash), author, and Jimmie Boles, wife of Superintendent Tom Boles, 1934. Albright collection.

editor of the Louisville *Times*, Richard Lieber, head of Indiana's state parks, and I spent almost an hour with the President in late December 1937.

At one point, Mr. Roosevelt mentioned the feud many years earlier between Forest Service Chief Pinchot and Interior Secretary Ballinger that had culminated in the firing of both by President Taft in 1909. Roosevelt seemed to imply that Ballinger had been the villain in the feud.

"President Taft thought that whatever might have been wrong about the timber transaction was the fault of both Ballinger and Pinchot," I interjected. "So he relieved both of them of their jobs. But there were similar problems involving cabinet members in earlier years."

A couple of other examples of apparent malfeasance in prior administrations were discussed. Then Lieber said, "And how about Homer Cummings?" (Roosevelt's Attorney General, who was currently being criticized in the press for an alleged wrong decision.) The President tilted his head back and laughed in acknowledgment of Lieber scoring a point.

When we got down to the serious business, it was apparent that Roosevelt was well aware that it was Pinchot's influence that had prevented the transfer of the Forest Service from the Department of Agriculture to Interior. The President wanted us to figure out how to offset Pinchot's influence and see to it that there would be enough votes in favor of a Department of Conservation to assure that a reorganization would not be blocked by Congress. "You fellows go and see what you can do about it," the President said as the meeting ended. We went over to the Cosmos Club for dinner and a long discussion, but couldn't come up with a satisfactory solution. We finally adjourned agreeing that if anyone had a good idea of how to win the fight, he should communicate with the others, or else we should drop it. That was the end of our effort.

The national forests never were put back into the Department of the Interior. But during his entire time as Secretary, Ickes continued to press for a Department of Conservation. Although it was not achieved, many of the elements that would have been included in it were transferred to the Interior Department due to Ickes' unceasing work. He got the Biological Survey from the Department of Agriculture and the Bureau of Fisheries from the Department of Commerce. The Bureau of Mines, which had been lost to Commerce in the 1920s, was returned to Interior. And he formed the Fish and Wildlife Service. He also organized the Soil Conservation Service in Interior. One day while Ickes was out of Washington on an official trip, however, Agriculture Secretary Henry Wallace had it transferred to Agriculture, and Ickes never got it back.

Although I privately supported Ickes' plan for a Department of Conservation or a Department of Natural Resources, I did not do so publicly. During the Park Service years I had always maintained good relations with the Forest Service, and now my duties with U.S. Potash also required that I have a good working relationship with the Forest Service.

Ickes was a diligent ally in our efforts to bring the Jackson Hole lands purchased by John D. Rockefeller, Jr. into the national park system. For me, completing the establishment of an adequate Grand Teton National Park remained a top priority and an ideal to which I continued to dedicate a great deal of time and energy for a number of years.

One of the major obstacles to getting the Jackson Hole land added to the park was the Bureau of the Budget's refusal to allow Teton County some form of federal compensation for the tax revenues they would lose if the Rockefeller lands became public. A compromise bill submitted in 1934 to extend the boundaries of the park contained a provision to reimburse Teton County for the lost taxes for a twenty-year period. But when the Bureau of the Budget came out against the tax provision, the bill failed.

Many influential people in Jackson and Jackson Hole continued their strong opposition to park enlargement, and a new Wyoming congressman, Frank Horton, who had won his office by campaigning against excessive government regulation of use of federal lands, introduced a bill to abolish Grand Teton National Park. I worked with Rockefeller associates Harold Fabian, Kenneth Chorley, and Vanderbilt Webb to thwart the Horton bill, and on business trips to Washington made calls on members of Congress. The bill never even came to a vote.

It was discouraging to see so many years pass and so many of the minor skirmishes fought and won without apparent progress toward achieving the Grand Teton Park enlargement. I was especially disappointed that the good people of Wyoming could not understand the necessity of protecting for future generations one of the greatest segments of our nation's heritage. However, in 1939, I went back to the Grand Teton area for the first time since leaving the Park Service, and what I saw revived my hope. Thanks to the CCC, all the dead timber had been cleared away from Jackson Lake, Rockefeller's people had succeeded in removing many of the dilapidated buildings and bill-

Grace and Horace Albright, 1972. Albright collection.

boards, and the whole region looked more beautiful than I had ever seen it.

By 1940 the Park Service had decided that getting the Jackson Hole lands into an enlarged Grand Teton National Park was not feasible, and they began seeking temporary protection for the area by getting the President to establish a national monument through executive action, an idea supported by Secretary Ickes.

Rockefeller was at the same time becoming somewhat discouraged by the years of delay in completing his dream of saving the Jackson Hole lands for the public. A considerable financial drain was also involved in the taxes he paid every year on the thirty-two thousand acres he was holding. In November 1942 Rockefeller wrote to Ickes:

> I have definitely reached the conclusion, although most reluctantly, that I should make permanent disposition of this [Jackson Hole] property before another year has passed. If the Federal government is not interested in its acquisition, or being interested, is still unable to arrange it on the general terms long discussed and with which you are familiar, it will be my thought to make some other disposition of it, or failing in that, to sell it in the market to any satisfactory buyers.

Neither Rockefeller's aides nor I believed he was actually planning to dispose of the land. We felt he was just trying to prod Ickes, or perhaps provide the Secretary with an argument he could use to persuade the President to issue an executive order declaring a Grand Teton National Monument. Rockefeller and Ickes met in late December and then sought a meeting with President Roosevelt. When presenting the idea of the national monument to the President, Ickes warned Roosevelt that if he took the action he probably would be strongly criticized by Congress. President Roosevelt decided to go ahead anyway, and on March 15, 1943, he signed Executive Order 2578, proclaiming the establishment of Jackson Hole National Monument. The action placed more than 220,000 acres in the National Park Service — about 100,000 acres taken from the Teton National Forest, more than 31,000 acres of water, including Jackson Lake, 39,000 acres of other public lands, 1,400 acres of state lands and almost 50,000 acres of private land, including the 32,000 owned by Rockefeller.

The reaction in Jackson Hole and among the state's congressional delegation was immediate and angry, and many of the local newspapers blasted Roosevelt and Ickes. Wyoming Representative Frank Barrett introduced a bill to abolish the new monument. This was a battle I had to get into, and I worked nights and weekends writing confidential letters against the Barrett bill, and even spent two weeks in Washington in 1944 lobbying members of Congress. I got the American Planning and Civic Association, of which I was then president, to adopt a position backing the monument. I was also able to get Ray Lyman Wilbur, former Republican Secretary of the Interior, to issue a statement that presidents Coolidge and Hoover had both supported preserving the Jackson Hole lands. When presidential candidate Thomas E. Dewey, governor of New York, made a speech in Wyoming suggesting that the federal government should not reserve any more land in the Teton area, I immediately phoned friends on the Republican National Committee and suggested that Dewey not discuss this issue until I could get information to him. Dewey did not mention the issue again.

Despite our work, Barrett's bill was passed by Congress just before Christmas of 1944. But it was vetoed by President Roosevelt, who had just been reelected for his fourth term. That was not the end of the opposition to the monument, however, and for another six years I continued to work toward the permanent solution of adding the monument lands to Grand Teton National Park. In 1945 Governor Dewey appointed me to the Palisades Interstate Park Commission. I also became friendly with Herbert Brownell, a political adviser to Dewey. When Dewey ran against President Truman in 1948, my call to Brownell was enough to prevent the Jackson Hole lands from being raised as a campaign issue.

Barrett became chairman of the House permanent subcommittee on public lands in January 1947, and reintroduced his bill to revoke Roosevelt's creation of Jackson Hole National Monument. Again I did some quiet maneuvering, enlisting prominent people to talk to members of Congress. The bill eventually died.

Meantime, there were continuing efforts to settle the differences over tax policy and find a compromise by which Jackson Hole National Monument could be abolished and legislation be enacted to incorporate the lands into Grand Teton National Park. In 1950, a compromise agreement was worked out that satisfied the Wyoming congressional delegation, state and federal officials, local land owners, and most conservation groups. It provided that most of the national monument (except for nine thousand acres in the southeast section that would be transferred to the National Elk Refuge and the Teton National Forest) would become part of the national park. Teton County would be allowed a descending schedule of tax reimbursements over a twenty-five year period to offset tax losses, and existing grazing rights within the park would be continued for the lifetime of the leaseholder and heirs. The National Park Service and the state agreed that in order to administer the overpopulated elk herd, Wyoming hunters could be deputized as temporary park rangers to kill surplus animals inside the park boundaries. The compromise plan also stipulated that a provision would be legislated prohibiting a President from ever again using executive action to establish new national monuments in Wyoming except by express authorization of the Congress. We were saddened by these compromises, especially the animal-cropping provision, which was a thinly-disguised way of permitting some sport hunting in the park. But it was the price we had to pay.

A bill co-sponsored by Wyoming senators Lester C. Hunt and Joseph O'Mahoney was passed by Congress in September 1950 with little opposition and was signed by President Truman. It enlarged the boundaries of the Grand Teton National Park to take in most of the national monument lands. At last the complete Grand Teton National Park was a reality.

Final protection of the Jackson Hole lands was a great satisfaction for John D. Rockefeller, Jr., then seventy-six. It had been twenty-five years since that summer day in 1926 when I had shown the Rockefeller family the Jackson Hole lands that needed to be added to the national park system. After passage of the act, Rockefeller wrote to me, "The recent transfer of property in Washington must have brought you hardly less satisfaction than it brought me. What a pleasure it has been to work with you in this matter over the years, as well as in so many other park matters."

Part of the last decade of the Jackson Hole struggle had taken place during World War II, a particularly difficult time for the National Park Service. In 1940, after seven years of leadership of the Park Service, Director Cammerer's health was failing, and the physician advised that he retire. With great reluctance, Cam stepped aside. There was a vacancy in the office of the regional director in Richmond, and Secretary Ickes transferred him to that post and appointed as director Newton B. Drury, the executive director of the Save-the-Redwoods League, who earlier had declined Ickes' offer to be my successor.

I had nothing whatever to do with these appointments, but I was sure that Newt Drury, who had been a classmate of mine at Berkeley and a good friend, would be a strong, dedicated Director — which he was. Drury had to face many difficult problems, some due to the fact that he first had to cope with New Deal agencies concerned with the Depression, and then with World War II. Secretary Ickes, compelled to yield space in the Interior Department building for war agency use, transferred the Park Service and several other bureaus to Chicago. So Drury had little contact with the Secretary's office or the Congress for several years. Many of his staff and field employees joined the armed services, appropriations were substantially reduced, and he had to resist proposals to utilize national park resources for demands of the war.

A few of Drury's and my mutual friends may have wondered if we held opposing views on certain national park policies. I think both of us felt that we were in as near perfect agreement as two men engaged in natural resource conservation could be. Drury had apprehensions that in certain parks such as Yosemite, too many people would seek to visit them at the same time, and there would be damage to park features from overuse. I thought this might happen, but only in the distant future. Also, Drury was opposed to any exotic entertainment in connection with guidance and interpretation of park features. This rarely happened and never impaired a park feature.

An example that worried Drury, but not me, was the singing of the hymn "Rock of Ages" in Carlsbad Caverns National Park at a monumental stalagmite which stood at the terminus of the tourist-guided trip around the largest room, seven hundred feet underground. Its size, proportions, and color made it a popular attraction and it was called the "Rock of Ages." When a party reached this magnificent feature, they were often invited to sit around its base, looking back at the great room they had just seen. The guide or a ranger would then give a short statement about the park, and suddenly all the lights would be extinguished and the cavern would be in complete darkness. A few moments later, from a point a half-mile back on the trail, the first verse of "Rock of Ages" would be sung by rangers or a quartet from the town of Carlsbad or a group from a church choir or even a lone singer.

As the singers advanced along the trail, lights were turned on behind them, with more lights turned on at the end of each verse. And when the last verse was sung near the great stalagmite, the cavern room was fully lighted. It was an emotional experience that brought tears to the eyes of many visitors.

Drury ordered Superintendent Tom Boles to stop the practice of the hymn singing and lights going on and off. But Boles, who believed the ceremony added greatly to the visitors' park experience, did not comply with the Director's order. Drury finally got exasperated and transferred Boles to Hot Springs National Park, despite outcries from New Mexico congressmen. Boles retired from the Park Service soon afterward.

Drury remained as Director until early 1951. When he resigned, a longtime associate of mine, Arthur E. Demaray, was appointed Director. He had come from the U.S. Geological Survey to join our ad hoc park administration team in 1916, then gradually worked his way up to the position of deputy director. He was making plans for retirement when then Secretary of the Interior Oscar Chapman decided to recognize Demaray's long service and outstanding accomplishments by making him Director. Demaray delightedly accepted, but limited his tenure to only one year, after which he proceeded with his retirement.

Conrad L. Wirth, who succeeded Demaray, served from 1951 to 1964, longer than any other Director. His distinguished thirty-year career in the Park Service included supervision of several hundred CCC camps, and he became especially known for Mission 66, the ten-year park improvement program completed in 1966. In his excellent book *Parks, Politics, and the People*, Wirth tells about getting President Eisenhower's personal approval of the Mission 66 proposal after making a slide presentation in the Cabinet Room at the White House.*

My ties to Washington remained strong, as I served on a number of commissions and committees. At first I declined the request of Ickes' replacement, Julius A. Krug, to join the Secretary's Advisory Board on National Parks, Historic Sites, Buildings and Monuments. I felt it better that I just continue as an informal advisor, as I had done with Ickes. I accepted the invitation to become a member of the

* Conrad L. Wirth, *Parks, Politics, and the People* (Norman: University of Oklahoma Press, 1980).

National Minerals Advisory Council set up by Secretary Krug, and became its chairman in 1948. (In 1952, after Conrad Wirth became director of the National Park Service and my friend Oscar Chapman was Interior Secretary, I did accept an appointment for a six-year term on the Secretary's parks advisory board, and served on its history committee, reviewing recommendations for additional National Park Service historic sites.)

In 1948 I was appointed by Herbert Hoover, chairman of the Presidential Commission on Organization of the Executive Branch of the Government, to serve on the commission's task force on natural resources. The task force was chaired by former governor of Wyoming Leslie Miller, and included former governors John J. Dempsey of New Mexico and Ralph Carr of Colorado, as well as Dean Samuel T. Dana of the School of Forestry and Conservation at the University of Michigan, President Gilbert White of Haverford College, President Isaiah Bowman of Johns Hopkins University, and Donald H. McLaughlin, president of Homestake Mining Corporation. We prepared a report recommending a Department of Conservation, but Hoover and the other members of the commission did not accept this initiative.

About this same time, by a fortunate series of coincidences, I had a part in founding a major new conservation organization and a national conference on natural resources. I had been working with some conservation organizations which were trying to interest the Ford Foundation in giving them financial support, and because I knew Rowan Gaither and Chester C. Davis of the Ford Foundation executive board, I was asked to head the group going to Pasadena to meet with foundation people. My group suggested that the foundation hire Charles W. Eliot II, who had been a member of FDR's Natural Resources Planning Board, to look into the funding of conservation efforts. Eliot was hired, but nothing happened. When I was in Pasadena a few months later, Davis asked me to have lunch with him and Eliot and Robert M. Hutchins, who was on the board of directors of the Ford Foundation. Hutchins readily agreed that the foundation should be supporting conservation activities, and asked me to prepare a funding proposal and secure the endorsement of about twenty-five national conservation leaders.

One of those I contacted for support was William S. Paley, president of the Columbia Broadcasting System, who had been chairman of President Truman's Materials Policy Commission, which had made

Author and granddaughter Susan Ford Isaacson with Medal of Freedom, 1980.

its report on natural resource and minerals availability in the waning days of the Truman administration. Paley had formed an organization called Resources for the Future to try to follow up on his commission's recommendations, but it existed only on paper, so he offered to turn over his organization to us as the group to be funded, and the Ford Foundation gave us one hundred thousand dollars to pursue conservation efforts.

We were still working on our program ideas when Ford foundation officials suggested that we undertake a White House conference on natural resources, and gave Resources for the Future (RFF) $150,000 more to cover conference expenses. Our group had already been considering such a conference, similar to President Theodore Roosevelt's White House Conference of 1908, but the Ford Foundation's suggestion came when we did not have our organization complete, and confronted us with an immediate, very large project.

We persuaded John A. Hannah, president of Michigan State University, to chair the conference, and decided to see if we could get presidential approval for a White House conference on natural resources. Twenty-five conservation leaders joined me as sponsors of the new organization and the conference, and I was elected as the first president of Resources for the Future.

Shortly after Dwight D. Eisenhower's election, I arranged for Hannah and myself to meet with the President-elect while he was staying at the Commodore Hotel in New York. Eisenhower was enthusiastic when we explained about the conference, and said it certainly could be a White House conference. He even told us about a report he had prepared years before on minerals availability for General Douglas MacArthur, then chief of staff of the army. As we got up to leave, Ike turned to me and said, "Would you excuse me if I keep Dr. Hannah for a few minutes?"

Leaving Hannah behind with Eisenhower, I stopped in to meet with Sherman Adams, the former governor of New Hampshire, who was soon to become chief of staff at the White House, and told him about our meeting and Ike's approval of the conference. Those few minutes got our conference into a lot of trouble. Eisenhower's reason for detaining Hannah after our meeting was that he wanted to offer him the position of assistant secretary of Defense. Hannah accepted, and we had to find a new chairman, which we did in the person of former congressman and budget director Lewis Douglas. My talk with Sherman Adams also produced problems. Adams looked at the list of people on our board, and some of the people connected with the Ford Foundation, and commented that they were all "New Dealers." That comment made me angry, and I replied, "I don't care, they are ideal men for our work. If they were New Dealers what difference does it make? This conference will be held in the Eisenhower administration. If you want to fuss about New Dealers, put me in that category too, because I helped organize the CCC." Adams laughed and said, "let's forget it."

But he didn't. The first thing I knew, Adams had advised Eisenhower not to have anything to do with the conference. We went ahead anyway without calling it a White House conference, and the President attended briefly and made some welcoming remarks at the first day's luncheon. The Mid-Century Conference on Resources for the Future, held at the Shoreham Hotel in Washington, D.C. the first week of December 1953, was a definite success, with 1,600 people in attendance. It helped alert the public to the need for conservation of minerals, land utilization, wilderness preservation, and better natural resources management. It also gave impetus to Resources for the Future, which became the leading conservation organization studying natural resource issues. Soon after the conference I was able to get out of the presidency of RFF, which was becoming a full-time job, and Reuben Gustavson, chancellor of the University of Nebraska, was selected as the new president. I served as chairman of the board of directors until 1962.

In 1956, after twenty-three years as vice president and then president of United States Potash, I retired. Grace and I moved back to California, and I cut down on my conservation activities somewhat, especially the lobbying in Washington for national park causes. Over the years, however, I have maintained contact with all of the Park Service directors and many other officials and park superintendents.

At a dinner given in my honor in 1959 in Washington, and attended by eight hundred people, University of California President Robert Gordon Sproul announced that the Regents of the University had appointed me a Regents Lecturer in Berkeley. So the winter and spring of 1961 found me in Berkeley teaching conservation for one semester.

Because of my long-time interest in Theodore Roosevelt's contributions to conservation, and my service as a trustee of the Theodore Roosevelt Memorial Association, Roosevelt family members and friends asked me in the early 1960s to undertake a leadership role in bringing the birthplace of Theodore Roosevelt in New York City and his home at Sagamore Hill on Long Island, New York, into the national park system as historic sites. I arranged to have the areas visited by Park Service Director Wirth, who helped me obtain a promise from Secretary of the Interior Stewart L. Udall to visit the sites. Early in 1962, Secretary Udall spent a day with Director Wirth and me, first at Sagamore Hill and then at the reconstructed birthplace at 28 East 20th Street in New York, and said he would back the legislation to bring the sites into the system. He did so, Congress promptly approved them, and President John F. Kennedy signed the legislation on July 25, 1962.

Grace and I made six extensive overseas trips in 1950, 1952, 1960, 1963, 1965, and 1967, visiting twenty countries. As often as possible I met with national park and conservation officials at the countries we visited to talk about what they were doing about national parks and historic preservation. (The national park idea, which started at Yellowstone in 1872, had spread throughout the world by the 1930s. While superintendent of Yellowstone, I had met with visitors from many nations who had come to the United States to find out how they could establish national parks or improve them in their own countries.)

It has been a great satisfaction to see how the national park idea has spread around the world. In 1960 I attended the General Assembly of the International Union for Conservation of Nature and Natural Resources (IUCN) in Poland and met with members of the IUCN

Parks Commission. I participated in the First World Conference on National Parks in Seattle in 1962, attended by sixty-two nations.

The one hundredth anniversary of the founding of Yellowstone National Park in 1972 was the busiest year of my retirement. In January, soon after my eighty-second birthday, Grace and I were invited to the White House for a dinner President Nixon gave to award the Medal of Freedom to both Dewitt and Lila Atcheson Wallace, publishers of the *Readers Digest*, and good friends of mine. In March we flew to New York and Washington for Yellowstone anniversary events, and in August we attended another anniversary ceremony and conference at Yellowstone and then went to Grand Teton National Park for the Second World Conference on National Parks, with more than eighty nations represented.

Other conservation activities included service on the Palisades Interstate Commission (1945–1961, as previously noted), and thirty-seven years on the board of trustees of Jackson Hole Preserve, Inc. The Preserve, established by John D. Rockefeller, Jr. to look after Rockefeller land holdings for conservation and affiliated purposes, was now headed by Laurance S. Rockefeller. I also served on the board of Colonial Williamsburg for twenty-three years (1935–1958), and was the member of the board with responsibility for liaison with the National Park Service. These latter two boards had offices in Rockefeller Center, New York, the same location as my United States Potash offices, which made my participation easier.

I even took on one new conservation activity after my retirement. In 1964, at the age of seventy-four, I was appointed to the board of trustees of the Pacific Tropical Botanical Garden. The following year, on the way home from our fiftieth anniversary vacation trip to the Far East, Grace and I visited the garden, and I found myself elected chairman of the board. I made additional trips to the garden in 1968 and 1971 before resigning as board chairman.

I have continued my membership in the Camp Fire Club of America, the Boone & Crockett Club, the Sierra Club, the National Audubon Society, the National Parks and Conservation Association, the Nature Conservancy, the National Trust for Historic Preservation, the Death Valley 49ers, and the Los Angeles corral of the Westerners.

In 1985 — at the age of 95 — as I complete this telling of events surrounding the founding years of the National Park Service, I am no longer able to make trips to visit the parks, although I took part in an environmental conference at Santa Monica Mountains National Recreation Area in 1984. But I still keep busy at my typewriter, corresponding with friends all over the world, sending a letter to a congressman, an official, or an editor when I think it will do some good, and writing articles for various periodicals. I feel very fortunate that I have frequent visits from rangers, superintendents, and Park Service officials. I also have family connections to the Park Service. My granddaughter, Susan Ford Isaacson, is a seasonal ranger at Kings Canyon National Park, where her husband, Scott, is a permanent ranger. My nephew, Stanley Albright, is an associate director (operations) of the Park Service. So the tradition and involvement of the Albright family in national parks lives on.

I have had a long and full life, and a wonderful sixty-five-year marriage. The two great tragedies of my life have been the death of my wife, Grace, in 1980, and the loss of my son, Robert Mather Albright, who died in 1950 at the age of thirty-one. But there have been great satisfactions, too. I still have my daughter, Marian Schenck, my four grandchildren and ten great-grandchildren, and Robert's widow, Mary Gower Albright, a vice president of CBS, all living within four hundred miles from me. I had the honor and privilege of working with Stephen Mather, learning from him, and being able to organize the Park Service in 1917 and 1918 when Mather was ill; starting the civilian administration of Yellowstone National Park and being its superintendent for a decade; helping to start the CCC; getting the military parks and historical areas into the national park system; and seeing Grand Teton National Park achieve its destiny. Through it all I had the help of countless dedicated and talented associates and employees without whose support these things could not have been accomplished.

The National Park Service was built upon the foundation laid during those early years, and I am confident that the competence and dedication I see in today's Park Service people will serve the American people well in the future as in the past. The national parks remain our country's greatest natural treasures. The National Park Service must continue, in the words of the founding act,

> To conserve the scenery and the natural and historic objects and the wildlife therein and to provide for the enjoyment of the same in such manner and by such means as will leave them unimpaired for the enjoyment of future generations.

Index